AGING, DURATION, AND

The rapid onset of dementia after an illness, the development of gray hair after a traumatic loss, the sudden appearance of a wrinkle in the brow of a spurned lover. The realist novel uses these conventions to accelerate the process of aging into a descriptive moment, writing the passage of years on the body all at once. *Aging, Duration, and the English Novel* argues that the formal disappearance of aging from the novel parallels the ideological pressure to identify as young by repressing the process of growing old. The construction of aging as a shameful event that should be hidden – to improve one's chances on the job market or secure a successful marriage – corresponds to the rise of the long novel, which draws upon the temporality of the body to map progress and decline onto the plots of nineteenth-century British modernity.

JACOB JEWUSIAK is a Lecturer in Victorian literature at Newcastle University. His work has appeared in the journals *ELH, Textual Practice, Novel: A Forum on Fiction, SEL, Victorian Literature and Culture, and Nineteenth-Century Gender Studies.*

CAMBRIDGE STUDIES IN NINETEENTH-CENTURY LITERATURE AND CULTURE

Nineteenth-century British literature and culture have been rich fields for interdisciplinary studies. Since the turn of the twentieth century, scholars and critics have tracked the intersections and tensions between Victorian literature and the visual arts, politics, social organization, economic life, technical innovations, scientific thought – in short, culture in its broadest sense. In recent years, theoretical challenges and historiographical shifts have unsettled the assumptions of previous scholarly synthesis and called into question the terms of older debates. Whereas the tendency in much past literary critical interpretation was to use the metaphor of culture as 'background', feminist, Foucauldian, and other analyses have employed more dynamic models that raise questions of power and of circulation. Such developments have reanimated the field. This series aims to accommodate and promote the most interesting work being undertaken on the frontiers of the field of nineteenth-century literary studies: work which intersects fruitfully with other fields of study such as history, or literary theory, or the history of science. Comparative as well as interdisciplinary approaches are welcomed.

A complete list of titles published will be found at the end of the book.

AGING, DURATION, AND THE ENGLISH NOVEL

Growing Old from Dickens to Woolf

JACOB JEWUSIAK

Newcastle University

CAMBRIDGE
UNIVERSITY PRESS

CAMBRIDGE
UNIVERSITY PRESS

University Printing House, Cambridge CB2 8BS, United Kingdom

One Liberty Plaza, 20th Floor, New York, NY 10006, USA

477 Williamstown Road, Port Melbourne, VIC 3207, Australia

314-321, 3rd Floor, Plot 3, Splendor Forum, Jasola District Centre, New Delhi - 110025, India

103 Penang Road, #05-06/07, Visioncrest Commercial, Singapore 238467

Cambridge University Press is part of the University of Cambridge.

It furthers the University's mission by disseminating knowledge in the pursuit of education, learning and research at the highest international levels of excellence.

www.cambridge.org
Information on this title: www.cambridge.org/9781108713221
DOI: 10.1017/9781108615501

First published 2020
First paperback edition 2021

A catalogue record for this publication is available from the British Library

ISBN 978-1-108-49917-0 Hardback
ISBN 978-1-108-71322-1 Paperback

To my wife
Myrto

Contents

Acknowledgments

Writing a book means confronting duration in an unusually direct way, pulsing between a feeling of never-ending deferral and the urgency of deadlines. Thinking about time requires a great deal of it, and without the support of friends, family, colleagues, and institutions, I would not have been able to complete this book.

I am immensely grateful for the generous and insightful criticism of Rachel Ablow, who read through drafts of this work in a very early form. Danny Hack also spent a great deal of time reading through my work and providing helpful feedback. Linda Hughes provided guidance at an early stage of my career and continues to have an impact on my current work. I owe each of them a huge debt of gratitude for modeling the rigor and professionalism that I strive for as a scholar.

My thanks to Mary Mullen for providing detailed and invaluable feedback on Chapter 5, and to John MacNeill Miller for his conversation and camaraderie at past NAVSA conferences. Also, thank you to the editors of *Nineteenth-Century Gender Studies*, who published my first article when I was a still a graduate student. A heavily revised version of that article appears in this book as Chapter 3.

I owe a great debt to my friends and colleagues, who provided the intellectual and emotional support that make writing possible: Joe and Maria Aldinger, Jacob Bodway, Richard Cardenas, Jeremiah Crotser, Anne Greenfield, Deborah Hall, Allen Harshaney, Ubaraj Katawal, Melinda Mejia, Donna Sewell, Marty Williams, and Paul Wingo. And to my new colleagues at Newcastle University, especially Ella Dzelzainis, Kirsten MacLeod, and Michael Rossington, for answering a seemingly inexhaustible well of questions.

In 2013 I received the Donald Gray Prize from the North American Victorian Studies Association for an article-length version of Chapter 2, which originally appeared in *NOVEL: A Forum on Fiction*. Without this award, I'm certain that this book would have been written differently – less confidently, with more compromises, and more slowly. Supporting early career researchers – through awards, generous feedback, and funds – helps scholars feel like their contribution matters to an intellectual community that can feel heavily invested in gatekeeping and exclusivity.

I was also fortunate to receive a summer stipend from the National Endowment for the Humanities to support work on Chapter 6. This award was crucial in freeing up the summer months for finishing the book.

To my family in Chios – Stamatis, Fragkoula, and Maria – our time together in the summer has always been a period of nourishment and rejuvenation. A great deal of writing took place in my little chair in the living room, so I want to thank you all for opening your home to me. My thanks to Cindy Gibson for inspiring kindness and generosity wherever you go. To Michelle Astley for having a loving and gentle heart.

What would this book be without my father, Pops Jewusiak? I am sure that without your great patience and indefatigable optimism it would not exist. You have been my mentor, my biggest fan, and my friend. You are a hero. Without your constant support this project would have collapsed many times over.

Finally, this book is dedicated to my wife, Myrto Drizou. You have been by my companion since graduate school, when we were both freezing in our underheated apartment in Buffalo, NY. You have read this manuscript more times than I can count. When I think of growing old it is always with you – two durations jointly extending into the future.

Abbreviations

CC	Charles Dickens, "A Christmas Carol," in *A Christmas Carol and Other Stories* (New York: Modern Library, 2001), pp. 1–107
Cinema	Virginia Woolf, "The Cinema," in *Selected Essays*, edited by David Bradshaw (Oxford University Press, 2008), pp. 172–6
Clock	Charles Dickens, *Master Humphrey's Clock*, vol. 1. (London and New York: Chapman and Hall, 1840)
Cranford	Elizabeth Gaskell, *Cranford* (Oxford University Press, 2011)
DC	H. G. Wells, *In the Days of the Comet* (New York: Century Co., 1906)
Diary	Virginia Woolf, *The Diary of Virginia Woolf*, edited by Anne Olivier Bell. 5 vols. (San Diego: Harcourt Brace, 1977–84)
Dorrit	Charles Dickens, *Little Dorrit* (London: Penguin, 2003)
Elvesham	H. G. Wells, "The Story of the Late Mr Elvesham," in *The Country of the Blind and Other Selected Stories*, edited by Patrick Parrinder (London: Penguin, 2007), pp. 120–36
Food	H. G. Wells, *The Food of the Gods: And How It Came to Earth* (New York: Charles Scribner's Sons, 1904)
FT	Thomas Hardy, "Fellow-Townsmen," in *Wessex Tales* (Oxford University Press, 2009), pp. 86–135
Geriatrics	Ignatz Nascher, *Geriatrics: The Diseases of Old Age and their Treatment, Including Physiological Old Age, Home and Institutional Care, and Medio-Legal Relations* (York, PA: Maple Press, 1914)
Great	Charles Dickens, *Great Expectations* (London: Penguin, 1996)

Letters	Elizabeth Gaskell, *The Letters of Mrs. Gaskell*, edited by J. A. V. Chapple and Arthur Pollard (Cambridge, MA: Harvard University Press, 1967)
MC	Charles Dickens, *Martin Chuzzlewit* (Oxford University Press, 2009)
Nature	Élie Metchnikoff, *The Nature of Man: Studies in Optimistic Philosophy* (New York: G. P. Putnam's Sons, 1905)
Orlando	Virginia Woolf, *Orlando* (New York: Harcourt Brace Jovanovich, 1956)
Prolongation	Élie Metchnikoff, *The Prolongation of Life: Optimistic Studies* (New York: G. P. Putnam's Sons, 1908)
Shop	Charles Dickens, *The Old Curiosity Shop* (London: Penguin, 2000)
TM	H. G. Wells, *The Time Machine: An Invention: A Critical Text of the 1895 London First Edition, with an Introduction and Appendices*, edited by Leon Stover (Jefferson: McFarland, 1996)
Veil	George Eliot, *The Lifted Veil and Brother Jacob* (Oxford University Press, 2009)
Waves	Virginia Woolf, *The Waves* (New York: Harcourt Brace Jovanovich, 1959)
WB	Thomas Hardy, *The Pursuit of the Well-Beloved and The Well-Beloved* (London: Penguin, 1997)
WW	H. G. Wells, *The War of the Worlds* (London: Penguin, 2005)
Years	Virginia Woolf, *The Years* (New York: Harcourt Brace Jovanovich, 1965)

Full details of all other works cited in the text and notes are given in the bibliography.

Introduction

Aging, Duration, and the English Novel theorizes duration and the conventions of realism through an analysis of representations of old age and aging, especially through the way novelists plot the development of characters over time. Instead of conceptualizing old age as a state or a stage, this book analyzes the entanglement of narrative duration with biological and cultural accounts of the human lifespan, privileging temporal continuity over the sedimentation of life into categories such as youth, adulthood, and old age. This critical reorientation demonstrates the potential for age studies to address what both Catherine Gallagher and Caroline Levine have identified as the most undertheorized aspect of the novel form: its duration.[1] The Victorian novel, I argue, constructs a modern sense of duration by grafting the biological process of aging onto the era's most elongated form, which shapes and is shaped by the imagination of how a body endures through time. Critical attention to the temporal form of the novel reveals a series of political problems related to aging, which I analyze through aspects of nineteenth-century literature and culture such as aging masculinity, "redundant" women, queer sexuality, and dystopia.

This book reads duration on the surface of the body and in literary description rather than in hidden depths. Many scholars – from Gerard Genette to Nicholas Dames – account for duration by excavating it from the reader's passive experience of narrative, as a kind of rhythm that keeps time in the background of reading. In contrast, I draw attention to the surface of the text as the representational plane where novelists make descriptions move and provoke the reader's imagination of passing time. My case studies – surveying work from Charles Dickens, Elizabeth Gaskell, Thomas Hardy, H. G. Wells, and Virginia Woolf – suggest that aging served as a way for novelists to reflect on the relationship between the length of their novels, the protraction of plot, and the continuity of duration. These authors deploy a set of literary conventions to evade the difficulty of representing aging: the rapid onset of dementia after an illness, the development of gray hair after a traumatic loss, the sudden appearance of a wrinkle in the brow of a spurned lover, the shocking realization that one is old. Across the realist novel, the duration of aging continually falls out of the attempt to represent it, greatly accelerating the process of aging or writing the passage of years on the body all at once. By doing so, the novel mediates between the body and time, producing narrative coordinates for mapping progress and decline onto the temporalities of nineteenth-century British modernity.

Novelists like Elizabeth Gaskell embody this modernity in the way age writes itself onto her characters, drawing out the temporal contingency of social bonds that appear timeless and sacred, such as that between parents and children. In Gaskell's story "The Crooked Branch" (1859), the middle-aged couple Nathan and Hester Huntroyd are surprised by the birth of Benjamin, who matures into a scheming and greedy young man. Exploiting his parents at every turn, he eventually cuts off communication with his family when they run out of money to lend. Shocked by his son's ingratitude – and worried that Benjamin might be dead – Nathan lapses into an illness that accelerates his aging: "Nathan got up again, an older man in looks and constitution by ten years for that week of bed" ("The Crooked Branch," 250). Exemplary of the way realist literature represents aging, this passage collapses Nathan's maturation into a brief, retrospective sentence – a narrative acceleration that dilates one week into ten years of aging. As aging diminishes in narrative time – its duration compressed into a brief interval of description – it gains the ability to signify something else: for example, Nathan's grief about the dissipation of Benjamin or the breakdown of deference to one's parents and elders. However, my book restrains the impulse to treat aging as a symptom of something deeper. For many critics, the process of growing old fades into the background of a larger hermeneutic agenda, reproducing at the level of argument the cultural repression of aging. I ask the following questions instead: why does aging often serve as a signifier for something else? What forms – literary, biocultural, political – contain and make legible the becoming of aging?

These questions about the semiotics and form of aging introduce a largely unhistoricized problematic of Victorian literature and culture: the conversion of duration into length. Where the process of aging tends to be hypostatized into discrete divisions – such as "young," "old," "fifty-three," and so on – narrative does the opposite by conjuring a sense of duration from events that have been placed side by side or in a causal relationship. Put into this relationship, aging and narrative illuminate a category error, where length stands in for duration, contiguity for continuity, causality for becoming. The novel therefore trains readers to skip over the duration of aging, transforming it into a shocking moment of revelation: "I can't believe I'm old!" or "After her terrible illness, she looked twenty years older." The formal disappearance of aging from the novel parallels the ideological pressure to identify as young by repressing the process of growing old. Indeed, the construction of aging as a shameful event that should be hidden – to improve one's chances on the job market or to secure a successful marriage – corresponds to the rise of industrial capitalism and the long novel, which jointly redefine duration away from temporal continuity and toward sheer length and quantifiable intervals. The very bulk of the novel, like the temporal rationalization of the workday, becomes a signifier for duration itself.

Almost all Victorian novels represent individuals who mature because aging plays a significant role in conferring an aura of reality to the development of characters. The tacit connection between aging and development arises from what I call the novel's *temporal realism*, or the conventions that create readerly consensus about the relationship between the duration of a novel and the reality of passing time. Though the realist novel may skip ahead many years at a chapter break or grind to a halt during long description, it nonetheless creates a sense of correspondence between narrative and real time. Thus, as I contend in Chapter 1, temporal realism naturalizes a formal substitution, where the novel's extended length stands in for the representation of duration. It is precisely because we usually conceive of the realist novel as the most elongated of forms that realism's bypassing of duration so potently naturalizes the eventful time of modernity: time that is meaningful insofar as it is composed of shocks and epiphanies. The length of the novel comes to stand in for duration itself and serves as a kind of ideological training that devalues slow and uneventful time. In this way, the realist novel relies upon a representational paradox where the sense of duration arises alongside the vanishing of temporal continuity.

The nineteenth century codified many modern attitudes toward aging, as the rationalization of the workforce, debates about the rights of women, and the expansion of empire defined new roles for the elderly while making previous roles obsolete. The development of the industrial economy occurred alongside rapidly changing expectations about the workforce. Writing on behalf of the Fabian Society, George Turner laments in his "Case for State Pensions in Old Age" that wages "of men from forty-five years upwards show a gradual and persistent decline. The roughest forms of labour are the first to suffer; but in skilled trades where deftness of handiwork is the first condition of efficiency and of continued employment, the attainment of fifty-five years of age is usually accompanied by a reduction of earnings" (3). For many women during the nineteenth century, domestic service offered employment for those who did not marry or became widows. Yet, as sociologist Jill Quadagno writes in *Aging in Early Industrial Society*, "there was considerable prejudice against hiring servants over the age of 45" (147). The modernization of the marketplace privileged a youthful workforce and excluded the aged from the narrative of progress that defined the early to mid-Victorian imagination. Obscured by the pervasiveness of youthful metaphors and plots, growing old was pushed to the margins of an era that defined itself through the productivity of industry and the virility of empire.

As senescence became increasingly marginalized, it was not overwritten by the Victorian era's most powerful plots – the *Bildungsroman* and the marriage plot. As I discuss in Chapters 2 and 3, these plots unfold by channeling the chaotic energies of youth into the normative containers of middle-class employment and domestic life. They often conclude with the maturity of the protagonist, suggesting a teleological arc that ends with adulthood. But we know that, if we are lucky, life goes on after middle age. This remainder of life – unstructured by the popular plots of the nineteenth century – serves as a site for formal experimentation and political contestation. In *The Coming of Age*, Simone de Beauvoir writes that being "relegated to the fringe of humanity means escaping from the obligations and the alienations that are its portion; most old people do not take advantage of this opportunity, but it is held out to a certain number and some do grasp it" (487). While old age often occupies a marginal place in modernity, it attains a special ability to critique it, providing a temporal vantage point that many novelists use to reflect upon a rapidly changing social and economic world.[2]

While the dominant plots of the nineteenth century followed an upward trajectory that often culminated in marriage and adulthood, many fin-de-siècle novels deployed plots that declined toward separation or death. These plots of decline, exemplified by Thomas Hardy's naturalist novels and H. G. Wells's dystopic science fiction, did not externalize old age as something "other" to the happy outcomes of the youthful plots of development. Instead, they internalized senescence, turning it into a way of understanding the individual's relationship to the entrapment of social contexts. Chapters 4 and 5 suggest that discourses such as the evolutionary biology of aging and degeneration theory fed into fears that England was becoming an elderly nation beset by youthful threats from outside.

The novel's formal omission of the duration of aging corresponds to an ideological exclusion of old age from Victorian literature and culture. This double exclusion – the exclusion of aging from the form of the novel and the exclusion of old age in Victorian literature and culture – does not merely reflect the bias of an ageist society. The very marginalization of age allowed novelists to use it as a figure for critical distance itself, providing a symbolic means of grappling with the naturalization of modern temporalities, including the accelerating pace of everyday life and the crystallization of significance into epiphanies. By doing so, the analysis of aging and old age draws out issues central to the emerging modernity of the nineteenth century that I consider below: the capitalist stratification of the lifespan into zones of more or less value, the threat of a parasitic, elderly demographic, and the emergence of a class of elderly men and women as a social problem.

Capitalist Stratification of the Lifespan

In "Time, Work-Discipline, and Industrial Capitalism," E. P. Thompson identifies a shift in the relation between time and work. Where pre-industrial labor was defined by "task-orientation" – or the completion of necessary jobs, such as milking cows – industrial capitalism placed more emphasis on the employee's time: "not the task but the value of time when reduced to money is dominant" (61). For Thompson, industrialization arose alongside the value of increasingly exact intervals of time and a workday that was parceled out into stages, a socioeconomic transition that was made possible through an array of temporal technologies: "the division of labour; the supervision of labour; fines; bells and clocks; money incentives; preachings and schoolings; the suppression of fairs and sports" (90). In this regimented temporal ecosystem, "all time must be consumed, marketed, put to *use*; it is offensive for the labour force merely to 'pass the time'" (90–1). As intervals of time became smaller and the measuring instruments more precise, wasted time became a threat to productivity. To minimize this newly empty time, employers adopted measures such as clocking in and managerial surveillance.

The changing relation between time and work in industrial societies greatly affected the sociocultural understanding of the human lifespan. The rationalization of the day into intervals of work, rest, and leisure exemplified the wider nineteenth-century trend toward identifying and valuing units of time. The human lifespan was no exception. The development of industrial capitalism occurred alongside a growing emphasis on chronological age in determining the competency of workers. Quadagno cites the following notice from the Barrow Steel Company, published in 1898:

> From this date forward please note that no men are to be engaged who are known to have any defects, such as the loss of a limb, defective sight or hearing. Further, no men to be engaged in any department who are older than fifty years of age. Any man already in the employ of the company in the excess of this age may be retained, but in case of their leaving they are not to be reengaged! (quoted in *Aging in Early Industrial Society*, 139)

By setting an age limit to employment, the manager of the company illustrates the increasing significance of chronological age across the capitalist economy. Quadagno goes on to describe how "employers in some industries refused to pay the aged wages equal to those of younger workers" (141). Elderly workers were often employed under "hour" work to complete odd jobs, thus preserving the higher pay scale for the younger employees. As the temporal discipline of the workday allows for the identification and elimination of wasted time, a corresponding discipline of the lifespan results in devaluing – both economically and culturally – the later years of a worker's life.

The capitalist stratification of the lifespan forms the subtext of many Victorian novels that represent the miseries of work and unemployment in late life and takes center stage in Anthony Trollope's *The Fixed Period*. In this novel, a former British colony called Britannula implements a law of compulsory euthanasia at the age of sixty-seven and a half (Trollope was sixty-seven and eight months old when he completed the novel). As the first doomed individual nears the time of commitment to the Necropolis – where he will live in peace for a year before being destroyed – the people of the island begin to have second thoughts. The victim appears in good health: "his hair was beautifully white, had fewer of the symptoms of age than any old man I had before known. He was tall, robust, and broad, and there was no beginning even of a stoop about him" (37). Before Crasweller meets his end by the hand of the state, the English arrive in a warship and force Britannula to revoke the law, taking the zealous President John Neverbend back to England.

Neverbend narrates *The Fixed Period* from his exile, spending a great deal of time defending the law. His apologia illustrates how assumptions about old age were linked to a conceptualization of the lifespan as marked off by zones of utility. He emphasizes "the costliness of that old age which is unable in any degree to supply its own wants" (4). Describing people over the age of sixty-seven as a relentless drain on the economy, Neverbend understands old age as a period of abject dependence on the productive work of the rest of society. His thinking takes a utopian turn, positing the elderly as the demographic Other that must be repressed to enable a flourishing polis: euthanizing the elderly "would keep us out of debt, make for us our railways, render all our rivers navigable, construct our bridges, and leave us shortly the richest people on God's earth! And this would be effected by a measure doing more good to the aged than to any other class of the community!" (8). In "Let the Reader Think of the Burden" Andrea Charise writes that in Trollope's novel the "aged body – in both its individual and its demographically conceived senses – becomes an avatar of literal and figurative cost" (10). In *The Fixed Period*, the elderly serve as the scapegoats for a lack of economic growth – a stagnant portion of society that impedes the youthful progress toward a new and better future.

As the title *The Fixed Period* suggests, the novel draws attention to the idea of fixedness and ossification – a trait often ascribed to the elderly, but here shown to apply to the statistical imaginary and bureaucratic machinery of the state. The modern state, Trollope implies, ascribes value to abstract units of time rather than the living experience of individuals past their mid sixties. The demographic imagination transposes delimited life stages onto the dynamism of human development. These categories do not reflect reality so much as create it; for example, once interred at the Necropolis, the once robust Crasweller ages quickly to reflect the expectations of decrepit old age. As labor becomes temporally rationalized into intervals, so too the lifespan becomes segmented into "periods": "in the interests both of the young and of those who do become old when obliged to linger on after their 'period' of work is over" (4). Trollope's novel underlines the close links between the modernization of the workforce and the utility of growing old by showing how the construction of static "periods" takes precedence over the complex duration that underlies them. As these periods allow for ever greater control over the workday and aging employees, duration recedes into economic and existential insignificance.

Construction of a Parasitic Elderly Demographic

The concept of a homogeneous elderly population arose alongside the modern push to classify and record information about the social body.[3]

Adolphe Quetelet's influential *A Treatise on Man and the Development of his Faculties* (1842), for example, draws together an unprecedented amount of data to craft generalizations about "average man" or the "normal state" against which the individual can be compared (99). The fact that some individuals have more or less vigor in old age requires comparison with an average. Quetelet's work appeared alongside the development of institutions such as the almshouse, state pensions, and social surveys that, as Stephen Katz writes in *Disciplining Old Age*, "converged in constructing the elderly population as a homogeneous group, characterized by supposedly uniform dependencies and liabilities" (49). In Katz's Foucauldian narrative of how modernity disciplines the elderly into a subject for power and knowledge, institutions construct the aged as a group with predictable characteristics. Yet the generalizations that support modernity's administrative and bureaucratic networks inspire a way of viewing age as strangely devoid of duration. Though the Old Age Pensions Act of 1908 assigned the age of seventy as the threshold for retirement, a temporally uncontainable aspect overspills the boundaries of who counts as old and who does not. The idea of constructing identity around a number – of attaching significant qualifications such as "retirement age" to sixty-five or seventy – conceals the continual process of aging, making chronological age a more reliable index to reality than the temporality of transformation upon which it is projected.

Reducing the elderly into a homogeneous population turns them into a demographic threat that some novelists represent in the form of monstrosity.[4] For Karen Chase, sexually "desiring old people are redrawn as fearsome creatures ... What are witches and vampires but old men and women who are starved for the life force of others, for whom 'youth' is the elixir of life, the semen which produces, or reproduces life in aged and decrepit individuals?" ("'Senile' Sexuality," 134). As Chase goes on to suggest, the vampire narrative "reflects the face of age imagined by those who worry that persistent and unsatisfied sexual energy would produce a monster that outlives his time by stealing libido from youths" (134). Elderly sexuality exists at the expense of youth, whose sexual choices have been narrowed by the "abnormal" appetite of the older generation. The language of Bram Stoker's *Dracula* registers the disgust of the Count's uncannily renewed youth:

> There lay the Count, but looking as if his youth had been half renewed, for the white hair and moustache were changed to dark iron-grey; the cheeks were fuller, and the white skin seemed ruby-red underneath; the mouth was redder than ever, for on the lips were gouts of fresh blood, which trickled

> from the corners of the mouth and ran over the chin and neck. Even the deep, burning eyes seemed set amongst swollen flesh, for the lids and pouches underneath were bloated. It seemed as if the whole awful creature were simply gorged with blood; he lay like a filthy leech, exhausted with his repletion. (53)

Later, when Harker first encounters Dracula in England, he sees the Count "observing the pretty girl" in the street (155). Chase's argument about elderly sexuality also applies to the economic world, as the battle for secure and well-paid employment pits older employees against their younger counterparts. Margaret Gullette observes that the elderly are "held responsible for an increasing portion of the national crises (fiscal deficits, high youth unemployment), serving as a scapegoat, a bogeyman, a mass of hysterical projections" (*Ending Ageism*, 5). The perceived monstrous appetite of older people pertains less to the reality of individual experience and more to a rising sense of demographic dread.

For Nicholas Daly, in *The Demographic Imagination and the Nineteenth-Century City*, the rise of a "demographic imagination" occurs alongside an increase in life-expectancy made possible by advancements in "medicine, sanitation, transport, and agricultural productivity" (1). He writes that across the nineteenth century "ageing and longevity become a recurring source of interest ... and, by the end of the century, in keeping with demographic trends, we begin to find longer fictional lives" (4). In *Demography and Degeneration*, Richard Soloway identifies a widespread anxiety regarding the declining birthrate in England, illustrating its connection to the emerging discourse of degeneration and weakening of the body politic. As demographic explanations become more persuasive, they also become more terrifying: "The proliferation of unofficial investigations by individuals and organizations in the new century indicated how quickly demographic considerations were becoming a focus of wider apprehensions about the changes already occurring in British society and the problems and challenges that lay ahead" (8). The rising number of elderly citizens formed the demographic corollary to the declining birthrate. The *Westminster Review*, for example, lamented England's tenuous global power at the beginning of the twentieth century by comparing the nation to an older individual: the country "has grown old, her national vitality is exhausted. She has arrived at the stage of senile decay."[5] The demographic trends of a declining birthrate and increasing elderly population translated to an image of a country declining into decrepit old age and sapped of its vitality.

Gender and the Age Question

The construction of aging is entangled with codes related to gender. As Susan Sontag points out, the double standard relating to gender becomes more entrenched in old age, as expectations about age-appropriate behavior diverge widely. For example, while older men often marry younger women without social consequences, an older woman marrying a younger man may lead to scandal. In *The January–May Marriage in Nineteenth-Century British Literature*, Esther Godfrey argues that the young bride is not always a victim and, in fact, can leverage age to "redistribute authority between husbands and wives" (5). She also acknowledges that "Older woman and younger man relationships do occur in nineteenth-century literature, although they are much less frequent and generally feature much smaller differences in age" (208). A great deal of critical attention has been paid to how gender affects younger characters in the nineteenth-century novel, particularly with respect to the *Bildungsroman* and marriage plot. Much less attention has been paid to the role of aging masculinity and femininity in the novel. Analyzing how the novel constructs and deconstructs spaces for older men and women draws out the temporal contingency of gender, which is not only a static construction – such as the coquette, the dandy, or the paterfamilias – but a performance that must be maintained or revised over time.

Older women formed a major topic of discussion during the nineteenth century. After the 1851 census that revealed a surplus of women in England, the spinster – already excluded from the hegemony of the procreative Victorian family – came to represent a drain on the economy. Through the hard life of his characters Alice and Virginia in *The Odd Women* (1893), George Gissing provides an image of the spinster aging beyond her society's meaningful narratives: "Their loneliness was for life, poor things. Already they were old; and they would grow older, sadder, perpetually struggling to supplement that dividend from the precious capital – and merely that they might keep alive" (38). Gissing's idea of spinsterhood suggests a suffocating constriction of personal and professional possibilities: contrary to the view of aging as the accumulation of experience, Gissing implies that for women the world grows smaller as they grow older. However, Rhoda – the New Woman of the novel – attempts to create opportunities outside the married woman–spinster dichotomy. As she devotes her life to educating women rather than seeking out a future husband, the normative values associated with age cease to apply: "Thirty-one or fifty-one is much the same for a woman who has made up her mind to live alone and work steadily for a definite object" (44). While *The Odd Women* goes on to illustrate the tenuousness of Rhoda's position in the face of hegemonic views of sexuality, Gissing demonstrates how the value ascribed to age relates directly to the way culture – and the conventions of the novel – determine the success or failure of a woman's life.

Gissing shows that the values associated with age shift with context. While Alice's and Virginia's bodies quickly deteriorate to reflect the identity of an old maid, Rhoda remains immune to this decline by pursuing interests outside the feminine milieu. Margaret Oliphant's *Hester* also challenges many of the beliefs about aging femininity, not by placing Catherine Vernon outside the dominant system, but by illustrating her success within it. In the plot of *Hester*, a woman saves a failing bank twice – the second time while she is retired and past sixty-five years old. The narrator carefully negotiates between what age has taken away and what it adds: "Sometimes it [old age] may mean the extreme of age, decrepitude and exhaustion: but sometimes also it means a softer and more composed middle age – a lovely autumnal season in which all the faculties retain their force without any of their harshness" (23–4). The logic of compensation also plays out in the narrator's description of Catherine's appearance: "Her face was not without lines, for that would be to say that it was without expression; nor did she look too young for her age: but her eye was not dim, nor her natural force abated. She had a finer colour than in her girlhood, though the red was not so smooth, but a little broken in her soft cheek. Her hair was white and beautiful, her figure ample, but graceful still" (25). In this novel, aging takes the form of credit and debit – a temporal balancing of accounts that reflects Catherine's fiscal acumen in the world of banking.

Oliphant acknowledges that the deck is stacked in favor of the young: "If the young but held out, even the most unwise and the most cruel, they must win in the end" (380). Yet the inevitability of youth's victory does not diminish the triumphs of old age. When Catherine stabilizes the bank, she does so as the youthful managers impotently scramble for answers: "It was not without a half contempt that she saw the overpowering of their young faculties by that which to her was nothing. There are so many things in which youth has the best of it, that age has a right to its dolorous triumph when that comes" (419). Doubly excluded from the masculine world of finance by her gender and age, Catherine nevertheless uses her senescent compensations – her experience and calmness – to redress a crisis that others find overwhelming. In this way, the novel stresses that Catherine succeeds not merely *in spite of* her double exclusion, but *because of* the insights offered by her position as an elderly woman.

Aging also affects nineteenth-century masculinity by entailing an emasculating dependence on others. Yet many authors find immense imaginative possibilities in the state of dependence. Near the end of George Eliot's historical novel *Romola*, for example, the elderly character Baldassarre blankly watches the Arno flow before him. Abandoned by his son Tito to languish in Turkish slavery, disavowed when freed from bondage, this once powerful scholar waits absentmindedly for a stray carrot so that he can feed himself. But when the unconscious body of his son floats before him, Baldassarre springs into action, rescuing Tito and placing his body on the bank of the river. As Tito's eyes quiver, Baldassarre delights in his son's recognition. For it is then that he "pressed his knuckles against the round throat [of Tito] and knelt upon the chest with all the force of his aged frame" (516). Though the Victorians often code old age negatively as decline, Baldassarre's combination of feebleness and ferocity suggests that aging masculinity occupies a more complex place in the Victorian imaginary than critics have yet acknowledged. For while Tito's youthful scheming absorbs much of the novel's attention, it is Baldassarre who ultimately has the upper hand.

The Temporal Limits of Age Studies

By placing aging at the center of a study of the Victorian novel, this book provides an account of duration that is historically specific and tethered to bodily affect. Yet *Aging, Duration, and the English Novel* also aims to reorient the field of age studies away from the implicit stasis of a term like "age" toward the temporal dynamism of what Chris Gilleard calls "aging studies."[6] I turn to Bergsonian duration to defamiliarize the process of aging that often takes on terrifying aspects – of obsolescence, excess, and dependence – in nineteenth-century modernity and the novels that represent it.

The systematization of the study of old age occurred at the beginning of the twentieth century, as Élie Metchnikoff and Ignatz Nascher developed the fields of gerontology and geriatrics, respectively. The emergence of these fields marked a turning point in the study of age, situating it as a subject worthy of scientific and medical analysis. I go on to discuss these two figures in the final chapter of my book, as they provide some retrospective insight into the study of age in the nineteenth century. While old age was not completely ignored by physicians in the nineteenth century, it did not inspire the same enthusiasm as work on adulthood or, increasingly, childhood. The relative absence of old age from the most stimulating medical developments of the nineteenth century both reflected and reinforced the cultural neglect of the elderly, who were objectified as a demographic problem that needed solving. This marginalization of old age had a powerful effect on the plots that were available to structure human development over time. It was as if a whole portion of the lifespan was missing, distorting the relationship between the aging body and time. As childhood became ever more important, from the works of Rousseau to Freud, time stopped at middle age – the dusky interval of old age was often ignored or relegated to the margins of the cultural field.

In his influential account of human development, *Identity and the Life Cycle*, Erik Erikson reorients Freudian analysis – usually so interested in the development of the child – toward the hinterlands of old age. He argues for a view of aging based on the "epigenetic principle": "this principle states that anything that grows has a *ground plan*, and that out of this ground plan the *parts* arise, each part having its *time* of special ascendancy, until all parts have arisen to form a *functioning whole*" (53). Erikson privileges the view that the human organism develops through a series of stages, with each stage defined by the predominance of a certain trait: "One might say that personality at the first stage crystallizes around the conviction 'I am what I am given,' and that of the second, 'I am what I will.' The third can be characterized by 'I am what I can imagine I will be.' We must now approach the fourth: 'I am what I learn'" (87). Drawing on Freudian models of childhood, Erikson suggests that each stage has a set of specific challenges that – if not confronted and mastered – will arise as symptoms later in the individual's life.

After the publication of *Identity and the Life Cycle* in 1959, Erikson and his wife Joan collaborated to write *The Cycle Completed* in 1982, claiming in it that "the role of old age needs to be reobserved, rethought" (64). As the authors mention several times, entering old age changed their perspective on the life cycle, a fact that the book reflects through its increased attention to the values associated with senescence. They also add a ninth stage of life – ranging, approximately, from one's eighties to nineties – that addresses the physical and psychological transformations that occur in the ninth decade of life. For this stage of life, the authors invert the normal predominance of syntonic affects over the dystonic ones. Unlike other stages of life where, for example, trust comes before mistrust, the ninth stage marks the only zone that defaults to the negative pole. Seemingly as a way of annexing positive attributes to aging, the authors deploy the term "gerotranscendence" as a way of describing a worldview dominated by wellbeing, "oneness," and lack of interest in material things (126).[7] While some gerontologists continue to work with the concept of gerotranscendence, the term implies a problematic withdrawal from the reality shared by the rest of adult society (126). Gerotranscendence exemplifies the problems of thinking of the life cycle in terms of stages, as old age achieves positive attributes only when conceptualized outside the zone of maturity and, by extension, the real.

According to Simon Biggs, Carroll Estes, and Chris Phillipson, the Eriksons' view of aging represents a modernist view of the lifespan, which emphasizes the stability of identity across time. In contrast, postmodern views emphasize an emancipatory fluidity of identity as one grows older: as the authors write, "we are faced with a surplus of commodities and images that defy coherent structure, thus forcing a continuous series of choices about identity and age."[8] Many postmodern accounts insist on age identity as a performance rather than a biological necessity, drawing out the tension that arises between the appearance of years on the body and the individual's subjective sense of age. Much recent work in the field of literary age studies historicizes aging as a way of deconstructing the biological essentialism of age stages and celebrating the multifarious performances of age. For example, Karen Chase's *The Victorians and Old Age*, Devoney Looser's *Women Writers and Old Age in Great Britain, 1750–1850*, Susannah Ottaway's *The Decline of Life*, and Teresa Mangum's "The Unnatural Youth of the Old 'New Woman'" demonstrate the cultural significance of the repressed narratives of the elderly. While these scholars historicize and denaturalize the lifespan, the temporality that accompanies aging does not usually receive the same critical treatment, and the duration of growing older remains an uncritical given of most analyses. As I explain at the end of Chapter 1, the category of "old age" provides a heuristic value in defining how the social value of the individual changes over time. My book does not attempt to nullify the concept of stages, and thus ignore their historical and cultural importance, but rather to invert the epistemological priority of age over aging.

The significance of this shift in method becomes clear when we analyze how other scholars address the relationship between aging and time.[9] In *Aged by Culture*, Margaret Gullette provides a forceful critique of identity as pre-existing or transcending duration: "Theorists rightly propose that we possess multiple selves. But so far that means only synchronic, simultaneous selves, bumping hips. These multiples look pretty static from the point of view of age studies. We can be multiple not just simultaneously but . . . *sequentially*" (126–7). While Gullette adds a temporal dimension to the formation of identity, her metaphors ultimately channel into the same view: simultaneous selves "bumping hips" do not differ in kind from identities arranged "sequentially." The first view privileges contiguity and the second causality; in both cases the connective tissue that links these selves across time falls out of the account. Helen Small also provides an important account of time in *The Long Life* by developing the implications of Derek Parfit's philosophy on old age. Small observes that a bias toward the near future informs many bad decisions about the welfare of our future self; for example, we may choose to smoke as a teenager without thinking about the consequences when we become fifty years old. For Small, "thinking more seriously about old age might operate as a check on" the "irrational bias toward the near" (153). Small's elaboration of Parfit's argument entails viewing one's future self as disconnected from one's present self, as a self that requires care to thrive. By parceling out the lifespan into different stages or "selves," however, we run into the problem of the duration that cuts across them. By emphasizing the stability of one's *age* rather than the becoming of one's *aging*, the reality of the transition slips between our fingers.

Aging, Duration, and the English Novel builds upon the work of these scholars by providing a theory of the duration of aging that resists the sedimentation of life into analytical categories: a project that Henri Bergson calls for in *Creative Evolution* when he writes, "We have only the imaginary stops 'child' and 'man,' and we are very near to saying that one of these stops *is* the other" (313). An account of aging's duration allows the critic to posit the continuity between youthful and elderly selves without falling into the reductive claim of age stages. Duration also provides a temporal ground for the postmodern view of aging, which emphasizes the performance of age identity. Though the postmodern view liberates the individual from an essential, biological age, these performances still result in a series of stops, whether an older person performs the cultural codes associated with youth or vice versa.[10] Critical attention must be directed away from the result of the performance and toward the interval of duration that links one to another – away from the completed spectacle of age and toward the slow, barely perceptible transformations that never cease working, from birth to death. As John Macnicol writes in *Neoliberalising Old Age*, "this consumption-rich postmodern old age only applies to an elite of wealth retirees – possibly only the top 5 per cent. Again, the notion that identities could be endlessly reinvented and that medical technologies could reshape the ageing body as part of this was far-fetched"

(10). Attending to duration enables a more nuanced account of aging that locates significance not only in the performance of age identity, but also in the temporal span that links each performance. This draws out the significance of aging for marginalized individuals, for whom growing older does not always culminate in the emancipatory production of new identities, but in a dreary repetition of familiar roles. Thus, the analysis of duration asserts the dignity of aging as lack of perceptible change, which critics often ignore in favor of more radical transformations, whether it takes the form of an invigorating, late-life romance or the transformations of dementia.

My use of the term duration derives from the work of Bergson, who argued throughout his oeuvre for the importance of distinguishing between time as a series of mathematical points (diachronicity) and time as true duration. True duration is synchronic, in the sense that it "forms both the past and the present states into an organic whole" (*Time and Free Will*, 100).[11] In order to represent duration as "succession without distinction," Bergson draws on a lexicon of change and becoming: he asks us to imagine the "notes of a tune, melting . . . into one another" and a "mutual penetration, an interconnexion and organization of elements" (*Time and Free Will*, 101, 100). Later, he compares it to the unrolling of a spool, a spectrum of feeling, and an infinitely small piece of elastic (*Creative Mind*, 137). Yet duration's unboundedness and synchronic intensity often becomes fixed into the lockstep of diachronic measurability. The fact that the term diachronic serves as a synonym for duration underlines the success of the conversion: "We instinctively tend to solidify our impressions in order to express them in language" (*Time and Free Will*, 130). To recover duration requires an act of *intuition* in which one submerges into the heterogeneous, continuous flux of becoming – an immediate relation to passing time that is categorically different from *understanding*. We understand time by spatializing it – by delimiting duration into an interval of determinate length. We intuit time by installing ourselves within it, feeling it pass. Not surprisingly, it is easier to communicate our understanding of time rather than our intuition of it.

Moments of critical age awareness – a term I use to refer not merely to the realization that one is old but that one is aging – constitute acts of Bergsonian intuition through which we install ourselves into the duration of our lives. An intuitive awareness of one's aging does not accord with the static, retrospective accumulation of one's life represented by chronological age. Rather, it takes on a stereoscopic consciousness of time passing, a temporal thickness and elasticity, a superadded awareness of one's bodily transformation through time. In its representation of characters who endure through time, the novel form encourages readers to immerse themselves in complex narratives that extend over long intervals of time. Yet in approximating duration in this way, the novel also reveals something of its temporal lack. This missing element, when length stands in for duration, plays a significant role in defining the modern experience of aging as rationalized, stage-based, and shocking: an experience that occurs, like the past tense of realist narrative, to a remote, earlier version of one's current self.

Chapter Summaries

This book begins with a theoretical account of aging as a way of staging the historical narrative charted in subsequent chapters. The first part of this narrative analyzes the early to mid-Victorian era, from the New Poor Law in 1834 to the 1860s, to draw out a tension between the push toward reform and the older individuals left out of the narrative of improvement. The optimism of these years was made possible, in part, by excluding old age from the plots novelists used to represent it. The second part turns to the growing pessimism at the end of the Victorian era, which arises not from marginalizing old age, but from using it as a figure for an exhausted century. While this has the effect of making old age central to fin-de-siècle narratives, senescence also gains new, negative connotations: traits such as vampirism, exhaustion, and dependence become more culturally visible as they take on narrative importance. The third part identifies another shift for old age in the beginning of the twentieth century. Where old age had been excluded from the major plots of the early Victorian era and internalized by the plots at the end of the century, modernism turned to old age as a figure for the lack of plot. In the shadow of the war, the tacit assumption that one would live to be old could no longer be taken for granted.

Chapter 1, "Aging Theory," theorizes the relationship between narrative, time, and aging. The first section draws on the idea of surface reading to argue for renewed attention to the effects of aging. By drawing aging to the surface of the body and its representation in the novel, my approach resists the modern tendency of repressing the duration of aging. The second section draws together the diachronic analyses of narrative theory with the metaphysics of Henri Bergson and Gilles Deleuze, contending that the reader's temporal encounter with the materiality of a text's discourse serves as a tacit reminder of the reader's own aging, and narrative temporality reflects to the reader the very duration that falls out of his or her experience of aging. The final section suggests that the novel's realism naturalizes a crisis model of character development by positing life-changing events as a part of "everyday" reality. As realism relies upon a model of change where duration surprisingly disappears, it diminishes the role of aging in the development of subjectivity over time.

Chapters 2 and 3 analyze the marginalization of old age in key mid-Victorian plots, such as the *Bildungsroman* and the marriage plot. "No Plots for Old Men" argues that old men and aging raised a problem for Charles Dickens's literary project: the novel's difficulty of representing temporal continuity over long spans of time. For the old man, the meaningful plots of the nineteenth century – such as the *Bildungsroman* or the marriage plot – are behind him. An object of little narrative interest from the perspective of these plots, the old man is continually activated in Dickens's novels, setting up a competition between the natural death he staves off and the closure of the narrative in which he is enmeshed. By examining three of Dickens's early novels – *The Old Curiosity Shop*, *Martin Chuzzlewit*, and *A Christmas Carol* – I show how old men are excluded from the youthful plot of development central to the bewildering progress of a modernizing society. No longer the subject of the plot and yet bound by the pressures of ambition, the elderly male engages in a narrative compulsion that underlines the tremendous imaginative power of what has been left behind by both the realist novel and the modernity it represents. In this way, the old man serves as the site through which Dickens addresses an impasse of the novel form, where its duration is marked by its inability to faithfully represent the texture of passing time.

Chapter 3, "Life After the Marriage Plot," examines how the women of Elizabeth Gaskell's *Cranford* preserve a temporal zone from the dual threat of patriarchy and modernization. The late-life romance between Miss Matty and Mr. Holbrook – a marriage plot without the possibility of marriage – generates narrative interest because it follows a set of temporal rules that originate from within Cranford rather than conforming to conventions about age and romantic love from outside the community. The superannuation of persons relates to a similar crisis in the marriage plot, which no longer reflects the experience of the older characters it purports to organize. Thus, I read *Cranford*'s representation of other forms of media – such as storytelling, the newspaper, and the letter – as a reflection on the formal obsolescence that takes place within the larger narrative economy of the novel. What emerges is a reconceptualization of the utility of what is "old," insofar as the women of Cranford reterritorialize the obsolete as a particularly feminine challenge to the temporality of modernity. For Dickens and Gaskell, the aged body challenges and revises the narratives of modernity that privilege capitalist accumulation.

Where the previous two chapters critique the triumphant plots of high Victorian optimism, Chapters 4 and 5 focus on old age in the context of fin-de-siècle pessimism. In Chapter 4, on Thomas Hardy's *The Well-Beloved*, "A Wrinkle in Time," I argue that the sexual escapades of an aging artist subvert the naturalist plot of decline. Instead of modeling the human lifespan on a parabola that begins with youthful possibility, reaches its apex in adulthood, and declines into senescence and death, *The Well-Beloved* demonstrates the opening of queer, non-normative desire as one ages. This chapter examines the discourses of evolutionary biology and geology as providing the late nineteenth century with non-linear models for the human lifespan. These scientific models, I argue, have a narrative counterpart in the counterfactual, or the imagination of what might have occurred in the past but did not. The use of counterfactual thinking in narrative enables Hardy to construct an ambivalent attitude toward the aging of his protagonist, who inverts the horizon of possibility away from the future toward a past that he struggles to remake.

My next chapter, "The Technology Age," focuses on H. G. Wells's scientific romances. The volatile modernity that Wells represents pivots on a failure of sympathy between the young and the old, generating the deeply ambivalent conditions by which generational antagonism arises alongside modernity's technological and social progress. Drawing on the work of Charles Booth and tracts by the Fabian society, I illustrate how socialist arguments for a universal pension depend upon youths imagining the older person they one day will become. Analyzing works such as *The Time Machine*, *War of the Worlds*, *Food of the Gods*, and *In the Days of the Comet*, this chapter highlights the multi-temporality of the banal process of aging. In this regard, science fiction provides insight into the reality of aging in a way that conventional literary realism cannot.

Chapter 6, "Gray Modernism," argues that modernist experimentation with narrative form draws theoretical and disciplinary inspiration from the invention of gerontology and geriatrics as a science. During the twentieth century, aging becomes the subject of clinical interest, a temporal pathology detachable from the body it affects. Similarly, for modernist novels like Virginia Woolf's *Orlando*, duration becomes separable from the highly charged aesthetic moments it contains. Though Orlando lives through many centuries, she does not grow old; instead, her greatest transformation occurs when her gender instantaneously switches from male to female. The novel creates a divide between the systems of duration and aging on the one hand, and the momentariness and constructedness of identity on the other. By breaking with the conventions that link duration and objective, shared time, Woolf situates aging in an ironic temporality that disrupts the forward press of years.

Aging, Duration, and the English Novel concludes by comparing the affordances of cinema and the novel as they relate to the representation of aging. Emerging near the end of this study's historical focus, cinema offered new formal possibilities for capturing the process of growing old. Returning to the question of duration through a discussion of Woolf's, Bergson's, and Deleuze's writing on cinema, this section teases out the formal arguments about narrative explored in the previous chapters. In fact, the comparison between cinematic and textual narrative underlines this book's thesis: that the affordances of form structure historically specific possibilities – affective, social, and political – for older people. The afterword also affirms an expanded version of this thesis by arguing that age – as a biocultural process – serves as a form with its own ability to organize human life and read texts. For the novels analyzed in this book, the mutually reinforcing hermeneutic between the representation of age and aging's inescapable embodiment of time serves as a fulcrum point for the politics of access: of who counts as a human being deserving of care and who does not.

CHAPTER 1

Aging Theory

The Surface of Aging

While characters of different ages appear in most novels, the process of aging rarely rises to the level of representation. It is a convention for the realist novel to use events such as illness or trauma to speed up the aging of its characters. In George Eliot's *Scenes of Clerical Life* (1857), the childless Sir Christopher plans to settle his property on his nephew, the handsome Captain Wybrow. Yet Wybrow dies abruptly from a heart condition, dashing Sir Christopher's hopes for the future. Grief ages him overnight:

> It was the first time Mr. Gilfil had had an interview with him [Sir Christopher] this morning, and he was struck to see how a single day and night of grief had aged the fine old man. The lines in his brow and about his mouth were deepened; his complexion looked dull and withered; there was a swollen ridge under his eyes; and the eyes themselves, which used to cast so keen a glance on the present, had the vacant expression which tells that vision is no longer a sense, but a memory. (150)

Occurring just after the traumatic event of Wybrow's death, Sir Christopher's aging takes a mere twenty-four hours to write itself onto his body, shocking the chaplain with the sudden intensification of the signs of old age: lines deepen, the complexion dulls, eyes swell. Such bodily transformations are coupled with the character's modified relation to temporality: his "keen . . . glance on the present" gives way to a "vacant expression" that signifies his absorption in memory and the past. The present loses meaning for the aged Sir Christopher, which corresponds to the way that the narrative compresses the duration of his aging into the brief interval of a single day.

Aging has happened, but rarely happens. Oscar Wilde's *The Picture of Dorian Gray* (1890) exemplifies this aspect of the narrative representation of aging. Throughout the novel Dorian's age (and his vices) do not appear on his body but on his portrait, painted by his admirer Basil Hallward. Dorian passes most of his life without the usual wrinkles and gray hairs associated with growing older, retaining his youthful appearance and beauty. Yet he is miserable. After years of debauchery, Dorian destroys the painting that absorbs the depredations of time and sin. But rather than setting him free from the past, this action causes the repressed years to flood back in an instant: "When they entered, they found hanging upon the wall a splendid portrait of their master as they had last seen him, in all the wonder of his exquisite youth and beauty. Lying on the floor was a dead man, in evening dress, with a knife in his heart. He was withered, wrinkled, and loathsome of visage. It was not till they had examined the rings that they recognized who it was" (177). Dorian's transformation occurs with the cutting swiftness of the knife's blade, cleaving his youthful persona and his elderly one in a moment. The sudden onset of age makes him unrecognizable to the servants who saw him daily.

Though most novels do not represent aging with the fantastic swiftness of *The Picture of Dorian Gray*, Wilde's example illuminates the conventional ways Victorians represented characters growing older. In George Gissing's *The Odd Women* (1893), a novel intensely concerned with how age impacts societal expectations, the middle-aged Edmund Widdowson suffers with jealousy regarding his young wife. As a result of the strain, in "the three of four months since his marriage, he seemed to have grown older; he no longer held himself so upright" (168). Another example occurs near the end of the novel after about two years of marriage: "when out of doors [he] seldom raised his eyes from the ground; grey streaks had begun to brindle his hair; his face grew yellower and more deeply furrowed" (362). Though Widdowson does not age with the same fatal instantaneity as Dorian, the effect produced by the prose is the same. As Widdowson's unhappy marriage accelerates his aging, Gissing contracts the duration of aging into moments of retrospective description.

Thus, the present tense of aging continually slips into the past, as something to be excavated and kept at a critical distance rather than experienced immediately. The realist novel's default third-person, retrospective narration slots the aging of its characters into the recovered past, able to show the effects of aging only after it has already occurred. The extended length of novels makes them especially adept at repressing the duration of aging. In Charles Dickens's *Great Expectations* (1861), for example, the final chapter skips ahead eleven years and registers the bodily changes that occur to Pip's father-in-law Joe, who is now "a little grey," and his beloved Estella, who has lost "the freshness of her beauty"

(*Great*, 482–3). The aging of the characters, which forms the most important plot development at this final stage of the narrative, retreats quietly between the chapters. Reflecting on the novel form provokes the bewildered question that arises at moments of critical age awareness: where did the time go?

The attempt to represent aging as a process is rare, and often extraordinary when the author attempts it. In Robert Louis Stevenson's *The Strange Case of Dr. Jekyll and Mr. Hyde* (1886), the process of aging becomes monstrous. Jekyll's potion enables him to indulge in his repressed desires by giving him another body, allowing Hyde to debauch himself without affecting Jekyll's reputation. One of the central transformations between the two characters relates to age: while Jekyll is "a smooth-faced man of fifty," Hyde appears as a "comparative youth" with "light step, leaping impulses and secret pleasures" (12, 49). Hyde is not a monster, but merely a man without social accountability – a trait that Stevenson emphasizes by suturing antisocial behavior with the unboundedness of youth: "I felt younger, lighter, happier in body; within I was conscious of a heady recklessness . . . a solution of the bonds of obligation, an unknown but not an innocent freedom of the soul" (44). Hyde quickly fills the blank slate of youth with a bloody act of murder.

The reader eventually witnesses the transformation of Hyde into Jekyll through Dr. Lanyon's posthumous testimony. Observing Hyde quaff the mixture, Lanyon writes: "as I looked there came, I thought, a change – he seemed to swell – his face became suddenly black and the features seemed to melt and alter – and the next moment, I had sprung to my feet and leaped back against the wall, my arm raised to shield me from that prodigy, my mind submerged in terror" (41). While Lanyon's language adopts an appropriately ominous tone for the dreadful transformation, this scene can also be read as a simple commentary on the process of growing older. The swelling and darkening features mark the passing of time accelerated to the point where its effects become visible in the present moment. The horror that such transformation causes in the observer arises not from splitting one man into two, but from drawing to the surface of the body the latent metamorphoses of aging itself.

H. Rider Haggard's *She* (1886) also concludes with a spectacular scene of accelerated aging when Ayesha leads the two male protagonists to a flame that grants eternal life. When Ayesha enters the flame for a second time it reverses her immortality: "she *was* shrivelling up . . . smaller and smaller she grew; her skin changed colour, and in place of the perfect whiteness of its lustre it turned dirty brown and yellow, like an old piece of withered parchment . . . the skin was puckered into a million wrinkles, and on the shapeless face was the stamp of unutterable age" (257). Observing the rapid aging of Ayesha occur before his eyes, the narrator exclaims that "nobody ever saw anything like the frightful age that was graven on that fearful countenance . . . and let all men pray they never may, if they wish to keep their reason" (257). Together, the examples from Stevenson and Haggard illustrate the horror of making age a visible process. Moreover, the narrator of *She* warns that registering the duration of aging goes against reason, a claim that receives added support from the fact that both Stevenson and Haggard turn away from realism to more fantastic modes of representation (though, as I will discuss in Chapter 4, Thomas Hardy also experiments with ways to represent a wrinkle in the process of development). Whether aging is elided or made terrible, Victorian novels continually attest to the imaginative difficulty of representing someone growing old.

Aging challenges the temporal limits of representation. In *Dreaming by the Book* Elaine Scarry asks, "How do writers get us to move pictures in our minds?" (76). This question proves difficult to answer, since it is in the nature of movement to continually shift ground. Her book takes an unconventional approach by relying on thought experiments that enlist the reader's imagination for support. She asks the reader to imagine a bird in flight and experiment by imaginatively placing filters over the event, such as gauze, which enable the reader to better picture the movement (76). However, movements such as aging occur "slower than perceptible motion" (172). In this case, Scarry argues that many authors bring growing older "within the radius of our compositional powers" by combining the development of the human body with the blossoming, wilting, and budding of the vegetable world (173). The imagination of movement always involves the imagination of something else, whether through the act of layering a film over the movement or imbricating one process with another.

Scarry's argument helps to clarify how narratives represent aging. While it is easy to imagine a human who is young or old, it is much more difficult to imagine a person in the *process* of aging. If one imagines an adolescent aging into adulthood and on to old age, she will find it difficult to image this process as a seamless, continuous movement. Rather, the body that she imagines will probably go through a series of stages that progress in a linear manner. Each image settles into progressively more aged glimpses of the individual, approximating the movement of a flipbook animation rather than the "melt[ing] and alter[ing]" we observed earlier in the case of Hyde's transformation. The temporal continuity of an individual life resists representation, and aging is usually registered narratively as a past event recounted in the present. From these examples, we observe a tendency in narrative to skip over the duration of aging, a tendency that is reinforced by the form's difficulty representing it. The discourse of age gravitates toward completed states. Thus, in a surprising reversal, one of the most intimately continuous experiences of human life – our aging – is continually translated through discourse into a sequence of snapshots.

Recent attempts at addressing duration, by critics such as Nicholas Dames and Amit Yahav, look to music – in the form of rhythm, repetition, and bodily feeling – to reconstruct how the novel "absorbs characters and readers into shared durations."[1] In their respective studies, Dames and Yahav argue that duration is a deep structure of narrative that is communicated through the reader's passive absorption of sentence level units. Sue Zemka writes in *Time and the Moment in Victorian Literature and Society* that duration "goes underground, and finds a home in the novelistic unconscious, that is to say, in reading time itself" (218). But the examples of aging I am interested in do not occur at a deep, structural level but on the surface of representation. When a novelist wants the reader to see a character age, she wants the description to move. The critical move of extracting a hidden duration from the depths of experience reinstates the remoteness of duration – the suspicion that duration merely allows experience to be temporally quantifiable in the way that a metronome beats out time in the background of a musical piece. To analyze duration as temporal depth addresses only one of its dimensions and has the unfortunate consequence of rendering duration's surface effects – the simple appearance of change, transformation, and movement – into an epiphenomenon of a more real and yet inaccessible structure.

As Stephen Best and Sharon Marcus write in "Surface Reading," the introduction to their 2009 special issue of *Representations*, surface reading provides a methodological alternative to approaches that assume "the most interesting aspect of a text is what it represses" (3). Best and Marcus "take surface to mean what is evident, perceptible, apprehensible in texts; what is neither hidden nor hiding . . . A surface is what insists on being looked *at* rather than what we must train ourselves to see *through*" (9). For these authors, the dichotomy of surface and depth is replaced by a monism of surface, so that "underneath surface there is only more surface" and that "depth is continuous with surface and is thus an effect of immanence" (8–9, 11). Symptomatic reading and the hermeneutics of suspicion translate the surface of the text into a deceptive, ideological layer that the critic must heroically overcome to reach "the truth that the text conceals" (17).

In her article "Close but not Deep: Literary Ethics and the Descriptive Turn," Heather Love attempts to avoid literary criticism's latent humanism by grounding her reading in the practices of description inspired by sociology. "Good descriptions," Love writes, "are in a sense rich, but not because they truck with imponderables like human experience or human nature. They are close, but they are not deep; rather than adding anything 'extra' to the description, they account for the real variety that is already there" (377). Depth is not only something that critics reveal, but something that they produce "by attributing life, richness, warmth, and voice to texts" and thus reproducing an "unacknowledged but powerful humanism" (388).

In reacting against the ideology critique that has become synonymous with literary criticism, Best, Marcus, and Love take the argument a step too far. Reclaiming the surface as a site worthy of close attention does not necessitate the additional move of eliminating depths. In *The Limits of Critique*, Rita Felski takes a skeptical view of surfaces, questioning whether "the metaphor of the surface is the best way of capturing the merits of the new directions they canvass. After all, the oscillation between surface and depth is a very familiar theme within aesthetics, a matter of complementary rather than mutually exclusive approaches" (55). The removal of depths, moreover, involves relinquishing one of the most powerful tools of literary criticism – the distance that enables criticism itself. Positing the distinction between surfaces and depths does not require giving up on surfaces altogether. Though the surface has long been associated with the superficiality of the commodity and the culture of instant gratification, some philosophers provide ways of complicating the surface–depth binary. Bergson's philosophical method of intuition, which I discuss in the introduction as how one "installs" oneself into duration, serves as a particularly powerful way of theorizing surfaces and depths together. He writes that

> the forces which work in all things we feel within ourselves; whatever may be the inner essence of what is done, we are of that essence. Let us then go down into our own inner selves: *the deeper the point we touch, the stronger will be the thrust which sends us back to the surface.* Philosophical intuition is the contact, philosophy is this impetus. Brought back to the surface by an impulsion from the depth, we shall regain contact with science as our thought opens out and disperses. (*Creative Mind*, 103; emphasis added)

Here, Bergson defines the gap between subject and object through the way analysis proceeds from depths to surfaces. The deeply introspective movement of intuition does not merely result in hidden knowledge of one's self, but redirects the philosopher back to the surface of things. As Elizabeth Grosz writes in "Bergson, Deleuze and the Becoming of Unbecoming," "If one reaches deeply enough, one finds a continuity with the surface, one rebounds directly to things in their immediacy" (8). For Bergson, the goal is not to arrive at knowledge of either surfaces *or* depths, but to find significance in the fluid relationship between the two terms, figured here as a kind of elasticity that causes the individual to swing from depth to surface with a force equal to the intensity of the original intuitive impulse.[2]

Inspired by Bergson and the Stoics, Gilles Deleuze makes a theory of surfaces integral to understanding the relationship between the body, time, and sense. In *The Logic of Sense*, by inverting Plato's association of the body with surfaces and ideas with depths, Deleuze reconfigures the surface as the site where sense is produced. At the "incorporeal limit" of the surface, however, sense does not arise merely from bodily causes but as a "surface effect," in the double sense of causation and difference (in the way an optical effect produces a secondary impression distinct from the elements that form it) (7). He writes that "sense, *the expressed of the proposition*, is an incorporeal, complex, and irreducible entity, at the surface of things, a pure event which inheres or subsists in the proposition" (19). To show how sense emerges from the surface, Deleuze references the way authors represent a battle:

> they "see" the battle and make their heroes "see" it. But it is above all because the battle *hovers over* its own field, being neutral in relation to all of its temporal actualizations, neutral and impassive in relation to the victor and the vanquished, the coward and the brave; because of this, it is all the more terrible. Never present but always yet to come and already passed, the battle is graspable only by the will of anonymity which it itself inspires. (100)

The sense of the battle does not coincide with its representation but "*hovers over*" it. The temporality of narrative representation prevents the final arrival of sense, which remains in the liminal time of the "never present but always yet to come and already passed." The congealing of sense, its fluidity and expansiveness, arises at the soft membrane between the body's depths and the bewildering infinity beyond the surface: "Sense appears and is played out at the surface ... in such a way that it forms letters of dust" (133). As in Deleuze's description of the battle, the representation of aging leaves behind something of its becoming as it slides into the past tense of narrative. Yet the sense of aging "*hovers over*" the description. While a focus on reading into the aging of characters makes aging about something deeper – for example, the sudden appearance of gray hair referring to a character's marital unhappiness – the surface of aging conjures the inarticulate feeling that characters grow older.

Across the Victorian novel, the duration of aging is either represented as a completed process or, when the author abandons realism, accelerated through fantastic means. Paying renewed attention to the surface of aging rather than the depths – to locate the duration of aging with the description rather than structural elements that invisibly constitute it – demonstrates that aging is not a process that occurs behind the scenes, but right in front of us, on us, and in us. While this process is an integral part of life, many would rather not acknowledge it. The modern turn away from aging – to ignore or forget it – culminates in moments of shock, where one suddenly realizes the significance of passing years in a flash. The sudden onset of age (which is, in fact, not sudden at all) arises alongside the novel's emphasis on moments of insight or epiphany. Despite the novel's celebration of the everyday, it channels the reader's attention to crises and revelation, a naturalization of Walter Pater's advice in *Studies in the History of the Renaissance* to "burn always with this hard gem-like flame, to maintain this ecstasy" (120). While the novel might seem too prosaic for Pater's momentary aesthetics, the form's paradoxically eventful everyday inspires a major change in the reader's relation to his or her quotidian reality. The duration of aging slides deeper and deeper from the surface of representation, a reality of one's existence that must be excavated for it to appear at all.

Duration and the Discourse of Aging

While the duration of aging fades into the background of realist narrative, the reader still *feels* that characters grow older. In most novels, the characters develop by gaining knowledge through their experiences, and it takes time for these experiences to register a substantial transformation in the character's personality or worldview. Yet this model remains tethered to the assumption that what matters most are deep, tectonic shifts in character. The surface level transformations of processes such as aging remain a superficial background against which these deeper changes occur. Drawing on narrative theory to analyze George Eliot's *The Lifted Veil* (1859), I argue that the materiality of discourse – the number, length, and arrangement of printed words on a page – serves as a surface that reflects the reader's duration back to them. While literary criticism often treats the time of reading as an empty byproduct of making sense of a narrative,

I suggest that this duration plays a crucial role in the reading process by entangling the affects of narrative temporality with the aging body of the reader.

In *Narrative Discourse*, Gérard Genette identifies the difficulty of representing the continuity of duration as a "paradox" of subsequent narration: "it possesses at the same time a temporal situation (with respect to the past story) and an atemporal essence (since it has no duration proper)" (223). According to Genette, the duration of narrative is an effect produced by the asymmetry between story and discourse, or the time that passes within the narrative and the time it takes to read. Where the story refers to the content of the narrative, the discourse refers to the formal, linguistic units that compose it. Narrative duration accelerates or slows down according to the variations in rhythm: a narrative can skip ahead twenty years in the span of one line or dilate an instant over the course of thirty pages of description. Thus, when Genette refers to duration he does not mean a unified temporality, but a fractured one that arises at the intersection of story and discourse.

Yet the problem of measurement remains. If narrative temporality arises by juxtaposing story and discourse, there must be some standard that enables the reader to extract a meaningful duration from this relation. For Genette, the reader imports this measurement from his or her lived experience of time, specifically the time of reading itself: "The narrative text," he writes, "has no other temporality than what it borrows, metonymically, from its own reading" (34). The collision of real and fictional temporalities produces what he calls pseudo-time: one hour passing in the story has meaning because it takes a longer or shorter amount of real time to read. During the process of reading, the narrative's duration takes on existential shape through its relation to the duration of reading itself. It is as if the duration of the text becomes clearer as the reader's own time is obscured by the engrossing act of reading. Rooted in the act of reading, the ability to measure discourse confers temporal legibility on the story.

The entanglement of human time and narrative forms a central question for Paul Ricoeur, who writes in *Time and Narrative* that "time becomes human time to the extent that it is organized after the manner of narrative; narrative, in turn, is meaningful to the extent that it portrays the features of temporal experience" (3). For Ricoeur, the reciprocal relation between narrative and human life plays out through a dynamic process of emplotment (as opposed to the fixed structure of plot). Emplotment, or what he calls "mimesis$_2$," is the "configuring operation" that mediates between "mimesis$_1$" and "mimesis$_3$" (53). While mimesis$_1$ constitutes the prefigured time or social givens before the text, and mimesis$_3$ constitutes the refigured time of the reader after the text, emplotment is the text itself that both shapes and is shaped by the temporal situation that precedes and follows it. Like Genette, Ricoeur asserts that narrative becomes temporally intelligible through the "joint work of the text and reader"; however, Ricoeur places less emphasis on the structural arrangement of linguistic units and more on plot's intervention between the reader and time. Through its ability to draw "a configuration out of a simple succession," Ricoeur claims that emplotment explains how a series of events (x_1, x_2, x_3. . .) coalesces into the unified whole of the text.[3] However, the teleological movement of emplotment from mimesis$_1$ to mimesis$_3$ posits duration as a mere temporal mediator between these representational stages. Placing duration at the center of a theory of emplotment – as interpenetrating rather than linking the different levels of mimesis – causes Ricoeur's model to lose some of its structural lucidity, but greatly enriches his account of the reciprocal feedback between human temporality and narrative.

In order to theorize how duration cuts across the three levels of mimesis – the time of the world, the time of the text, and the time of the reader – I turn to Bergsonian metaphysics, which inverts the ontological privilege of stasis and position by prioritizing movement, process, and becoming.[4] This turn enables an account of narrative and time that departs from the diachronic sequencing of stages toward a synchronic model of expansion and contraction.[5] One of Bergson's most powerful examples of duration takes human aging as its subject. In *Creative Evolution*, Bergson writes that growing older does not progress in a series of stages – from an infant, to child, to adolescent, to adult and so on – but arises from "an unbroken continuity between the evolution of the embryo and the complete organism" (18). He examines climacterics like puberty and menopause not as crises that mark the beginning of a new stage, but rather as changes that are "in course of preparation at every instant from birth, and even before birth, and that the aging up to that crisis consists, in part at least, of this gradual preparation. In short, what is properly vital in growing old is the insensible, infinitely graduated, continuance of the change of form" (19). The duration of the human life is not marked by ruptures, whether biological (puberty) or cultural (sixty-five marking retirement age), but shot through in its entirety with past and future qualities. A forty-five-year-old man is just as much the man he was at thirty and the child he was at five. Moreover, he is also just as much the man he will be at fifty-five as the man who will eventually die. As Deleuze puts it in *Bergsonism*, "Bergsonian duration is, in the final analysis, defined less by succession than by coexistence" (60). While singling out a specific life stage can be useful for analysis (for example, in making medical generalizations for a certain age group), the duration of life escapes when it is parceled out diachronically.

If duration is not *useful*, why does Bergson labor so hard to understand it? According to Bergson in *Creative Evolution*, creativity arises along the temporal axis of duration. When we assert that a child becomes a man, we place two stable forms in a sequence, but we do not draw out the duration between them. In this case, "we can no longer conceive how evolution is possible, for rests placed beside rests will never be equivalent to a movement" (312). Terms like infancy, adolescence, and middle age emerge when someone projects these positions "along the continuity of progress" (312). The problem arises when these imaginary positions take on an ontological priority over the transformation they rest upon. Bergson inverts the common assumption that stability and positionality are more real than fluidity and transformation:

> life is an evolution. We concentrate a period of this evolution in a stable view which we call a form, and, when the change has become considerable enough to overcome the fortunate inertia of our perception, we say that the body has changed its form. But in reality the body is changing form at every moment; or rather, there is no form, since form is immobile and the reality is movement. What is real is the continual *change of* form: *form is only a snapshot view of a transition*. Therefore, here again, our perception manages to solidify into discontinuous images the fluid continuity of the real. (302)

The human sensorium does not register the changes that occur to the body in real time. Nevertheless, such constantly occurring changes culminate in perceptual thresholds that mark a "change." The recognition of a difference obscures the duration that incites it, cultivating a view that posits reality in "discontinuous images" rather than "fluid continuity" (302). Privileging position over change has the consequence of constructing a view of the human lifespan as one delimited by age-appropriate actions. When narrative elides the duration of aging it participates in this larger philosophical and cultural thrust to contain passing time in static models.

Bergson's turn toward a metaphysics of becoming implies a great deal of skepticism toward representation. In *Creative Evolution* he writes that "The most living thought becomes frigid in the formula that expresses it. The word turns against the idea" (127). Deleuze's development of Bergson's ideas follows suit. In *Difference and Repetition*, by emphasizing the passivity involved in the experience of duration – or what he calls the "living present" – Deleuze claims that an immediate experience of passing time is "sub-representative" (72, 84). Representation "fails to capture the affirmed world of difference" because the "prefix RE- in the word representation signifies this conceptual form of the identical which subordinates differences" (55, 56). When it comes to duration, for example, an infinite number of representations will not accurately reproduce the immediacy of duration itself – the representations will be "distorted, diverted and torn from its centre" (56). The movement that Bergson and Deleuze place at the center of their philosophy cultivates a view of representation that falls perpetually short of its task.

If representation fails to align temporally with the represented – if the representation of aging, for example, fails to capture the duration that defines it as a process – why does the reader still *feel* that characters grow older? To answer this question, I turn to George Eliot's *The Lifted Veil*, a novella intensely interested in the relationship between affect, knowledge, and time. In this first-person narrative, the narrator Latimer develops the ability to see into the future and read the thoughts of other people. Despite his wealth and abilities, he finds no joy in life. As he approaches his prophesied death, he bitterly reflects on his wasted life: a childhood without fatherly love, the death of his brother, and a failed marriage. Latimer's omniscience, as Charles Swann observes, reflects that of the third-person realist narrator in so many nineteenth-century novels.[6] In this narrative about narrative, Eliot infuses the duration of the telling with the anguished revelation of her protagonist – where each word not only signifies linguistically, but also cumulatively, as a graphic utterance of pain.

After Latimer recovers from a severe illness, he hears his father utter the word "Prague" and immediately experiences a vivid presentiment of the city he had never visited. He believes this might be the beginning of a poetic sensibility, but quickly learns that this vision reveals the occurrence of future events, which he later confirms by comparing his prophetic imagination to the real city. Latimer's description of his prevision draws together different temporal modes: "I remembered distinctly the gradual breaking-in of the vision upon me, like the new images in a dissolving view, or the growing distinctness of the landscape as the sun lifts up the veil of the morning mist. And while I was conscious of this incipient vision, I was also conscious that Pierre came to tell my father Mr. Filmore was waiting for him" (*Veil*, 13). The phrasing "gradual breaking-in," "dissolving view," and "growing distinctness" emphasizes the process of becoming over the solidity of past, present, or future. The scene illustrates a palimpsest-like double consciousness, as the present moment cleaves into the simultaneous experience of a future-present. Such temporal gymnastics – Latimer relates his memory of a future event in the past tense as it emerged in his (then) present experience – reflects the Bergsonian notion that duration is not merely a facet of the present but an interpenetration of past, present, and future.

In addition to prevision, Latimer has insight into the thoughts of other people in his proximity. He becomes disgusted by the petty jealousies and vulgar egoism that underlie the graceful demeanor of those closest to him. Yet the thoughts of Bertha, the object of Latimer's youthful infatuation, remain a mystery. Despite her foul treatment of him, Latimer falls deeply in love with Bertha because she offers the excitement and suspense of not knowing. Yet Latimer *should* know better. After viewing a painting by Giorgione "said to be a likeness of Lucrezia Borgia," Latimer has a vision in which the image of the "cruel-eyed" woman in the painting maps onto Bertha. When she touches his arm "a strange intoxicating numbness" passes over him as a scene from his future life unfolds. As it gradually appears, Latimer learns that Bertha "was my wife, and we hated each other" (*Veil*, 30). Despite this certainty, after his prevision Latimer "felt a wild hell-braving joy that Bertha was to be mine" (*Veil*, 30). He learns about his future marriage and Bertha's treacherous character but ignores the latter information. He has learned the future, but he does not yet understand its meaning.

The Lifted Veil exposes this temporal gap between knowledge and understanding. Latimer's knowledge of what will happen does not help him determine the best course of action in the present. This epistemological interval or lag is rooted in the very processes of the body. In *The Physiology of Common Life* (1859), published the same year as *The Lifted Veil*, George Henry Lewes dismantles the notion that images are transmitted immediately to the brain: "Even on the supposition that images are formed on the retina . . . as the *cause* of the sensation – these images cannot be transmitted *as* images to the brain . . . it is the sensation which is transmitted, not the image" (277). What one *sees* is not the cause, but the byproduct of a chain of physiological mediation. The body translates the object of perception into a language that the brain can then interpret into a visual sensation. Thus, perception is the effect of a mediating process by which an original image is converted into sensation. Lewes calls this process "decomposition." He also refers to this as the subjective nature of vision: "We can no longer suppose that we see the objects themselves. Our visual sensations are simply excited states of our sentient organism" (282). By emphasizing the process of bodily mediation as the primary component of vision, Lewes renders what seems like an instantaneous process – the movement of the image into the brain – into a temporal process of decomposition and re-absorption. The bodily intervention between the image and the brain allows Lewes to explain a number of problematic visual phenomena related to the afterimage: the fudgy colors left behind when one closes one's eye after rubbing them or the lingering outline of letters when one looks away from a dazzling sign.[7]

By skipping over the duration between the present and the future, Latimer's prevision elides the epistemological interval between perception and understanding, removing the aging of the body from matters relating to knowledge. He claims that "We learn *words* by rote, but not their meaning; *that* must be paid for with our life-blood, and printed in the subtle fibers of our nerves" (*Veil*, 52). Meaning depends upon a painful interval of processing that Latimer links explicitly to the life blood and fibers of the body. One arrives at true understanding only through the depredations of time, which leave its mark on the increasingly mutilated body: "There is no short cut, no patent tram-road, to wisdom: after all the centuries of invention, the soul's path lies through the thorny wilderness which must be still trodden in solitude, with bleeding feet, with sobs for help, as it was trodden by them of old time" (*Veil*, 21). If a twenty-year-old suddenly acquired the knowledge of his seventy-year-old self, he would still lack the duration of aging to make sense of this knowledge. Growing older is an epistemology that sinks into the body, relating not to information as such, but to the individual's ability to interpret it.

Against the duration of the body, Latimer holds up the temporality of his own narrative: "The course of our life which I have indicated in a few sentences filled the space of years. So much misery – so slow and hideous a growth of hatred and sin, may be compressed into a sentence!" (*Veil*, 51–2).[8] Latimer laments the way language condenses the sufferings of a lifetime into "neat syntax" and "well selected predicates" (*Veil*, 52). Yet as Neil Hertz points out in *George Eliot's Pulse*, "If narration is only loosely mimetic of real time, if it is capable of such condensations, it can also accomplish equally affecting dilations" (60). Though he critiques the brevity of language, Latimer belies his canny understanding of how narrative manipulates time in other ways, drawing out the duration that he was unable to register when he was younger. As I argued above, Latimer fails at interpreting the future because he understands it as a separate temporal zone from the present, rather than one that is continuous with the present and the past. He asks the reader to "imagine this double consciousness at work within me, flowing on like two parallel streams which never mingle their waters and blend into a common hue" (*Veil*, 21). But his prose continually unites these two temporal streams, transposing one on top of the other in a formal approximation of duration's continuity.

Because of Latimer's foresight, every word in *The Lifted Veil* syncs with the duration of Latimer's life. He begins the story by forecasting his own death: "I forsee when I shall die, and everything that will happen in my last moments . . . Just a month from this day, on the twentieth of September, 1850" (*Veil*, 1). The novella ends on the day of reckoning: "It is the 20th of September 1850. I know these figures I have just written, as if they were a long familiar inscription. I have seen them on this page in my desk unnumbered times, when the scene of my dying struggle has opened upon me . . . " (*Veil*, 67). Signaled by the final ellipsis, the end of the narrative marks the simultaneous death of the narrator. In this way, *The Lifted Veil* constructs a narrative that is coterminous with the bodily death of the narrator: it is as if Latimer dies with pen in hand, and we must consider every word as an artifact composed in time. In other words, while we read about the events that occurred in Latimer's life (the retrospective narrative), we also chart another narrative that progresses word by word, moment by moment, to Latimer's death. Though Eliot leaves her characteristic realism behind in *The Lifted Veil*, its narrator's fantastic ability to see the future allows her to demonstrate the way that all narratives, even third person ones, conceal the double temporality of their narrating. And here Genette's distinction between story and discourse time becomes useful: for while the story time tends to dominate the attention of readers, it is the time of the discourse – the reading itself – that sinks into their flesh.

The narrator of *The Lifted Veil* complains about the temporal limitations of narrative even as he deploys them to represent the duration of the body that fails him. The novella's insistent doubling of temporal experience, both in Latimer's simultaneous experience of present and future and the narrative's retrospective and "to-the-moment" orientation, illustrate how duration arises through the imbrication of multiple times. Narrative draws out this duration by layering the time of the story with that of the reader, making the body's aging an important point of reference when language conjures the effect of passing time. Though the story's time radically differs from our own, we understand it through a tacit comparison to the way we pass through time. As George Eliot writes in her meditation on realism in *Adam Bede*, "with a single drop of ink for a mirror" we apprehend ourselves slowly growing older with each word (5).

Temporal Realism

The Lifted Veil illuminates the role of aging in mediating between the time of the story and the time of discourse, and the novella's fantastic subject matter allows Eliot to identify the formal techniques that narrative deploys to construct the effect of duration. We discover that the duration of narrative takes on a double life. As the temporality of the story borrows from the reader's lived duration it becomes increasingly convincing. But as the reader becomes more absorbed in the narrative she becomes less aware of her own duration that feeds into it. Arising from this antinomy of reading, the materiality of the discourse reflects the reader's duration back to them. Aging returns in a different form in its discursive immediacy, rooted in the materiality of printed words that take time to consume. This theory of reading and the surface of the novel posit duration at the level of discourse and assert that its intelligibility depends upon the body's aging. As I will go on to show, this poetics of duration provides a new framework for analyzing the novel's realism, which maps a youthful orientation toward temporality onto the lifespan of the characters within the narrative. A necessary condition for the feeling of reality in a novel arises from a consensus about the temporal conventions of narrative and their anchoring in biocultural processes of aging.

Many critics in the second half of the twentieth century privileged modernist experimentation over what they viewed as the aesthetically inferior and politically stultifying realism of the nineteenth century. However, a series of books published in 1999, including Nancy Armstrong's *Fiction in the Age of Photography*, Harry Shaw's *Narrating Reality*, and J. Jeffrey Franklin's *Serious Play*, showed how realism was not guilty of the charges that theorists attributed to it: that realism was referentially naïve or that it merely reinforced the dominant ideology. Reestablishing realism's formal complexity set the groundwork for a series of recent studies that focus on how specific aspects of Victorian culture shaped the way nineteenth-century novelists imagined the real: Richard Menke's "telegraphic realism" refers to the relation between a burgeoning information ecology and the representation of the everyday world; Tanya Agathocleous's "cosmopolitan realism" addresses the relation between urban networks and the social; and Rae Greiner's "sympathetic realism" shows how fellow-feeling was an important feature of the novel form.[9] The work of these scholars illustrates the dynamic and rich nature of Victorian realism, which expands or contracts to fit within the parameters of almost any defining term.

To address the aspect of realism most pertinent to the study of aging and time, I use the term *temporal realism* to refer to the conventions that solicit the reader's belief that the time represented in the story corresponds with how time passes in the real world. As Elizabeth Deeds Ermarth argues in *Realism and Consensus in the English Novel*, realism works by consensus: "The consensus not only establishes an agreement of meanings; it literally establishes the continuity of time. This continuity in time, common sense might object, is what makes collective agreements possible" (54). The first principle of temporal realism is that time can only pass in one direction. Like the reader, characters cannot travel back in time to fix a mistake or travel into the future to discover what happens next. The second rule is that time cannot stop or accelerate – despite subjective discrepancies, all characters in the novel abide by the same objective temporality, enabling a social world knitted together through shared time. These rules, however, are offset by the form of the narrative, which continuously contradicts them. Though characters are locked into a linear chronology, the narrator has analeptic and proleptic liberty. Where characters share an objective temporality, the narrator can stop time to describe a scene or simply skip years from one paragraph to the next. A narrative that overuses these techniques might be criticized for poor pacing, but it still adheres to the tenets of temporal realism.

The term temporal realism isolates a tension between the novel's content and form: while the narrator can carry the reader back and forward through time, at a faster or slower pace, the realism of the story depends on its characters passing through time in a manner consistent with how the reader believes it passes in the real world. Reading for temporal realism problematizes the way that we understand novelistic time. We can take Benedict Anderson's influential account of the novel and simultaneity as an example. He argues in *Imagined Communities* that the sense of simultaneity inherent in the novel form – that "acts are performed at the same clocked, calendrical time, but by actors who may be largely unaware of one another" – serves as a "precise analogue of the idea of the nation, which also is conceived as a solid community moving steadily down (or up) history" (26). The realization that subjects pass through time alongside other subjects (that may or may not be aware of each other) serves as the foundation for the imagination of a collective identity to which one belongs. Yet the novel must represent simultaneous events diachronically: if event A occurs at the same time as event B in the story, one event must nevertheless be represented before the other in the narrative discourse. While the novel can conjure the effect of simultaneity, the prose cannot represent two things at once unless the original representation is supplemented in some way (for example, with a subordinating conjunction like "meanwhile"). The reader's experience of simultaneity in the novel results from a retrospective addition to a previous representation. Temporal realism enables the novel to posit the simultaneous occurrence of events at the level of content while presenting them to the reader as a diachronic sequence.

Though it seems at odds with duration, the example of simultaneity illuminates the way temporal realism mediates between the reader's experience of form and content, converting a formal arrangement of words into a temporal effect that convincingly stands in for the experience of real temporality. As the dominant literary mode structuring the representation of time and narrative, temporal realism plays a significant role in shaping the cultural understanding of aging. In what follows, I analyze two aspects of temporal realism that were especially significant in constructing modern attitudes toward aging: mimesis and the everyday.

Duration and Mimesis

In temporal realism, the novel's story accords with the reader's beliefs about how time passes in the real world. In this sense, narrative is temporally mimetic at the level of character and action. Many theorists and critics view realist mimesis as a deceptive means of indoctrinating the reader into dominant or repressive ideologies. As David Lodge puts it in *After Bakhtin*, "part of the problem is that realism is a literary effect that works by disguising its own conventionality," reinforcing the status quo by sidestepping the reader's defenses (121–2). The most influential arguments in favor of this position derive from the Foucauldian tradition, which reveal the many ways that power insinuates itself into the institutions of modern society. D. A. Miller crystallizes this position in *The Novel and the Police*, in which he argues that the novel's realism serves as the means of gathering the reader's consent to the current milieu. Once the reader agrees to realism's mimetic claim to represent the world as it really is, power sneaks in through the back door, conditioning the reader to reproduce the social relations represented or merely implied in the novel.

For Harry Shaw in *Narrating Reality*, however, it "is difficult to cast realism as either a stupid or a manipulative genre without making its readers seem chumps" (33). The subversive reinforcement of power that forms the basis of many Foucauldian critiques "suggests that the general, global, abstract schemes we bring to reality have a total power to construct reality for us in advance of our encounters with it" (33). This view results in "a certain enslavement" and "a hemming-in of the reader," who becomes passively interpellated by the text that he or she reads (31). Moreover, reading bifurcates into amateur and expert forms, where "Expert reading becomes synonymous with unmasking, and . . . any other experience of the realist text sinks to the level of mass hypnosis" (34). This diagnosis anticipates the arguments of the surface theorists that I cite above, as Shaw's critique of realism bears a family resemblance to the theorization of the surface as a site of affective intensity. Both positions empower the reader: for while mimesis succeeds or fails based on its ability to accord with reality, this does not imply a reader who mistakes one for the other.

Yet in turning away from Foucauldian coercion, Shaw pushes aside elements of the novel that serve more than just the function of reproducing ideology. He condemns the view of "realism ... as a kind of training ground whereby readers learn to perform, and to accept as natural, practices that promote the continuation and extension of power" (23). While the novel as a "training ground" has taken on negative connotations in post-Foucauldian scholarship, this training is not always indoctrination, nor is it always unconscious or subversive. Many readers actively consume novels for exactly this reason, as a kind of training for the social world in which they participate, in a way that runners train to become faster or politicians practice oratory to persuade their audience. In *The Realistic Imagination*, George Levine writes that "Nineteenth-century realistic fiction tends to be concerned with the possibility of accommodation to established power, and yet, given its inevitable interest in character, it explores with at least equal intensity the possibility of resistance as well" (24). We cannot understand the significance of temporal realism without this ambivalent sense of training, both as an active exercise and as a passive programming.

While the time of the story adheres mimetically to the reader's expectations of real time, the form of the narrative is not limited by this requirement. When temporal realism garners the reader's agreement about the story's mimesis, it feeds back into the form of the novel – which bears no structural similarity with the representation itself – and functions to naturalize the literary techniques that create temporal effects. This has the consequence of rendering the formal techniques that construct duration invisible. Temporal realism encourages the reader to believe that a narrative has duration: characters mature, marry, and die, and dialogue marks out the length of conversations. Moreover, reading a novel absorbs the reader's time. Temporal realism works to erase the seams between the content and form, obscuring the very discourse that gives rise to the story. It succeeds when the reader perceives the duration of a story but does not think about its manifestation as words on a page.

Temporal realism effects the construction of aging by providing a scheme for the development of character over time. By unhinging the duration of narrative from the formal ground that gives rise to it, temporal realism redefines the continuity of duration as a diachronic sequence of intense moments of change. The very intensity of these moments of transformation alters the nature of the time that connects them, which loses its meaning as an axis of change. At the most extreme, duration becomes something to be passed over, a mere function of building suspense on one's way toward the meaningful events that constitute character.[10] Consider the trajectory of a *Bildungsroman* like that of Charles Dickens's *Great Expectations*, in which Pip's development as a character clusters into highly charged moments of revelation, of which the discovery of his benefactor looms largest. The most drastic growth in Pip's character does not arise from his everyday experiences but in the pivotal moment of truth. This has the effect of locating change with the momentary over the durable and suggests that the novel's representation of characters over long stretches of time trains readers to accept a model of development that occurs quickly in response to strong stimuli. Pip grows older throughout the novel, but his aging has little to do with his development as a character.

Though character development is more nuanced in George Eliot's novels than in Dickens's, she retains the emphasis on crisis. In *Middlemarch* (1871) Dorothea undergoes a major transformation when she learns that her recently deceased husband included a codicil in his will forbidding her to marry Will Ladislaw: "She might have compared her experience at that moment to the vague, alarmed consciousness that her life was taking on a new form, that she was undergoing a metamorphosis in which memory would not adjust itself to the stirring of new organs. Everything was changing its aspect ... Her world was in a state of convulsive change" (490). She recognizes, in a flash, her repulsion toward Casaubon while simultaneously becoming aware of "a sudden strange yearning of heart" toward Ladislaw (490). For Catherine Gallagher, this moment illustrates how "the narrator figures the transformation not as a gradual departure but as an abrupt metamorphosis" ("George Eliot," 70).

In *Middlemarch*, Eliot writes about how the interval leading up to a change often does not anticipate the change itself: "We know what a masquerade all development is, and what effective shapes may be disguised in helpless embryos" (83). This deterministic view of change as coded into the organism devalues the explanatory power of duration in the same way as the crisis model: in both, duration is the empty interval that must be overcome to achieve some real change. Moreover, Eliot's embryological metaphor also draws attention to the assumption about age and development that temporal realism helps to reify: that significant transformation happens to young folks rather than old ones.

When Erich Auerbach contrasts the Greek and Hebrew tradition of representation in the first chapter of *Mimesis*, he connects surfaces and depths to the way characters develop over time. The ancient Greeks, he writes, represented external phenomena "in a perpetual foreground"; this tradition privileged the surface as a site where important events occur (11). The orientation toward surfaces contributed to the removal of age from the representation of passing time: "So little are the Homeric heroes presented as developing or having developed, that most of them . . . appear to be of an age fixed from the very first . . . Odysseus on his return is exactly the same as he was when he left Ithaca two decades earlier" (17). The Hebrew tradition, on the other hand, finds meaning in the depths rather than the surfaces, trading description for hermeneutic complexity. Meaning is hidden and requires work to extract. As such, aging and development takes on a different role:

> Fraught with their development, sometimes even aged to the verge of dissolution, they show a distinct stamp of individuality entirely foreign to the Homeric heroes . . . the stern hand of God is ever upon the Old Testament figures . . . but he continues to work upon them, bends them and kneads them, and, without destroying them in essence, produces from them forms which their youth gave no grounds for anticipating. (18)

Contemporary criticism tends to read the nineteenth-century novel from the perspective of the Hebrew tradition, valuing the deep changes that occur to a character at the psychological or emotional level. Novels themselves reinforce this view, and the quote from Eliot above – about the unexpected developments that derive from the embryo – provides grounds for looking deeper into invisible and more real causes of transformation.

However, by drawing out the implications of temporal realism, we observe the legacy of the Greek tradition – a commitment to the surface that exists alongside and problematizes the novel's depths. The developing modernity of the nineteenth century channels attention and resources to unprecedented change, a tendency that the novel reflects through characters who undergo seismic shifts in personality and social standing. But the emphasis of modernity on transformation belies the subtle power of that which does not radically change. The duration that connects intervals of development becomes insignificant or invisible, a mere stepping stone toward the moment of crisis. This becomes especially clear when it comes to aging, as realism's temporal mimesis naturalizes the recognition of aging only after it has already happened rather than as a process that occurs continuously over time. An analysis of the duration of aging demonstrates that change occurs during spans of quiescence as well as at moments of crisis. Instead of plunging to the depths in search of a more real reality, the surface of representation rewards an enduring form of critical attention that is rooted in the biological rhythm of aging itself.

Affect and the Everyday

The interruption in chapter 29 of Eliot's *Middlemarch* – "but why always Dorothea?" – reveals some of the assumptions behind the realist novel's representation of the prosaic and everyday (278). The narrator protests "against all our interest, all our effort of understanding being given to the young skins that look blooming in spite of trouble; for these too will get faded, and will know the older and more eating griefs which we are helping to neglect" (278). For Eliot, realist representation of the everyday depends upon a tacit commitment to the conventionally interesting, which she aligns here with youth. A truer realism not only attempts to provide a fine-grained account of select individuals, but also expands outward to include those characters whom the realist novel portrays as minor. Old age becomes the very figure for this marginality, embodied by Casaubon's "blinking eyes and white moles" that other characters in the novel find "objectionable" (278). Eliot illustrates that much of what counts as a fit subject matter for realism depends upon the reader's affective investment in certain characters rather than a philosophical adherence to the representation of the everyday. In the previous section I argued that the novel's commitment to the quotidian belied its tendency to develop character through highly charged moments of crisis. Here, I will illustrate a corresponding privilege of strong over weak affects with regard to determining realistic content for the novel. The marginalization of aging as a process of slow, continuous transformation – so that it hardly seems like transformation at all – derives in part from the role that intensity and affect play in temporal realism.

The issue of affect can be illuminated by returning to a point I made in the introduction: that the representation of becoming loses something essential when it is fixed by critical analysis. When we analyze the everyday, it rises above its mundane status and loses the quality of everydayness that defines it as such. The analysis of duration constantly threatens to collapse its temporal extension into demarcated units of time. And aging follows suit, settling into reified stages (young, middle aged, old) rather than remaining a continuous process. But this leaves us with a paradox. How do we talk meaningfully about these terms when, the moment we attempt to do so, that which defines them vanishes?

The representation of processes such as aging remains intelligible because it retains the affect of becoming – the feeling of movement that arises from inert marks on a page. Eric Shouse writes in "Feeling, Emotion, Affect" that affect "is a moment of unformed and unstructured potential ... affect cannot be fully realized in language, and ... is always prior to and/or outside of consciousness." In what has become an influential and controversial example, Brian Massumi argues in *Parables for the Virtual* that affect arises in the "missing half second" "between the beginning of a bodily event and its completion in an outwardly directed, active expression" (29).[11] According to Massumi, our bodies respond to stimuli before our conscious mind can grasp them. Thus, choice and decision are rationalizations after the fact, which give the appearance as such because consciousness retrospectively adds itself into what were affectively overdetermined events. The body absorbs impressions before the mind can perceive them, resulting in a temporal gap that "is missed not because it is empty, but because it is overfull, in excess of the actually-performed action and of its ascribed meaning" (29).

Where the rationalization of duration, aging, and the everyday enables meaningful discourse, affect confers the plenitude of movement that defines them as a process. Massumi contends that the term affect allows us to combat a persistent myth about the everyday: that, in contrast to the change of rupture, "the everyday was the place where nothing ever happens" (1). Instead, we learn that the rupture provides a reductive narrowing of the environmental conditions that allow the novelist to persuasively assign a cause to transformation. The everyday, however, is not the empty counterpart to the meaningful rupture, but its teeming, irreducible background. By inverting the assumption that the everyday is empty while the rupture is meaningful, affect provides a model for aging as "continuous, like a background perception that accompanies every event, however quotidian" (36). Aging can be understood as what Massumi refers to as one's "sense-of-aliveness" that manifests as a "continuous, nonconscious, self-perception" (36). Yet, as I suggested earlier with respect to duration, once we become aware of our "sense-of-aliveness" it slips away; thus, Massumi calls for "a vocabulary . . . for that which is imperceptible but whose escape from perception cannot but be perceived, as long as one is alive" (36). The linked processes of aging, duration, and the everyday share this affective temporality, which crystallize in the practice of literary realism.

Affect also plays a significant role in Fredric Jameson's *The Antinomies of Realism*, in which he writes that the novel contains "two systems of temporality": one defined by the linear chronology of a past-present-future and the other defined by affect, or "the present of consciousness" (25). The temporality of affect is "an eternal present" that passes like a "sliding scale of the incremental, in which each infinitesimal moment differentiates itself from the last by a modification of tone and an increase or diminution of intensity" (36, 42). The realist novel fills out the everyday with affect, creating what Jameson describes as a "conviction as to the massive weight and persistence of the present as such" while distracting from "the deeper currents and contradictory tendencies within the social order" (145). Jameson suggests that criticism has been dominated by an approach to narrative that leaves out the affective half of the novel's temporal dialectic.

While terms like duration and the everyday reveal the workings of affect at the level of temporality and setting, aging is the principal figure through which affect works at the level of character. Aging is the existential form of duration, the embodied manner through which one passes through the everyday: it forms the background against which all character development occurs, but almost never rises to the level of analysis in its own right. The temporality of narrative as a forward moving, rationalized sequence and that of affect as an ever-present duration contest one another through characters who change in response to external events and yet cannot be exhaustively explained in this way. Some aspects of a character's development spill over. It is this additional change, the excessive transformation that cannot be explained by referencing causal relationships to external stimuli, that provides the basis for a study of realism and the affect of aging. Rather than treat aging as a symbol for something else, we must look directly at the springs of bodily affect as they resonate through time.

Aging to Old Age

While old age is an important focus in the following chapters of this book, it does not play a major part in my discussion of aging as a process. On the one hand, focusing on a specific stage in the human lifespan reinforces the bias against duration that I have outlined here. Too much attention, both literary and critical, has been directed toward specific age stages rather than the temporality that cuts across and binds them together. This has the effect of reifying stages such as youth, adulthood, and old age by making them appear more real than the passage of time upon which they are projected. In this way, these stages enforce normative behaviors based on factors such as chronological age, appearance, and functionality. While thinking in terms of stages provides the kind of objective data that inform useful projects such as medical research and pension plans, thinking exclusively in these terms reduces the intellectual and affective richness of growing older. To recover the duration of aging opens the lifespan to creativity and combats the notion that aging is a disease to be cured.

On the other hand, the concept of age stages plays a significant role in the Victorian imaginary, which is reinforced by the relationship between the human lifespan and the trajectory of the novel's most significant plots. It would be a mistake to abandon the concept of stage, as such a move would run counter to the historical importance of such conceptualization. The theoretical work in this chapter allows for a return to the concept of age stages from a newly critical perspective, leavening the analysis of old age with an awareness of aging's duration. For example, Chapters 2 and 5 will show how Charles Dickens and H. G. Wells challenge the cultural expectations of old age by strategically deploying the conventions of temporal realism; Chapter 3 will show how affect and the everyday enable the imagination of a more fluid alternative to the marriage plot; in Chapter 4, the idea of the surface will lead to an analysis of how Thomas Hardy represents passing time on the skin. My goal is not only to show how old age was unfairly stigmatized in the nineteenth century or how senescence served as a site of subversive potential, though both of these claims will emerge in my readings of different authors. Rather, instead of looking at old age as the subject of interpretation – as something to be extracted from the depths of the text – I treat it as a figure for interpretation itself, as a set of strategies for mediating between our experience in the world and its narrative representation.

While all stages of life contain their own orientation to the world, their own codes for understanding and creating meaning, old age provides an especially rich approach for the study of narrative and time. The positioning of old age as the final stage of the human lifespan gives rise to a series of stereotyped beliefs that correspond to narrative phenomena: that old age turns away from the future toward the past (retrospective narrative), that it tends to stasis rather than change (the novel's privilege of crisis over gradual development), that it is superfluous (realism's inclusiveness and excessive detail).[12] The theorization of duration alongside aging and narrative not only problematizes these assumptions but also provides the groundwork for elaborating new models for understanding how the Victorians fashioned their lives in culture and in the novel. The following chapters will propose these models in relation to Victorian novelists and show how this legacy translated into the modernist aesthetics of Virginia Woolf.

CHAPTER 2

No Plots for Old Men

Included in the collection *Sketches by Boz* (1836), Charles Dickens's melancholy story "Scotland-yard" chronicles "the advance of civilization" and "improvement" of the eponymous locale after the erection of a new bridge across the Thames in 1832 (88).[1] White tablecloths appear at the neighborhood eating place, the fruit-pie maker acquires the genteel moniker "pastrycook," and the "long song and the joyous shout" of the coal heavers no longer shake the roof of the public house (88–9). Alongside this improvement in manners materialize more visible signs of progress: the boot-maker adds a first floor to his business, a jeweler sets up shop, and the once frugal tailor hires a coterie of uniformed assistants. Yet near the end of this sketch appears the figure of an old man:

> Amidst all this change, and restlessness, and innovation, there remains but one old man . . . Misery and want are depicted in his countenance; his form is bent by age, his head is gray with length of trial, but there he sits from day to day, brooding over the past; and thither he will continue to drag his feeble limbs, until his eyes have closed upon Scotland-yard, and upon the world together. (89–90)

Set against the background of Scotland-yard's bustle, the anonymous old man is Dickens's way of representing that which has been left behind by the youthful narrative of development that modernizes the world around him. The old man endures alongside this meaningful development, asserting his own stubborn existence as proof that he is not only the excess of modernity, but also that which exceeds it.

Most critics assume that the developmental plots of modernity are concerned primarily with the maturation of youth. In what Franco Moretti identifies in *The Way of the World* as a central means of understanding the "bewitching and risky process" of modernity, the *Bildungsroman* relates the story of a youth who passes into adulthood amidst great struggle, eventually reintegrating into the society from which he or she has been alienated (5). In the English *Bildungsroman*, Moretti explains, "Youth acts as a sort of *symbolic concentrate* of the uncertainties and tensions of an entire cultural system," and so it must be overcome in the process of achieving a stable maturity (185).[2] Reaching a very different conclusion, Patricia Meyer Spacks nevertheless claims in *The Adolescent Idea* that for Victorian novelists like Dickens "the adolescent ... becomes a version of the self," a point of "predominant wistful identification" (195). For Spacks, overcoming the dangers of adolescent aggression and sexual energy merely results in "the necessity, the discipline, the sorrow of maturity" (217). Providing different accounts of the progression from youth to maturity, Moretti and Spacks represent a larger critical tendency to remove old age from developmental narratives. By overstating Dickens's fascination with the dynamism and vitality of youth, critics ignore his investment in that which follows the telos of development and maturity. In Dickens's novels this takes the form of the elderly man, who emerges as the byproduct of an unsuccessful attempt to represent modernity as complete or mature.

Appearing regularly in Dickens's early fiction, the aged male serves as a human reminder of what has been left behind by both the rationalization of plot and the modernization of the marketplace. As historians of old age have shown, the elderly were pressured out of work as industrialization took root in England. Jill Quadagno observes that "the work of the aged was marginal and sporadic" and "the labor market in general was more rigid for older people." Pat Thane adds that technological "change might erode the occupations old people could cling on to."[3] As young labor was increasingly privileged by manufacturers, cultural institutions such as the family had yet to adjust to the changing attitudes toward age. Ostensibly supported by male income, the idealized Victorian family structure was based on a tacit belief that the paterfamilias would be able to support his wife and children well into old age. While some individuals secured a pension by contributing to Friendly Societies, many working-class and some middle-class men staked their future on the uncertain prospect of being able to work late in life. The difficulties that old age presented for the integrity of the family were systematized by the passage of the New Poor Law in 1834. The uneven ability of family or kin to support elderly parents set the groundwork for this reform, in which the local and haphazard deployment of relief to the aged poor by the parish gave way to a more centralized and depersonalized model. Though critics are divided about the efficacy of the poor laws in distributing relief, few would argue with the fact that the workhouse was regarded with horror by the elderly.[4] The New Poor Law was symptomatic of the elderly man's exclusion from the cultural narratives he had helped to produce: his aged body revealed that the ideology of family and work were not universal truths but temporally contingent.

Jettisoned to the plotless fringes of society, the old man's existence provides a test case for how the Victorian novel represents and constructs the social margins. We tend to discuss marginality and the novel in terms of who is included or excluded, observed or ignored. Alex Woloch and Emily Steinlight have directed our attention to the novel as an elastic form that includes a surplus of human life that constantly threatens to overspill the bounds of representation. Both critics think of the excesses of the novel in spatial terms. For Woloch it is "the many" who "jostle for limited space within the same fictive universe"; for Steinlight the density of character presents the problem of "too many bodies to too little space" and the "mass of life that defies containment."[5] But the elderly man draws attention to the fact that the realist novel's aspiration to represent the social will always be burdened with a temporal compromise – that as the spaces enlarge to accommodate the swell of urban life, the time allotted to represent the characters becomes shorter. In other words, because so many characters appear in the Victorian novel there is simply *not enough time* to consistently represent the transformations that age registers on this multitude of characters.

The omission of aging is not only inherent in the novel's temporal form, but also in the bewildering progress of a modernizing society that suddenly finds itself irrevocably changed. In what follows, I argue that the old man lingers at the intersection of Dickens's attempt to represent modernity and the temporal limitations of his realism. Tending toward digression, stasis, and senile confusion, Dickens's old men resist the progressiveness and causality of linear plotting. Yet in the process of resisting, they create the conflicts that enable developmental narrative to unfold successfully. In *The Old Curiosity Shop* (1841), *Martin Chuzzlewit* (1844), and *A Christmas Carol* (1843), I identify a pattern of old men not only functioning as counterpoints to the developmental plots of youth, but also serving as imaginative catalysts for the literary reconfiguration of the social. Built into Dickens's realism is that discarded remainder, a narrative compulsion that continues in the afterlife of plot: an unplotted energy that threatens to nullify the very structures – of development, of modernity – that it has helped to realize.

Old Curiosities

Published in weekly parts between April 1840 and December 1841, *Master Humphrey's Clock* was intended as a collection of "sketches, essays, tales, adventures, letters from imaginary correspondents" organized "to diversify the contents as much as possible."[6] In the preface Dickens suggests that the new publication developed partly out of his concern that the reading public would become bored with the twenty monthly installments that made him famous (*Clock*, iii). If revitalizing the reader's attention was indeed the goal of Dickens's shift in publication strategies, it seems a strange choice for him to introduce his magazine through the character of Master Humphrey, who describes himself as a "mis-shapen, deformed, old man" and spends most of the first installment complaining about his difficult childhood and alienation from others (*Clock*, 3). As head of a club where elderly men meet regularly to share stories, Humphrey also serves as the frame for the stories that appear in the publication: in the first eleven numbers of *Master Humphrey's Clock* the perspective shifts between Humphrey's first-person narration in the present and the storytelling voice of the club's members.

Beginning in the fourth number of *Master Humphrey's Clock*, *The Old Curiosity Shop* quickly dominated the pages of Dickens's publication, eventually replacing the short and disconnected sketches with a continuous novel length project. It begins with Humphrey as a first-person narrator helping the young girl Nell find her way home. Nell lives with her grandfather Trent, a dealer in curiosities, who attempts to gamble her into "a fine lady" (*Shop*, 15). In order to fund his misguided ambition, Trent borrows money from the demonic Quilp, who eventually calls in his debt. Unable to bear his misfortunes, Trent becomes ill and demented, eventually agreeing with Nell that they should abscond from London. The rest of the novel follows the picaresque wanderings of Nell and Trent, and the attempts made to discover their whereabouts by Quilp and Trent's good-natured brother, known in the context of the novel as "the single gentleman." The novel is notable for the lack of development of its youthful protagonist: Nell is good from the beginning of the novel and she remains so until she dies. Instead, the youthful plot of development is displaced by the plotless wanderings of Grandfather Trent, whose old age serves as a metaphor for the restless energies of narrative at the impasse of closure.

Like almost every other character in the novel, Humphrey cannot stop thinking about Nell. After delivering the girl to her grandfather, Humphrey muses: "I had ever before me the old dark murky rooms . . . the faces all awry, grinning from wood and stone – the dust and rust, and worm that lives in wood – and alone in the midst of all this lumber and decay, and ugly age, the beautiful child in her gentle slumber" (*Shop*, 22). Imagining the youthful Nell framed by "decay" and "ugly age," Humphrey critiques the dusty objects of the curiosity shop owned by Grandfather Trent. However, he also gestures toward himself as the narrator and to the club of men – old curiosities themselves – who listen to the story. Humphrey's description of his own house in *Master Humphrey's Clock*, with its "worm-eaten doors," "moth and spider," and "staring portrait[s]" directly recalls the worm, decaying lumber, and grinning faces that he imagines terrorizing Nell (*Clock*, 2, 49). That *Master Humphrey's Clock* serves as the frame for *The Old Curiosity Shop* suggests that while "ugly age" is stigmatized through images of decay, it is also the imaginative conduit through which the reader's attention is channeled.

Writing about the aged in Dickens's work, Chase observes that the "elderly often appear as a kind of fiction in Dickens – a kind of specter – fading into impalpability" (*Victorians*, 36). Humphrey proves Chase's claim more literally than she probably intended it. Referring to himself repeatedly as a ghost or shade in the opening installment of *Master Humphrey's Clock* and disappearing from *The Old Curiosity Shop* after the third chapter, Humphrey draws attention to his own erasure from the text. Moreover, following the conclusion of *The Old Curiosity Shop*, in the forty-fifth number of *Master Humphrey's Clock*, he reveals that the first-person narrator of the first three chapters was, in fact, a fiction. To the surprise of his fellow club members and the readers of *Master Humphrey's Clock* since its publication, Humphrey claims that he was the irascible single gentleman, the estranged little brother of Grandfather Trent, who pursues Nell for over half of the novel with the desire to improve her fortunes. Robert L. Patten is representative of the critical response to Humphrey's late revelation when he says:

> Master Humphrey, misshaped, deformed, a recluse, has nothing in common with the haphazardly energetic Single Gentleman ... It is clear that Dickens, at the last minute, was straining his ingenuity beyond credible limits to provide some explanation of the novel's original title [Personal Adventures of Master Humphrey].[7]

But what if the discrepancy between the single gentleman and Humphrey is more than just Dickens's hackneyed repair for a broken *Clock*? From this perspective the vast difference between the two men is not an aesthetic blunder on Dickens's part but a means of representing the tremendous transformative potential of old age. Described as "growling and cursing in a very awful manner," the single gentleman suffers from "constitutional irritability and haste," and is referred to by the narrator variously as "the impatient gentleman" and the "restless gentleman" (*Shop*, 269, 292, 309, 355). In contrast, Humphrey claims that "retirement has become a habit with me," recognizing in his own step "the failing tread of an old man" (*Clock*, 1, 2). Not many characters are more constitutionally dissimilar than the single gentleman and Humphrey. However, this is precisely Dickens's point. The vast divide between the personalities of the two characters underwrites the physiological and emotional changes that occur over a lifespan. The single gentleman's impulsive and brusque manner has transformed into Humphrey's careful and monotonous reflections. This transformation not only suggests that the change between the two characters is one of obvious decay – that old age is a pathology to be feared and avoided[8] – but also the fertility of literary imagination: the creation of something different and new from the established patterns of the past.[9] Old age facilitates new perspectives even as the transformation from the single gentleman to Master Humphrey is represented as one of decline.

Grandfather Trent has this catalyzing effect on the imaginations of the characters of *The Old Curiosity Shop*. Though Nell has received the attention of readers since the novel's publication, the real motivation for the plot falls on the feeble shoulders of Grandfather Trent, who flees into the countryside when Quilp calls in his debts. Trent's frantic desire to get away from London lacks direction. When they first leave the house, he looks "irresolutely and helplessly" around him for guidance, and as Nell leads him out of the city the narrator observes that they "wandered they knew not whither" (*Shop*, 103, 105). When offered a place to rest early in their travels, Trent urges that they move blindly on, telling his granddaughter "Further away, dear Nell, pray further way" (*Shop*, 127). The plotlessness of the old man's uneasy wanderings has the surprising effect of intensifying the imaginative activity that provokes plotting in others. When Nell and Trent encounter the travelling Punchmen Short and Codlin, Short observes to his companion: "Have you seen how anxious the old man is to get on – always wanting to be furder away – furder away. Have you seen that?" (*Shop*, 145). It is the very fact that Trent has no more direction "than the man in the moon" that Short supposes "he has given his friends the slip, and persuaded this delicate young creetur all along of her fondness for him to be his guide and travelling companion" (*Shop*, 145). In response, Short constructs a plot of rescue, heroically returning

Nell to her friends in London; Codlin, on the other hand, imagines a plot where kidnapping and ransoming Nell results in a reward.

While most of the plots constructed by characters in *The Old Curiosity Shop* take Nell as the subject, it is the restless energy of the old man who inspires them. This energy is on display after Nell's death. Though Nell and Trent finally arrive at a quiet parish where they can live peacefully, the peace that pervades the atmosphere is that of death: the difficulties of the journey have stressed Nell's body beyond its limit and she eventually dies. Surviving his granddaughter and yet oblivious of her death, Trent "had some hope of finding her again – some faint and shadowy hope, deferred from day to day, and making him from day to day more sick and sore at heart" (*Shop*, 545). He falls into the habit "every day, and all day long" waiting at Nell's grave, "murmuring to himself, 'She will come to-morrow!'" (*Shop*, 546). Trent's reaction to Nell's death is suggestive not only of his grief but also of the difficulty of coming to terms with a plot that nears its end: he lapses into delusional repetition, and it is not long before the "broken hearted man" dies (*Shop*, 546). Without a plot of his own – his story is hinged to that of Nell – Trent stubbornly and pointlessly continues to exist, illuminating a narrative compulsion that survives in the afterlife of plot. Symbolizing that which is left behind by developmental plots, the old man also lives beyond them – a satellite that orbits around the gravity of Nell's corpse.

Grandfather Trent is not the only old man who is drawn to the corpse of Nell: the old sexton, the "bachelor" of the parish, the schoolmaster, and the single gentleman also cluster around Nell's deathbed at the end of the novel. James Buzard describes this tableau in "Enumeration and Exhaustion" as a "self-negating inventory of spent men gathered around the figure of Nell" (204). But what do these men hope to gain from their vigil? In his essay on *The Old Curiosity Shop* in *Notes to Literature*, Theodor Adorno claims that "The novel is nothing but the story of [Nell's] sacrifice" (173). For Adorno, Nell and her grandfather are "formed of the same materials, the two remain inseparable; neither could exist as an autonomous being, the child no more than the feeble-minded old man" (173). The path that the novel charts from Trent's guilt to Nell's sacrifice is the fated result of the "revolt from bourgeois society" that is staged over the course of their journey (173). In Helen Small's revision of Adorno's argument in *The Long Life*, youth and old age are distinct. In Small's account, while the novel still critiques industrial society, Nell's sacrifice is "upheld but also denied" (194). The sacrifice represents the philosophical "hope of a beyond" which is "exposed as the murderous proof that 'mere existence' is all we have"

(194). As youth takes on the burden of the aged, it is destroyed in the process of trying to guard against the nearness of death (198).

Old men show such interest in Nell's sacrifice because the stasis and discontinuity of her death – Nell is "mute and motionless for ever" – embodies a comforting suspension of the inexorable march toward their own demise (*Shop*, 540). Nell's death purchases relief for the aged men in the novel that is at odds with the tragic sentiment that Dickens clearly wanted to inspire in his readership. It is the inability of Nell's story to move forward that enables the pleasurable displacement of encroaching mortality. "When Death strikes down the innocent and young, for every fragile form from which he lets the panting spirit free, a hundred virtues rise, in shapes of mercy, charity, and love, to walk the world . . . In the Destroyer's steps there spring up bright creations that defy his power, and his dark path becomes a way of light to heaven" (*Shop*, 544). The narrator's mawkish reflections on death belie a therapeutic model of narrative activity – a "hundred virtues rise . . . to walk the world" and "there spring up bright creations" – that surfaces at the moment of most radical closure. While Adorno and Small argue that there is no "beyond" in *The Old Curiosity Shop* – of either bourgeois society or "mere existence," respectively – narrative continues in the wake of death, igniting the imagination of the old men who see in Nell's corpse a way of coming to terms with the ends of their own lives.

In *The Old Curiosity Shop* old men consistently use the plotlessness of another's death as a way to confront anxieties about encroaching mortality. When Nell and Trent retreat to the countryside, the first person to help them is an old gentleman who addresses his anxieties about death by comparing his own age to that of another: "He had changed . . . eighty-four [was] a great age, though there was some he had known that had lived to very hard upon a hundred – and not so hearty as he, neither – no, nothing like it" (*Shop*, 126–7). The gentleman takes comfort in two aspects of his reference. The chronological disparity between his own age and that of his example distances himself from the end that he fears. And the plotlessness of his allusion – to "some he had known that lived to very hard upon a hundred" – erases the context and narratability of human life. Rather than provoke existential terror, imagining other aged bodies in descriptive rather than narrative terms allows the old gentleman to mystify the forward progress of development that propels him to death.

The old gentleman's comparison performs the function of a popular genre of writing that recorded the lives of centenarians. One of the most popular of these works, James Easton's *Human Longevity* (1799), collects the names, ages, place of residence, and year of decease for 1,712 people over the age of 100. In the midst of Easton's many examples, there are some exquisitely drawn characters. For example, the description of Daniel Bull M'Carthy, who died in the year 1752 at the age of 111: "Of the county of Kerry, in Ireland. At the age of eighty-four he married a fifth wife, aged fourteen, and had by her twenty children, one every year; he was always very healthy, and never observed to spit" (36). One can easily imagine a slightly less prolific version of Daniel Bull M'Carthy appearing in the pages of a Dickens novel. The point of Easton's *Human Longevity*, however, is not to render old age exceptional, but to make it something commonplace and within the compass of the reader's experience. This effect is achieved partly by the form of the piece, which presents a series of discontinuous sketches that are meant to increase the reader's credulity through repetition and a highly idiosyncratic level of detail.[10] Thomas Wiggin, aged 108, made a "very fair corpse"; Dr. Glysson, aged 100, had hair that "very much resembled snow"; Agnes Milborne, aged 106, had "twenty nine sons and one daughter" "twenty of whom frequently followed her to church" (11, 24). Daniel Bull M'Carthy thus emerges not as an exception, but as the necessary remainder – that which is excessive and unaccountable – which is necessary for Easton's account of long-livers to seem comprehensive and credible.

Each entry in Easton's *Human Longevity* tells the story of a life in abbreviated form – one that compresses the narrative development of a life into a descriptive moment. As Amanpal Garcha shows in *From Sketch to Novel*, a similar kind of descriptive non-narrativity exists alongside the progressiveness and causality of novel plots. The predominance of descriptive prose and episodic narrative fragments of the nineteenth-century novel resist

> the forward drive of narrativity and the coherence of plot, and instead put[s] forth an alternative model of temporality – a model in which time is disorganized, nonprogressive flux and in which stability appears not through developmental, teleological plots, but only through the consistency and stasis of an author's style or distinctive voice. (42)

Garcha uses this tension between plot and discontinuity to suggest that "the pleasures of Dickens's early works . . . often lie not in his hopelessly melodramatic plots, but rather in the descriptive moments or digressive episodes that interfere with narrative's move forward" (45). *Human Longevity* contextualizes the nature of this pleasure, which is not affected principally by the knowledge that other people have lived longer than one's self, but structurally through the synchronic arrangement of long-livers in catalogue form. The very non-narrativity of the centenarian's life allows for the imaginative suspension of the teleological plot that organizes biological life.

As *The Old Curiosity Shop* nears its end, the old men in the parish grow increasingly sensitive to old age and death. This is particularly true of the old sexton, whose fear of death takes the aggressive form of displacing the weakness of age onto others. Tasked with digging a grave, the sexton requires the help of the parishioner David (another old man) because he is too feeble to dig the grave himself. Looking on as another man carries out his work, the sexton nevertheless projects debility onto his companion: "when the sexton . . . exchanged a remark with him about his work, the child could not help noticing that he did so with an impatient kind of pity for his infirmity, as if he were himself the strongest and heartiest man alive" (*Shop*, 406). When the sexton leaves the scene, David reciprocates when he observes to Nell that the sexton is "failing very fast. He ages every day" (*Shop*, 408). In the next sentence the narrator wryly observes: "And so they parted: each persuaded that the other had less life in him than himself" (*Shop*, 408–9). Seeing in each other the aged man that they fear for themselves, the sexton and David demonstrate how old age gives rise to a burst of imaginative activity that reframes the lives of other old men as exhausted past usefulness to the community. Unable to live up to the standards of Victorian masculinity – represented here by the inability to continue working digging graves – the sexton becomes increasingly sensitive about his age, evincing a deep-seated anxiety about lapsing into plotlessness of unemployment.[11]

Critics working on the issue of age in the nineteenth century agree that the aged man took on the characteristics of Victorian femininity. Thomas Cole and Claudia Edwards suggest that old men were closely associated with the feminine sphere during the Victorian era, and Teresa Mangum claims that old men were rendered absurd by being feminized). Lisa Hamilton makes an even stronger case, stating that "To be a man in decline was to become like a woman."[12] For the old man, fears of death were coupled with anxieties about the inability to live up to masculine expectations and the consequent loss of social and physical power.[13] While developmental narratives structure masculine experience – where youth develops into maturity and power – this does not account for how age enacts physiological changes that make sustaining this linear narrative untenable for old men. *The Old Curiosity Shop* reveals this pervasive bias toward youth even as it reinscribes old age as a central means of imaginative and literary transformation. What emerges from Dickens's experiment is a cadre of tenacious old men who recycle the youthful energies that surround them.

Narrative Inheritance

In the previous section I argued that aged men who are confronted with unemployment or the possibility of being physically unable to work embody a plotlessness that exists in tension with the developmental tendency of narrative. *Martin Chuzzlewit* inverts this problem by giving the elderly man a surfeit of resources in the form of inheritance, thus radically changing the role of the old man in the scheme of this novel's developmental plot. Spanning the city and countryside of England and America, the main plot of *Martin Chuzzlewit* is set in motion when the wealthy Old Martin disowns his grandson, Young Martin, after learning of the young man's intention to marry his servant and companion, Mary. While the focus of the plot is on Young Martin's development, this development is more a product of Old Martin's elaborate schemes than a process of self-willing on the part of youth. In setting his grandson on the path that will enable him to learn his lesson, Old Martin is carried along on his own improving journey. In the tension that arises between generations, *Martin Chuzzlewit* disables inheritance as a means of supporting masculine subjectivity in a society where male power is increasingly threatened by age; instead, the old man engages in acts of deferral that invest his aged frame with narrative control and social relevance.

Old Martin is introduced as suffering from a stomach complaint. Far from indicating his decrepitude, the illness highlights the old man's robust constitution: "He was, beyond all question, very ill, and suffered exceedingly: not the less, perhaps, because he was a strong and vigorous old man, with a will of iron, and a voice of brass" (*MC*, 24). Not registering the stereotypical signs of senile decay, Old Martin's body signifies his stubborn refusal to submit to the will of others: "this old man, and even his grip on the stout stick on which he leaned, were all expressive of a resolution not easily shaken, and a purpose . . . such as in other days might have survived the rack" (*MC*, 136). All the more odd, then, when Old Martin seeks refuge from the avaricious members of his family by moving in with his most villainous relative, the architect and arch-hypocrite Seth Pecksniff. As Young Martin has recently apprenticed himself to Pecksniff, Old Martin's sudden desire to cultivate ties with his relative triggers the removal of his grandson from the house. This serves as a ruse by which Old Martin can set his grandson free from the influence of Pecksniff, do penance for his own pride, and punish Pecksniff in the process.

Central to the success of Old Martin's performance of decrepit old age – which serves as the engine for the novel's plot – is a tacit belief that the inevitable progression toward the end of life is one marked by decay and debilitation. Early nineteenth-century medical discourse provides a suggestive blueprint. In "On the Climacteric Disease" Sir Henry Halford observes that "the stomach seems to lose all its powers; the frame becomes more and more emaciated ... the mind grows torpid and indifferent to what formerly interested it; and the patient sinks at last, seeming rather to cease to live, than to die" (7). As the body weakens so do moral qualities such as agency and will, leaving the elderly man in a state of passivity so complete that death itself lies outside his grasp. This sentiment is echoed by the author of the entry titled "Age" in the *Cyclopedia of Medicine*, who likens old age to the winding down of a watch, and by Thomas Andrews, who writes in *A Cyclopedia of Domestic Medicine and Surgery* that "the slightest fall, is sufficient to arrest some one of the vital functions, and death immediately arrives, as the last term of destruction of the functions and organs."[14]

Old Martin deceives others by making his demeanor correspond with the expectations of his visible old age. After just a short time at Pecksniff's the ill-mannered old man "had gradually undergone an important change": "he was comparatively subdued and easy to deal with" and "the colour of the whole man was faded ... He was less keen of sight; was deaf sometimes" (*MC*, 409). The narrator observes that he had a "blank and motionless expression which is not uncommon in the faces of those whose faculties are on the wane, in age" (*MC*, 572). The assumption that most characters make in the novel – that old age and decay go hand in hand – allows Old Martin to regain control of the plot by other means than the violent imposition of his will. The characters in the novel lament his collapse under the power of Pecksniff, but Old Martin has never been busier. Though rarely represented in the text, he surreptitiously motivates most of the events that move the plot forward to a satisfactory conclusion.[15] He asks Pecksniff to remove Young Martin before the hypocrite negatively influences him; he anonymously sends Martin twenty pounds when he needs money to travel to America; the money he uses to pay off Montague Tigg allows him to set up the "Anglo-Bengalese Disinterested Loan and Life Insurance Company"; and, among other things, he provides Tom Pinch with a job and orchestrates a meeting between Ruth Pinch and John Westlock, resulting in their engagement. As John Bowen observes in

Other Dickens, in *Martin Chuzzlewit* "the self is always dissolving into gesture and performance," and so it is for Old Martin, whose time performing the senselessness and torpidity of old age teaches him new ways to plot for others and achieve his ends (207).

However, Old Martin's end is not entirely clear. When he first moves in with Pecksniff, Old Martin tells him: "You and yours are to find that I can be constant, and am not to be diverted from my end. Do you hear?" (*MC*, 137). One cannot help thinking that Old Martin's "end" has a different meaning for Pecksniff, who greedily anticipates the old man's speedy demise. Around this slippage of the word "end" – as the eventual death of the old man or as the consummation of Old Martin's plots – pivots the development of *Martin Chuzzlewit*'s narrative. In the ongoing competition between narrative and biological closure, the end of the story constantly threatens to arrive too soon: "Old Martin's cherished projects, so long hidden in his own breast, so frequently in danger of abrupt disclosure through the bursting forth of the indignation he had hoarded up, during his residence with Mr Pecksniff, were retarded, but not beyond a few hours" (*MC*, 679). Embodied in the old man – "hidden in his own breast" – the success of Old Martin's project requires the discipline to hold the end at bay. But when is the right time for Old Martin to reveal his plot? As Sylvère Monod points out, when Young Martin returns from America, having almost died from trying to earn his fortune abroad, "nothing *is* said to explain why the moment of truth and revelation is further delayed."[16] Seemingly having achieved his end, with Young Martin a changed man begging for his grandfather's forgiveness, Old Martin nonetheless perpetuates the ruse.

The deferral of Old Martin's end is part of the novel's larger fascination with how development – for both the narrative and the characters – is wrought by the very means that forestall it. For example, the revelation of Old Martin's secret at the end of the novel seems to be brought about more by a crisis of narrative intensity than by the rationalization of narrative closure: "scattered as his purposes and hopes were for the moment, by the crowding in of all these incidents between him and his end; still their very intensity and the tumult of their assemblage nerved him to the rapid and unyielding execution of his scheme" (*MC*, 679). In this case, deferral paradoxically creates the conditions that enable the realization of his end: "the crowding in of all these incidents between him and his end . . . nerved him to the rapid . . . execution of his scheme." As Old Martin recedes into the background of the story, he deploys many of the techniques that we associate with the construction of a successful novel. Usurping linear progression for a more tortuous plot, Old Martin achieves his end through a circuitous route of delay.

Old Martin serves as a pattern for how other old men in the novel defer ends as a means of realizing them. For example, the text's dismissal of Anthony Chuzzlewit's ancient accountant, Chuffey, merely emphasizes the significance of the elderly man's revelation late in the novel. In the other major plot of *Martin Chuzzlewit*, the reader is led to believe that Jonas Chuzzlewit has murdered his father to expedite his inheritance. When Tigg Montague learns of Jonas's act, Tigg uses his knowledge as leverage against Jonas, forcing him to invest capital into his fraudulent business. Backed into a corner, Jonas murders Tigg. Shortly after, Old Martin accuses Jonas of killing his father, but before Jonas can be hauled off to prison the frail Chuffey comes to life: "The trembling figure of the old man shook with the strong emotions that possessed him . . . and with his gray hair stirring on his head, he seemed to grow in size, and was like a man inspired" (*MC*, 669). Chuffey reveals that Jonas's intended patricide was not successful. Discovering the poison in a drawer, Anthony only pretends to drink the liquid, dying soon after from grief and a broken heart. Exemplary of the dilatory effect of old men on narrative, Chuffey withholds his knowledge for most of the novel. As the vectors of narrative attention shift to Jonas, at a point of such intensity that deferral is no longer an option, the story bursts from Chuffey. As with Old Martin's revelation, the end (in this case the truth of Jonas's subplot) seems to derive from the fact that the story has been postponed for so long.

Chuffey's suppression of information quietly sets the plot of Jonas and Tigg Montague into motion. This plot is also grounded on the machinations of another old man, the proto-detective Nadgett: "He was a short, dried-up, withered, old man, who seemed to have secreted his very blood; for nobody would have given him credit for the possession of six ounces of it in his whole body" (*MC*, 385). The keyword for Nadgett, as it might be for all the old men in *Martin Chuzzlewit*, is "secret": "the whole object of his life appeared to be, to avoid notice, and preserve his own mystery" (*MC*, 505). As Nadgett tells Tigg after giving his report on Jonas, "It almost takes away any pleasure I may have had in this enquiry even to make it known to you" (*MC*, 509). For Nadgett, it is not so much the act of disinterring secrets that he enjoys – his surveillance leaves him with an "anxious face and bloodshot eyes" – but the condition of knowing something that others do not (*MC*, 673). Like both Old Martin and Chuffey, however, the protraction of the plot eventually yields to the crisis of necessity: with a "tone of regret in which he deplored the approaching publicity of what he knew," Nadgett brings Jonas's plot to a close while discharging his secret of any narrative importance (*MC*, 674).

The protraction of plots, the creation of new ones, and the harboring of secrets functions as an alternative source of power for the old men of *Martin Chuzzlewit*, one that is threatened by the closure and the revelation of secrets. Indeed, this narrative capital exists alongside the prospect of inheritance that looms over much of the novel, supplementing and in some cases replacing the function of wealth. The promise of inheritance and the power of money are widely acknowledged as the best way to ensure independence and respect for elderly people who might otherwise be pushed to the margins. Cole and Edwards state that "the elderly's bargaining power over the bequest of land, tools, and other economic assets, as well as trade skills, will safeguard their comforts until death." Thane adds that older people could command respect "by possession of property or high position." And Small claims that in *Martin Chuzzlewit* "The old recall and speak when the novel's moral scheme dictates, and even then their moral authority is awkwardly dependent not just upon their retention, or retrieval, of their mental powers but on their having access to the protection of wealth."[17]

However, far from implying the "protection of wealth," the core relationships in *Martin Chuzzlewit* suggest just the opposite: the older one becomes, the more the aged body is made to signify his or her resources. Money serves an ambivalent role in preserving the agency of the elderly, one that if taken too far has potentially dangerous consequences. Quadagno writes in *Aging in an Early Industrial Society* that while "Control of property gave the aged a good deal of power over their children . . . the disadvantage was that it created tensions between generations. There are many folktales describing fighting and even murder between parents and children" (14). The security provided by economic assets can quickly lapse into violence. Complaining to the father he will eventually attempt to murder for his inheritance, Jonas says "why don't you make over your property? . . . That would be natural to your own son, and you like to be unnatural, and to keep him out of his rights" (*MC*, 256). In the case of Old Martin and his grandson, while money does not act as the means of destroying their relationship, it also does not help in reconciling them. Old Martin claims that his money has brought him only "pain and bitterness": "I hate it. It is a spectre walking before me through the world, and making every social pleasure hideous" (*MC*, 36). It is upon this "spectre" that his relations project their attentions, anticipating the old man's demise and the wealth he will leave behind.

Reconciliation occurs instead through the other form of capital that old men wield in the novel: the hoarding of stories or information that results in the protraction of plots. It is a commonplace of the Victorian novel for the disruption of the linear trajectory of primogeniture to form the basis of the conflict, while the conferral of inheritance on the real heir signals resolution. But *Martin Chuzzlewit* de-emphasizes the role that money plays in the motivation of its protagonists: the novel is, after all, a sustained critique of selfishness. Old Martin laments, "I have so corrupted and changed the nature of all those who have ever attended on me, by breeding avaricious plots and hopes within them" (*MC*, 38). Money offers no protection. In fact, it turns one into a target. Old Martin responds to the proliferation of plots against him with one of his own, and his performance of decrepit old age allows him to influence Pecksniff and Young Martin as a means of realizing his goals. This plotting reinvests the old man with social power and narrative significance that exceed even that of wealth.

In *Martin Chuzzlewit* inheritance fails to inspire development because it channels desire almost exclusively toward the end. Such is the morbid trajectory of inheritance, in which the anticipation of death confuses one's normal sense of moral responsibility. In *Reading for the Plot*, Peter Brooks suggests that

> the paradox of the self becomes explicitly the paradox of narrative plot as the reader consumes it: diminishing as it realizes itself, leading to an end that is the consummation (as well as the consumption) of its sense-making. If the motor of narrative is desire, totalizing, building ever-larger units of meaning, the ultimate determinants of meaning lie *at the end*, and narrative desire is ultimately, inexorably, desire *for* the end. (51–2)

Placing meaning at the end of narrative turns the process of reading into an act of consumption – one where progress through the story does not register development (of the self, of meaning), but rather shrinkage and diminishment. When Old Martin cries out "A new plot; a new plot! Oh self, self, self!" he recognizes this link between selfishness and the teleology of plot (*MC*, 40). Moving forward is not development but death, and so looking forward to the prospect of inheritance in *Martin Chuzzlewit* results in Jonas's attempted patricide and eventual negation of self through suicide.

The deferrals enacted by the old men in *Martin Chuzzlewit* provide an alternative model of narrative where desire for the end has been replaced with the compulsion to suspend narrative progress. This dilatory compulsion opens a clearing for Young Martin's character to develop outside the coercion of teleological plots like that of inheritance. While the agency of the old man certainly plays a role in this development, within the broader context of Dickens's imagination he serves as the very figure of that postponement. Reflecting on Old Martin's altered state in the Pecksniff household, Mary says: "I have sometimes heard . . . that those whose powers had been enfeebled long ago . . . have been known to rouse themselves before death, and enquire for familiar faces once very dear to them; but forgotten, unrecognized, hated even, in the meantime" (*MC*, 575). Just so, Old Martin and Chuffey burst from their senescent stupor in spectacular fashion near the end of the novel. But no character better embodies the fearsome energies of age than Anthony Chuzzlewit on his deathbed: "battling for each gasp of breath, with every shrivelled vein and sinew starting in its place, as it were bent on bearing witness to his age . . . an old, old, shrunken body, endowed with preternatural might, and giving the lie in every motion of its every limb and joint to its enfeebled aspect, was a hideous spectacle indeed" (*MC*, 262–3). The trajectory of old age balks linearity: as with the aged sailor in Tennyson's *Ulysses*, just before the end we return back to the middle. It is this elliptical movement that gives old age a surprising power that is at once both terrifying and awesome.

The Afterlife of Plot

A close reading of the old men in *Martin Chuzzlewit* reveals that the success of the novel's plot has less to do with Young Martin's attainment of maturity than with opening channels where affect and resources can pass between generations. Dickens continues to develop this line of thought in *A Christmas Carol*, though here what is at stake is not familial relations – between grandson and grandfather – but the interiorized stages of one's own life. Already an old man at the beginning of the story, Ebenezer Scrooge is jerked through space and time by an entourage of spirits, who inspire him to change his miserly ways. Unlike the classical coming of age story, which depicts the development of youth, *A Christmas Carol* is a *Bildungsroman* for old age, where the pathos of the story lies not in the timeliness of maturity but in a change of heart that occurs before it is *too late*. Whereas in the conventional *Bildungsroman* youth develops into maturity through experience and education, Scrooge must forget the lessons he has learned over the course of his long life. The success of this project results in the dissemination of Scrooge's accumulated wealth through charitable acts at the end of the story. In *Season of Youth*, Jerome

Buckley's account of the Victorian *Bildungsroman*, "to 'make good' is to make money . . . Money therefore assumes a new and pervasive importance in the Bildungsroman" (21). But in *A Christmas Carol* "to make good" is inverted: the end of life is not the apotheosis of personal and financial development, but the opportunity of return and the subversion of the accretive logic of maturing capital that underwrites linear narratives of self-development.

Scrooge's transformation begins when he is visited by the ghost of his former partner, Jacob Marley. Enchained by his callous disregard for others while still alive, Marley warns Scrooge that "It is required of every man . . . that the spirit within him should walk abroad among his fellow men, and travel far and wide; and if that spirit goes not forth in life, it is condemned to do so after death. It is doomed to wander through the world . . . and witness what it cannot share, but might have shared on earth, and turned to happiness!" (*CC*, 23). The end of life does not result in abrupt termination but in a lingering consciousness that lacks the ability to effect a meaningful change in the surrounding world. The Dickensian hell is one where the damned wander meaninglessly amongst scenes of human misfortune. For the damned of *A Christmas Carol* the accumulation of resources has not enabled the reintegration into society that marks the ending of the classical *Bildungsroman*; instead, they inhabit an afterlife of plot where they repeat forever the alienating desire for personal gain.[18]

The hellish perpetuity of Dickens's afterlife is a fitting punishment for the individual who identifies self-development with capital's interminable maturation. As Franco Moretti writes in *The Way of the World*, capital represents a unique problem for the *Bildungsroman* because it closes off the possibility of concluding: "Capital, due to its purely quantitative nature, and the competition it is subject to, can be a fortune only in so far as it *keeps growing*. It must grow, and change form, and *never stop*" (26). *A Christmas Carol* literalizes this attribute of capital by putting the practices of misers into an imaginative context that underlines the terror of hoarding without end. To unhinge self-maturation from the maturity of capital, Scrooge must reinterpret the youthful journey that set the ground for his cynical worldview. Escorted by the Ghost of Christmas Past, Scrooge observes his young self alone and separated from his family during Christmas. He sees the magnanimity of his old employer, Fezziwig, and he watches the dissolution of his engagement to Belle, as his fears of poverty cause him to place the love of wealth above all others. Scrooge's youth results in a maturity that has determined the remainder of his life: "There was an eager, greedy, and restless motion in the eye, which showed the passion that had taken root and where the shadow of the growing tree would fall" (*CC*, 45). The recapitulation of Scrooge's past ends here: after this last, great conflict of his life, Scrooge's old age circles the desire for money with increasing intensity and futility. Scrooge merely grows older as his capital grows, and as such there is no story to tell.

But Scrooge's return to the past is more than just a didactic dramatization: it is an embodied renewal of the dynamic and haphazard energies of youth. When the Ghost of Christmas Past sardonically criticizes the generosity of Fezziwig, Scrooge takes offense and speaks "unconsciously like his former, not his latter self" (*MC*, 44). By moving between his "former" and "latter" self, Scrooge brings together the disparate perspectives offered by youth and old age. Such generational interplay is one of the defining characteristics of the Ghost of Christmas Past, who is described as:

> a strange figure – like a child: yet not so like a child as like an old man, viewed through some supernatural medium, which gave him the appearance of having receded from the view, and being diminished to a child's proportions. Its hair, which hung about its neck and down its back, was white as if with age; and yet the face had not a wrinkle in it, and the tenderest bloom was on the skin. (*CC*, 31)

The representative of past – a figure that we might expect to appear in the guise of old age – uncannily embodies the features of both the child and the aged man. The distinction between youth and age is continually subverted in *A Christmas Carol.* While the Ghost of Christmas Present begins its tenure as a giant in the prime of its life, it "grew older, clearly older" by the end of Christmas night (*CC*, 77). The boy and girl that huddle under its robe – allegories of ignorance and want – are similarly disfigured: "Where graceful youth should have filled their features out, and touched them with its freshest tints, a stale and shriveled hand, like that of age, had pinched and twisted them, and pulled them into shreds" (*CC*, 78). Written unequally on the bodies of the young and the old, age registers the social asymmetries of modern capitalism: where aged capitalists are locked into a terrifying perpetuity, the impoverished young are plunged into premature senescence.[19]

The compression of youth, adulthood, and old age into a single body merges the horror of a monstrous combination with the exuberant success of Scrooge's reformation. Waking up on Christmas day, he exclaims: "I am as merry as a school-boy," later adding "I'm quite a baby . . . I'd rather be a baby" (*CC*, 100). Avoiding the end that was not one – an afterlife tormented by the misery of others – Scrooge combines the financial means of old age with the reckless abandon of youth. Significantly, his first act of generosity is to enlist the help of a "delightful boy" who acts as his proxy in the purchase of a prize-winning turkey for Bob Cratchit's family (*CC*, 101). In his change of heart, it is as if Scrooge's aged frame requires a youthful surrogate into which his overflowing enthusiasm can be channeled. Other acts of generosity follow this one: he donates a large sum to the charity he had previously rebuked and raises Cratchit's salary. Scrooge's youthful revitalization is accompanied by the dissemination of his wealth, and further serves to destabilize the linear narrative of accumulating capital. He inhabits a temporal field that extends forward and backward simultaneously: signaling his reformation at the end of the story, Scrooge says twice "I will live in the Past, the Present, and the Future" (*CC*, 98–9). In Jesse Matz's reading, "The Art of Time, Theory to Practice," this means that Scrooge "has learned to perform the temporal diversity modern capitalism would destroy" (274). But in *A Christmas Carol* it is a very specific kind of temporal diversity grounded in sociocultural attitudes toward age, and the ability that age grants Scrooge to transgress the economic system in which he is situated.

Presented with the dismal prospect of his death by the ghost of Christmas future, Scrooge pleads: "Men's courses will foreshadow certain ends, to which, if preserved in, they must lead ... But if the courses be departed from, the ends will change" (*CC*, 97). In *A Christmas Carol* self-development is not a linear affair but a circuitous one that wraps around the past, the present, and the future: one does not progress to maturity and an independence secured by capital, but to an old age that is saturated by the reckless energies of youth and made permeable by outlets of distributed wealth. What makes *A Christmas Carol* more than a mere bourgeois fantasy, where social integration is accompanied by economic independence, is Scrooge's old age. As we approach the end of life, the rules that structure socioeconomic experience change. With some supernatural assistance, Dickens shows Scrooge that the goal of his life – the security offered by the accumulation of capital – decreases in importance in proportion to the amount of time that he has left to live. The spirits merely remind Scrooge of what old age enables him to do: as he is liberated from the economic necessity that compelled him to abandon his engagement to Belle, the proximity of old age to the end of life multiplies the possibilities available to Scrooge instead of closing them down.

Conclusion

In Dickens's novels the elderly man emerges as the discontent remainder of the developmental plot's teleology, bringing into relief the temporal limitations necessary to enable the expansiveness of realism. One of the ironies of the realist novel is that while its sheer length requires a great deal of time to read, the novel does a better job of representing the social spaces of modernity – the places where its characters work, interact, and gather – than it does representing the temporal continuity of an individual life. For example, while a novel like *Great Expectations* (1861) covers a great deal of time – the growth of Pip from a very young child to mature adulthood – much of Pip's development is carried out through what Gerard Genette in *Narrative Discourse* calls narrative ellipses: "where a nonexistent section of narrative corresponds to some duration of story" (93). Pip ages eleven years in the time that it takes to transition from chapter 58 to 59. Represented scenes of time passing tend to move at a much slower pace, with the human interest increasing as the temporal units become smaller. Pip's long descriptions of Satis House stall the forward movement of the story even as they occupy long stretches of the narrative discourse. Although adept at conjuring the illusion of vast and proliferating spaces, the realist novel does an inferior job of reproducing the texture of passing time over long spans.

The result is that the novel's representation of the social is one where aging – a context that all characters have in common – is strangely absent or relegated to the plotless fringes of the narrative.[20] The temporal discontinuities that inhere in the representation of any fictional life, whether in the form of compression or elongation, are marked out by Dickens's elderly men, who register the way that age attenuates the relation between men and the masculine values that shape their identity: the ability to work and be a productive member of society, the maintenance of patrilineal inheritance, and the accumulation of capital that secures independence and support for one's family. Such values were not only central to the construction of male subjectivities but also provided the ideological stimulus that ensured the smooth functioning of Victorian society. What elderly men allow us to see is a fault line at the heart of Victorian culture, where the white, male, middle-class subject is forced to cede power and inhabit a position of lesser influence in old age. This transition, Dickens implies, is occluded for the sake of maintaining a patriarchal social order, a sacrifice that finds its formal analogue in the novel itself: able to reproduce a complex and coherent social panorama, the novel is unable to faithfully represent the temporal continuity of something as mundane and essential as aging.

The elderly women of Dickens's novels provide an illuminating counterpoint. In *Little Dorrit* (1857) Mrs. Clennam expatiates her sins by "stopp[ing] the clock of busy existence," condemning herself to the life of an invalid by immobilizing her body for a dozen years (*Dorrit*, 361). In *Great Expectations* Pip observes that Miss Havisham's clocks are permanently set at twenty minutes to nine, and he begins to "understand that everything in the room had stopped, like the watch and the clock, a long time ago" (*Great*, 60). To a lesser degree, Mrs. Skewton of *Dombey and Son* (1848) attempts to stop time by prolonging the appearance of youth through cosmetics and by wearing the fashions of a young woman.[21] These women follow a regimen of preservation that keeps up the appearance of temporal stasis. "All seasons are alike to me," Mrs. Clennam tells her son, a sentiment that is echoed by Miss Havisham when she says, "I know nothing of days of the week; I know nothing of weeks of the year" (*Dorrit*, 49; *Great*, 62). The behavior of these women can be read as the result of the marriage plot's misfiring. Mrs. Clennam's terrible marriage with her husband, Miss Havisham's non-marriage to Compeyson, and Mrs. Skewton's attempt to attract sexual attention constitute social failures that exclude them from shared temporalities such as the seasons or calendar dates. For these women, to be outside the marriage plot is to shift from an existence where time's passage seems to matter to one where stasis and preservation becomes meaningful. As I will discuss further in the next chapter on Elizabeth Gaskell's *Cranford*, the experience of aging femininity provides a way of representing time after or outside marriage.

The aged characters of both sexes suggest that what is at stake with the elderly in Dickens's work is not only old age per se, but also that which has been left out in the process of getting there: aging. I have focused on elderly men because their response to old age illustrates the social consequences of omitting duration as a formal principle of the novel. Where the misfiring of the marriage plot results in elderly women who refuse to acknowledge the passage of time, Dickens's older male characters are subject to plots of ambition that no longer apply to their aged state. Instead of finding meaning in stasis, they engage in a narrative compulsion for which there is little need and for which there is no plot. They must negotiate between the modernity they wish to control and the past to which they seem to belong. Once occupying a position of cultural privilege, the elderly male subjects of my analysis find themselves in altered circumstances that raise questions central to the bewildering progress of a modernizing society: not the exuberant "what have we achieved?" but the sobering "what have we left behind?" In the realist novel's attempt to represent the development of a modernizing society there is always something left over, a temporal remainder that, like the aged man's existence, denies the comfort of a conclusion.

CHAPTER 3

Life After the Marriage Plot

Near the end of Elizabeth Gaskell's *Cranford*, the town doctor, Mr. Hoggins, follows through with his intention to marry Lady Glenmire, despite the withering disapproval of the Cranford society ladies. During the auspicious event,

> Mr. Hoggins looked broad and radiant, and creaked up the middle aisle at church in a bran-new pair of top-boots – an audible, as well as visible, sign of his purported change of state; for the tradition went, that the boots he had worn till now were the identical pair in which he first set out on his rounds in Cranford twenty-five years ago; only they had been new-pieced, high and low, top and bottom, heel and sole, black leather and brown leather, more times than any one could tell. (*Cranford*, 115–16)

As a bachelor, Mr. Hoggins's extraordinary boots underwent a continual process of repair. As a damaged heel is replaced with another, the cracked leather carefully patched together, and torn shoelaces exchanged with new ones, the boots lose bits and pieces of themselves while remaining recognizably the same. Much like the wear and tear that occurs to the human body over time, Hoggins's old boots display the patchwork of wrinkles and scars imprinted into the leather. However, a radical change occurs when he marries Lady Glenmire: the old boots are replaced by "bran-new" ones, breaking the thread of continuity that linked each repair to the previous one. So too, matrimony transforms the body of Lady Glenmire: "her face seemed to have almost something of the flush of youth in it; her lips looked redder, and more trembling full than in their old compressed state" (*Cranford*, 115). Marriage, in Elizabeth Gaskell's *Cranford*, represents this potential to disrupt continuity and posit a new – and distressingly unfamiliar – state of affairs. Though it rejuvenates the newlyweds, marriage also threatens the social hierarchy that binds together the women of Cranford, reducing the noble Lady Glenmire to a doctor's wife who takes the ungenteel name of Hoggins. Though Gaskell does not structure *Cranford* as a marriage plot, the novel is still very much *about* the marriage plot – what it binds together, disrupts, and leaves behind. For the elderly women of Cranford, the teleology of marriage competes with the nonlinearity of senescence as meaningful structures for organizing social life.

Since *Cranford*'s serial publication in *Household Words* between 1851 and 1853, critics have had difficulty reconciling the novel's episodic storytelling with the teleological arc of a conventional novel narrative. A reviewer in *Graham's Magazine* (1853) writes that while *Cranford* inspires "pleased attention" from the reader, "there is hardly any thing that can be called a plot" (448); similarly, Henry Fothergill Chorley in his review in the *Athenaeum* (1853) unflatteringly refers to Gaskell's novel as a "collection of sketches" where "there is hardly a solitary incident which is not of every-day occurrence" (765). In contemporary Victorian studies, Andrew Miller concedes in *Novels Behind Plate Glass* that *Cranford* displays a "conventional teleological structure" that coexists "with a cyclical movement, an alternative narrative form which emerges out of and represents the routines and material culture of everyday life" (93). Reference to circular, cyclical, or static models of time appear often in *Cranford* criticism, addressing a wide variety of issues such as memory, sympathy, and narrative repetition.[1]

As Barbara Adam points out in *Timewatch*, many different times structure an individual's experience – "time-frames, temporality, timing, tempo, a relation to the past, present, and future and ... clock and calendar time" (37). Adam suggests that the complexity of these times "cannot be expressed through the dualisms of cyclical and linear time": "cyclical time is neither the opposite of linear time nor separable from moments passing and recurring" (37, 23–4). The emphasis on linear time in Western culture, Adam argues, has caused us to lose "touch with our own cyclicality" (41). As a result, we project cyclicality onto the object of investigation as "other time" (41). When we think about the temporal experience of men and women according to the dichotomy of linear and cyclical time, women's time is typically collapsed into "other time." In *Doing Time*, Rita Felski further critiques this tendency, deriding the assumption that men are "encouraged to think of their lives in linear terms" while women's lives consist "of a series of fragments, not a carefully choreographed upward ascent" (21). These categorizations elide obvious similarities between how men and women experience time: "the realm of everyday life simply *is* repetitive, being largely defined by monotony, routine, and habit" (20). Thus, "the perception that cyclical time is a uniquely female province is highly misleading" (20).

The spinsters and widows of Cranford provide an alternative to the linear, progressive structure of the marriage plot without relying upon cyclical models of what the philosopher and literary critic Julia Kristeva calls "women's time." Talia Schaffer and Rachel Ablow provide new models for examining individuals who do not fit into the normative structure of the marriage plot. Ablow argues in *The Marriage of Minds* that while novelists like Charles Dickens privilege marital sympathy, for Emily Brontë the marriage plot "obscure[s] the utter powerlessness of married women" (45). According to Ablow, Brontë directs her critique at the limitations of the marriage plot, how it "depends on . . . our attachment to, identification with, and desire on behalf of some one central character" (48). By funneling the reader's attention to the privileged individual, the marriage plot renders most characters lesser objects of sympathy. As an alternative to the marriage plot's focus on the individual, Schaffer, in *Romance's Rival*, holds up the prospect of familiar marriage. Schaffer draws attention to the little-recognized, and yet pervasive, competitor to the romantic lover – the well-known and boring alternative suitor. This familiar lover, Schaffer notes, is "often significantly older," and embodies a different temporality from his romantic counterpart: "The romantic marriage lives in the present moment, collapsing past and future into one intense, immediate contact" while "familiar marriage relies on a shared past and anticipates a long future. It imagines love developing after marriage and it justifies itself by reference to benefits to come" (5–6). When the possibility of marriage rears its head in *Cranford* – between Miss Poole and the rector, Miss Matty and Mr. Holbrook, Lady Glenmire and Mr. Hoggins, or Mrs. Jamieson and Peter – it is usually of this familiar kind, sometimes realized but more often fading into the impalpability of gossip. In Gaskell's novel, the familiar marriage does not have a romantic challenger, allowing Gaskell to trace out the elderly lineaments of a narrative structure based on contentment rather than competition.

Yet *Cranford*'s contentment does not merely lapse into the temporality of utopian stasis. Making the marriage plot senescent – more familiar, without a romantic competitor – allows Gaskell to shift the tension usually posited between characters to the level of literary forms. In the affective excess left behind by a marriage plot that has been denied its usual strategies for generating interest, the formal structure of narrative – the *how* of its telling – becomes charged with an interest usually reserved for content. Genres such as the oral story and the newspaper illustrate different temporal possibilities for how narrative binds together the individual life with that of others. The newspaper, on the one hand, represents the invasively masculine temporality of modernity, which the women of Cranford recontextualize for the sake of conversation and reinforcing the bonds of the community. The Cranfordians also engage in what Gaskell codes as the feminine practice of storytelling. Yet even as storytelling forms the bedrock of Cranford's community, it also threatens to alienate the women from the world beyond its borders. As gendered literary forms in the textual economy of *Cranford*, the temporalities of the newspaper and the story are irreducible to either linear or cyclical models. Moreover, the two forms contribute to what I call "Cranford time": the aspiration to construct an alternative temporal zone outside of the forces of modernization through the attempt to displace the desire for ends with an interminable desire for more stories.

By continually raising and defeating the reader's expectations about marriage – of deploying a marriage plot without the possibility of marriage – Gaskell positions *Cranford* within the masculine temporality of modernization and yet hollows it out of content. Arguments regarding *Cranford*'s feminist intervention usually pivot on the perceived success or failure of Cranford's community in relation to the masculine world that threatens it. Critics like Patricia Wolfe and Nina Auerbach celebrate the closed community of Cranford as an alternative, feminine space that challenges the dominant ideology of the male sphere. Other critics, such as Martin Dodsworth, Audrey Jaffe, and Patsy Stoneman, are more skeptical of Cranford's autonomy, suggesting instead that the women form a "supportive sub-culture delimited by the dominant group."[2] To read *Cranford* as a fantasy of feminine empowerment that – successfully or unsuccessfully – is set against a male dominated world is to approach the novel from a predominantly spatial standpoint. Readings of *Cranford* that emphasize space tend to draw starkly gendered divisions; for example, Tim Dolin suggests in "Cranford and the Victorian Collection" that "it carries the Victorian orthodoxy of the separate spheres to its logical conclusion by imagining a world in which sexual division is so absolute as to be experienced as *geographical segregation*" (202; emphasis added). While Cranford is an emphatically feminine *place*, it is one that represents a much more complex approach to the way *time* is manifested by men and women. Its Amazonian exclusivity from the rest of England emphasizes Cranford's multi-temporality and the way the women adapt, or fail to adapt, to these new rhythms. The text that results – in its episodic, fragmented, and anecdotal irregularity – does not merely reflect the femininity of Gaskell's characters, but also their age. The superannuation of persons relates to a similar crisis in the marriage plot, which no longer reflects the experience of the characters it purports to organize. Thus, I read *Cranford*'s representation of other media – such as storytelling and the newspaper – as a reflection on the superannuation of form that takes place within the larger narrative economy of the novel. What emerges is a reevaluation of the utility of obsolescence, insofar as the women of Cranford reterritorialize the obsolete as a uniquely feminine challenge to the temporality of modernity.

The Duration of Contentment

Despite Miss Pole's many warnings against the institution, there are a surprising number of marriages in *Cranford.* Yet each marriage defies some expectation about its centrality to the narrative. When the orphaned Miss Jessie marries Major Gordon in the second chapter, she does not rise in narrative importance. Just the opposite: she disappears from the story, only to return briefly near the end of the novel. The marriage between Lady Glenmire and Mr. Hoggins – a controversial and monumental event – comes as a shock to the ladies of Cranford. Their courtship takes place along the margins of the narrator's interest, and there are none of the usual conventions – the coy glances and unexpected rendezvous – associated with their betrothal. Skipping over the preliminary signs of impending marriage, the two lovers simply announce their engagement. Similarly, the marriage between Jem and Martha occurs out of expediency, for the sake of giving the disenfranchised Miss Matty a suitable place to live. As the bewildered Jem responds to Martha's proposal: "It's that you've taken me all on a sudden, and I didn't think for to get married so soon – and such quick work does flabbergast a man" (*Cranford*, 132). Instead of protracting the vicissitudes of betrothal across the length of an entire novel, *Cranford*'s marriages have no time for plot.

In *Cranford*, the marriages that did not happen matter more than the ones that did. The love story between Miss Matty and Mr. Holbrook takes place in two parts: the past event of Holbrook's proposal and rejection, and the brief encounter between the two elderly lovers in the present. The passage of time renders the continued romance unable to end conventionally in marriage. When Holbrook sees Miss Matty in a fabric shop, the narrator observes that "He kept shaking her hand in a way which proved the warmth of his friendship; but he repeated so often, as if to himself, 'I should not have known you!' that any sentimental romance which I might be inclined to build, was quite done away with by his manner" (*Cranford*, 31). Moreover, when Mary Smith learns Holbrook's age from Miss Pole, she claims again that the romance is destroyed: "'He must be about seventy, I think, my dear,' said Miss Pole, blowing up my castle, as if by gunpowder, into small fragments" (*Cranford*, 31). Outside the conventional marriage plot (Miss Matty and Holbrook are now too old to marry), the romance continues to generate narrative because the end has ceased to matter as much as the story itself. A marriage plot without the possibility of marriage, the love story between Miss Matty and Holbrook defies the temporal conventions regarding age and romantic love.

The narrator captures the temporal disparity at the heart of the relationship between Miss Matty and Holbrook through the way she relates the story. Early in the chapter titled "A Love Affair of Long Ago," the narrator introduces "One of Miss Pole's stories" that "related to a shadow of a love affair that was dimly perceived or suspected long years before" (*Cranford*, 25). Instead of following this declaration with more explanation about the affair, the narrator launches into several unrelated anecdotes that cross the span of twelve full paragraphs. Stories about the problem of servants keeping lovers around the house, the way Miss Jenkyns and Miss Matty eat oranges, and the visit of Miss Matty's cousin Major Jenkyns all intervene between the announcement of the love affair and its elaboration, signaled by the narrator's statement: "And *now* I come to the love affair" (*Cranford*, 29). The narrator's italicization of "*now*" signals her awareness of the effects that withholding the story will have on the reader. This example of periphrasis, which occurs continually throughout *Cranford*, recalls the effect that occurs when, to quote Frank Kermode's *The Sense of an Ending*, "the end comes as expected, but not in the manner expected" (53).[3] The reader is kept at a distance from the story through the narrator's self-conscious deferral of desired information. In *Cranford*, the practice of storytelling displaces what Kermode calls the "hunger for ends and for crises" that propel conventional novel narratives, subverting the reader's assumptions about how the time of narration relates to the end of the narrative (55). The way the women of Cranford tell a story often matters more than the story's content, as the pleasure of forms – both literary and social – takes precedence over closure.

Storytelling is woven into the everyday lives of the Cranfordians: as Hilary Schor puts it, *Cranford* "conjures up a different (older) kind of storyteller: the anecdotal, intimate, immediate storyteller of village life." Storytelling draws upon a different temporality from the "linear or cataclysmic" models of historical transformation that Rita Felski argues "have been conventionally coded as masculine."[4] By attempting to displace the "end" toward which narrative moves, Gaskell draws attention to the youthful and masculine assumptions that inhere in the marriage plot's teleology. As she does so, she experiments with a narrative temporality that aspires to displace the reader's desire for the end with the desire for more *story*.[5] At the structural level, Gaskell uses techniques of storytelling to construct a dilatory form that displaces the reader's teleological desire in favor of a periphrastic mode of reading. At the level of content, this displacement occurs through the role of storytelling in consolidating the community around a shared temporal zone that sets them apart from everyone else.[6] The temporal displacements enabled by storytelling allow the women of Cranford a kind of ownership over their time that is not possible while under the coercion of the marriage plot.

In his essay "The Storyteller," Walter Benjamin analyzes the tension between the story and the novel. He likens the art of the storyteller to the "way the handprints of the potter cling to the clay vessel": as an "artisan form of communication," the story bears the traces of the storyteller herself, and produces meaning in the unique context in which it is told (92, 91). In contrast, the novel's "essential dependence on the book" liberates the author from the requirements of immediacy (whether figurative or literal) while obscuring the craftsman-like trace of the author's impression (87). The notion of proximity is at the heart of the distinctions that Benjamin notes between the two forms: "The storyteller takes what he tells from experience – his own or that reported by others. And he in turn makes it the experience of those who are listening to his tale. The novelist has isolated himself. The birthplace of the novel is the solitary individual" (87). The story and the novel differently position the individual within (or without) the community, as Benjamin observes that a "man listening to a story is in the company of the storyteller; even a man reading one shares this companionship. The reader of a novel, however, is isolated, more so than any other reader" (100). While the story unfolds during the immediacy of the shared moment, the novel supports an individual response to narrative.[7]

Benjamin's observation that reading a novel and listening to a story situate the individual in different ways corresponds with the reader's temporal experience of narrative. As Benjamin argues, the "novelist … cannot hope to take the smallest step beyond that limit at which he invites the reader to a divinatory realization of the meaning of life by writing 'Finis'" (100). However, the story's structural open-endedness suggests that "there is no story for which the question as to how it continued would not be legitimate" (100). A story "does not expend itself. It preserves and concentrates its strength and is capable of releasing it even after a long time" (90). Quoting the multiple and yet irreconcilable interpretations of a story from ancient Egypt, Benjamin concludes that the story "resembles the seeds of grain which have lain for centuries in the chambers of the pyramids shut up air-tight and have retained their germinative power to this day" (90). The open-endedness of the story replaces the novel's revelatory conclusion with the long pause and "germinative power" of indeterminacy.

The dynamic that Benjamin represents between teleological and periphrastic modes of narrative production maps onto the roles that the novel and the story play in *Cranford.* Characters associated with the novel and written texts are propelled to their own death; the deaths of these characters metaphorically stand in for the violence of "ends" in general and propulsive narrative specifically. When the avid reader of Charles Dickens, Captain Brown, is run over by a train while saving the life of a little girl, his act of heroism is qualified by the fact that he was reading a serial before his death: his obituary emphasizes that the "gallant gentleman was deeply engaged in the perusal of a number of 'Pickwick', which he had just received" (*Cranford,* 19). Even Miss Jenykyns confuses the Captain's cause of death, substituting "that book by Mr Boz" for the train (*Cranford,* 24). Though *The Pickwick Papers* is only associatively implicated in the Captain's death, Nina Auerbach points out that Dickens's *Dombey and Son,* specifically the scene where Carker meets his death by locomotive, also plays an allusive part.[8] Not unlike the propulsiveness of a train, Dickens's novels are teleologically organized in a way that *Cranford* is not. It is fitting, therefore, that Gaskell would later acknowledge in a letter to Ruskin that "The beginning of 'Cranford' was *one* paper in 'Household Words'; and I never meant to write more, so killed Capt Brown very much against my will" (*Letters,* 748). Captain Brown's premature death symbolically registers the danger of propulsive narrative to hasten ends that would be better off postponed.

Gaskell's rejection of teleology as a dangerous structure provokes her turn away from the novel's reliance on the marriage plot. Instead of concluding by uniting just two people, *Cranford* deploys the open-endedness of storytelling as a way of preserving a community of friends. When the women of Cranford are finally invited to visit Mrs. Jamieson's aristocratic – though poor – sister-in-law Lady Glenmire, the greatest sign that intimacy has been established between them is through the relation of "an anecdote known to the circle of her intimate friends": "As proof of how thoroughly we had forgotten that we were in the presence of one who might have sat down to tea with a coronet, instead of a cap, on her head,

Mrs. Forrester related a curious little fact to Lady Glenmire" (*Cranford*, 78). In the story, Mrs. Forrester's cat eats the lace she had been soaking in milk. Desperate to retrieve the item, she puts the cat inside Mr. Hoggins's top-boot and feeds it tartar emetic until it vomits. Those critics who try to account for this story tend to push it aside. In "Women Without Men at Cranford" Martin Dodsworth suggests that it represents the "triviality" of a "village society" that lacks the "true vitality" of the male (140). Taking a materialist approach, Christina Lupton argues in "Theorizing Surfaces and Depths" that the anecdote signifies "that textiles reward a closer look precisely because they are both texts and subjects of their own histories" (248). Such accounts ignore Mrs. Forrester's intention in telling the story, which has less to do with cats and lace than with creating intimacy. The content of the story takes a secondary role to the fact that it enables the incorporation of Lady Glenmire into Cranford's network of friends. Displacing the meaning of the story in this way also disables the teleological thrust of the narrative, as the point is no longer to reach the end of the story – the story ends where it started, with Mrs. Forrester in possession of her lace – but to enjoy the immediate and shared experience of the story itself.

By resisting the teleology of conventional narrative, Mrs. Forrester's story exemplifies *Cranford*'s larger embrace of what I call the duration of contentment. In contrast to the marriage plot, *Cranford* does not propel one toward a conclusion, but redirects attention to the pleasures of sharing time with another person (or, for the reader, the company of the novel). By doing so, it offers a model of social connection outside of the marriage plot's heterosexual and youthful focus. In *Between Women*, Sharon Marcus shows how "female friendship offered a vision of perfect reciprocity" to challenge the capitalist ethos of competition (4). Like female friendship, old age provides a way of thinking beyond the gendered, youthful binary of the marriage plot. Yet senescence draws attention to the temporal contingency of marriage's construction of identity. Excluded from the ubiquitous marriage plot, the elderly women of Cranford jointly construct a meaningful narrative of their experience by turning away from the temporality of plot and privileging instead the duration of storytelling. Rather than anticipate a future revelation, such storytelling eschews competition and places emphasis on the duration of contentment as a mode of relation with others.

Gaskell embeds the duration of contentment in the form of *Cranford* through the narrative's leisurely pace and digressions. The narrator interrupts moments of protracted description with statements like the following: "But I am getting on too fast, in describing the dresses of the company"; or, "I have wandered a long way from the two letters that awaited us on the breakfast-table that Tuesday morning" (*Cranford*, 74, 118). The whole of *Cranford*'s narration might be described as a reaction against "getting on too fast," of passing over those important details – what the narrator calls "fragments and small opportunities" – that become legible only when some time is taken to recognize that they exist in the first place: "the rose-leaves that gathered ere they fell, to make into a pot-pourri for some one who had no garden; the little bundles of lavender-flowers sent to strew the drawers of some town-dweller, or to burn in the chamber of some invalid" (*Cranford*, 17). By adopting a periphrastic style, Mary Smith confers meaning on overlooked actions by merely lingering upon them.

Even as the women of Cranford age beyond the conventions of the marriage plot, its structure of feeling continues to exert a powerful hold on their imaginations. As Miss Matty remarks, "for even if I did meet with any one who wished to marry me now (and as Miss Pole says, one is never too safe), I could not take him – I hope he would not take it too much to heart, but I could *not* take him – or any one but the person I once thought I should be married to, and he is dead and gone, and he never knew how it all came about that I said 'no'" (*Cranford*, 105–6). Excluding herself from matrimony while simultaneously registering her availability, Miss Matty finds significance in human relations other than marriage. As she asserts shortly after her comment above, "No one has such kind friends as I" (*Cranford*, 106). And, as the narrator's father exclaims in awe of Cranford's response to Miss Matty's misfortune: "See, Mary, how a good innocent life makes friends all around" (*Cranford*, 139). Aging past the marriage plot takes the gendered, binary model of marital dependence and replaces it with a non-hierarchical network of elderly dependence.[9] Even as this network codes dependence as mutually beneficial and outside the competition of capitalism, it also sets up a confrontation with the modern temporalities already reshaping the world outside Cranford.

Modernity and Age Obsolescence

To be outside the marriage plot was to be outside the dominant narrative of nineteenth-century modernity. The elderly spinsters and widows of Cranford attest to many of the difficulties of being left out of this structure. The gentle sarcasm of Mary Smith, the character-narrator of Cranford, posits a temporal gap between the unfashionable society of Cranford and the society of London: for example, observing an old woman who takes her "magnificent family red silk umbrella" to church on rainy days, Mary remarks, "Have you seen any red silk umbrellas in London?" (*Cranford*, 4). As the odd person out of the game of Preference, Mary notes, "Miss Barker provided me with some literature, in the shape of three or four handsomely bound fashion-books ten or twelve years old, observing, as she put a little table and a candle for the especial benefit, that she knew young people liked to look at pictures" (*Cranford*, 67). Though included within the Cranford community, the narrator sets herself apart from the other women because of her knowledge of fashion and, as we learn in Miss Barker's comment, her youth. Describing herself as "vibrat[ing]" between the industrial town of Drumble and Cranford, the narrator takes pleasure in the society of Cranford but views it from modernity's ironic distance (*Cranford*, 152).[10] However, in what follows, I argue that Cranford is not as out of touch with modernity as it might seem. By strategically recontextualizing what modernity considers obsolete, the women construct a narrative framework for recoding their own superannuation from the marriage plot.

In *The Gender of Modernity*, Rita Felski defines modernization as "the complex constellation of socioeconomic phenomena which originated in the context of Western development but which have since manifested themselves throughout the globe in various forms: scientific and technological innovation, the industrialization of production, rapid urbanization, an ever expanding capitalist market, the development of the nation, and so on" (12–13). The technologies of modernization import new temporalities into places unaccustomed to the rhythms of modernity. Wolfgang Schivelbusch, in *The Railway Journey*, shows the wide-ranging consequences of the railroad for the temporality of local communities: "The regions lost their temporal identity in an entirely concrete sense: the railroads deprived them of their local time . . . the temporal foreshortening of the distances that was effected by trains forced the differing local times to confront each other" (43). As the technologies of modernization shrink time, they also put pressure on local communities to adopt an increasingly homogeneous and rationalized discourse of time. Yet this process was not consistent. Even in the 1840s, the decade between when *Cranford* was published and when the events of the novel are thought to take place,[11] Schivelbusch notes that railway companies worked independently to institute "a new time on its own line" (43).[12] The resulting temporal complexity – a patchwork of local times crisscrossed by standardized railway times – suggests that modernity's acceleration and standardization of time challenged rural and suburban communities. The asymmetry between the time of modernity and that of Cranford is captured by the fatal speed of the locomotive as it hurtles through the village, crushing the beloved Captain Brown as he saves the life of a child. The railway represents a violent imposition of modern temporalities that Cranford is both unprepared and unwilling to confront, registering a youthful and masculine threat to the local community of elderly women whose affiliation is primarily to family, friends, and the people in their immediate proximity.

Yet modern temporalities are not always violent, nor are they always coercive. Like the railroad, the newspaper registers the trauma of modernity: as Schor notes, "Change in this novel is the world of the railways, and the railways mark not only a change in the ways of life but a change in ways of publication as well."[13] In contrast to their response to the railway, however, the women of Cranford recontextualize the newspaper for local concerns. Indeed, the steady rhythm of the periodical press contributes to Cranford's highly regimented temporality, even as the women are economically removed from its subject matter and uninterested in the newspaper's contemporaneity. Using the newspaper in unconventional ways, the Cranfordians stake out a temporal zone that serves as an alternative to the encroaching homogenization of masculine temporalities. As Felski argues, "women's interests cannot be unproblematically aligned with dominant conceptions of the modern, neither can they simply be placed outside of them."[14] The women of Cranford value the newspaper when it has been detached from its modern uses: its obsolescence allows it to circulate amongst the community of friends, stimulating the conversation that animates their everyday life.

The *St. James's Chronicle* serves as the reading of choice for the women of the village. Reporting on the actions of the aristocracy, the *Chronicle* was intended for the elite of England, even though, as Patricia Ingham observes in the notes to her edition of *Cranford*, such reading also attracted groups outside the upper class such as the clergy (243). While it may appear out of place for a group of poor, older women to turn to the *Chronicle* for entertainment, the newspaper appeals to the way that Cranfordians imagine themselves as – what the narrator sets off in quotations – a "genteel society" (*Cranford*, 26). Because the women of Cranford lack the money for individual subscriptions, they share the fees and trade the newspaper amongst themselves according to an established social hierarchy.[15] Mrs. Jamieson is the first to receive the paper, but her servant Mr. Mulliner consistently hijacks the *Chronicle*, thus delaying its dissemination:

> This very Tuesday, the delay in forwarding the last number had been particularly aggravating; just when both Miss Pole and Miss Matty, the former more especially, had been wanting to see it . . . Miss Pole told us she had absolutely taken time by the forelock, and been dressed by five o'clock to be ready, if the "St. James's Chronicle" should come in at the last moment. (*Cranford*, 74)

Part of the *Chronicle*'s appeal is in the timeliness of its information, so its postponed delivery disappoints Miss Pole and Miss Matty. For the Cranford ladies, whose financial limitations force them to share a subscription, the temporalities of the newspaper, such as the aspiration to contemporaneity, come with a prohibitory price tag.[16]

The delay of the *Chronicle* serves as a reminder of the material conditions that privilege the immediacy of personal contact over the imagination of community. Benedict Anderson claims in *Imagined Communities*, for example, that newspaper reading "is performed in silent privacy, in the lair of the skull. Yet each communicant is well aware that the ceremony he performs is being replicated simultaneously by thousands (or millions) of others of whose existence he is confident, yet of whose identity he had not the slightest notion" (35). For Anderson, the newspaper not only reports information about other people and events, but more importantly transforms the isolated experience of reading into a means of cultivating a national community. In Cranford, however, reading the *St. James's Chronicle* is sometimes a communal activity; for example, Mary Smith reads the *Chronicle* aloud to Miss Matty just before Miss Pole reveals the news of Lady Glenmire's engagement. In contrast to the solitary experience of reading that we associate with contemporary newspapers, the *Chronicle* tends to bring together the community through a network of sharing and communal interaction. As Matthew Rubery observes in *The Novelty of Newspapers*, this was not uncommon in the early nineteenth century: "News reading at the beginning of the century had been a largely communal activity by which a single issue was estimated to reach upwards of twenty readers through coffeehouses and public assemblies . . . Private reading would have been out of reach for all but the wealthiest individuals until the repeal of the stamp duty ushered in a century long process by which the listening public became a reading public" (6). In the many ways that the Cranfordians use newspapers, the tendency is not to imaginatively integrate with a larger national community, but rather to strengthen the local ties that bind the individual to her immediate group.

The rhythm of the *St. James's Chronicle*'s thrice weekly publication plays a significant role in structuring the economy of conversation in Cranford.[17] As Mark Turner suggests, this delay between installments organizes the time of readers and serves as "a form of social bonding": "During a weekly or monthly pause, readers were looking back at events that had occurred in previous installments and were projecting forward, thinking about the future of the narrative, and they were doing this together."[18] As Miss Matty observes, recalling the elderly women from her childhood, the *Chronicle* serves as a springboard for conversation: "They had the 'St. James's Chronicle' three times a-week, just as we have now, and we have plenty to say" (*Cranford*, 52). Striking the balance between having too much to say and not having enough, the *Chronicle*'s publication scheme not only provides the content for conversation, but also provides enough time between installments to talk about it.

Though not specifically mentioned as the cause, the *Chronicle*'s thrice weekly rhythm of publication helps to explain the otherwise arbitrary social rules that pace the everyday lives of the women of Cranford. Cranford time is defined early in the novel when the narrator explains the "rules and regulations of visiting and calls" by imagining a conversation that might occur for a young initiate in the community:

> "I dare say your mamma has told you, my dear, never to let more than three days elapse between receiving a call and returning it; and also, that you are never to stay longer than a quarter of an hour."
>
> "But am I to look at my watch? How am I to find out when a quarter of an hour has passed?"
>
> "You must keep thinking about the time, my dear, and not allow yourself to forget it in conversation." (*Cranford*, 4)

When considered in the light of the *Chronicle*'s publication, the rule that no more than three days may pass before returning a call makes more sense: three days ensures that enough time passes so that new content can inform conversation, but not so much that the articles lose their relevance. Even the brevity of the visit – a mere fifteen minutes – suggests that the length of conversation is appropriate for the length of a newspaper article. If the newspaper plays a role in structuring Cranford's experience of time, it also helps to construct a time that everyone in the community thinks about in the same way: "*We* kept ourselves to short sentences of small talk, and were punctual to *our* time" (*Cranford*, 4; emphasis added).

Cranford's desire for the newspaper hinges on its ability to mediate conversation and police the boundaries of their community. This is made clear when Miss Matty and Mary Smith transform the paper into walkways to defend Miss Jenkyns's new rug from the feet of her guests:

> We were very busy, too, one whole morning before Miss Jenkyns gave her party, in following her directions, and in cutting out and stitching together pieces of newspaper, so as to form little paths to every chair, set for the expected visitors, lest their shoes might dirty or defile the purity of the carpet. Do you make paper paths for every guest to walk upon in London? (*Cranford*, 15)

Miss Matty and Mary Smith ignore the content of the newspapers as they deconstruct the texts into something that has a new and very different significance from its original composition. The *content* of the paper transforms: from an account of things happening elsewhere and to other people, the newspaper takes on a material meaning as a pathway for Miss Jenkyns's guests. The narrator's question – "Do you make paper paths for every guest to walk upon in London?" – underscores the fact that the newspaper's reportage of others has been subordinated to the immediate concerns of the women's dirty shoes. The newspaper does not import a normative time into Cranford, so much as form the basis of a competing, local temporality dictated by the members of the community.[19]

Though the Cranfordians reject the normative temporalities of the newspaper – specifically the aspiration to contemporaneity and simultaneity that forge imagined links between the individual reader and the modern community – Cranford's temporality does not merely regress to cyclical patterns of non-socialized time. Attempting to protect Miss Jenkyns's new rug from the discoloration of the sun, Miss Matty and Mary Smith dismantle newspapers and place the leaves of paper upon the carpet:

> Oh the busy work Miss Matty and I had in chasing the sunbeams, as they fell in an afternoon right down on this carpet through the blindless window! We spread newspapers over the places, and sat down to our book or our work; and, lo! in quarter of an hour the sun had moved, and was blazing away on a fresh spot; and down again we went on our knees to alter the position of the newspapers. (*Cranford*, 15)

Seemingly unable to predict where the beams of the sun will fall, Miss Matty and Mary Smith exclaim in wonder at the natural rhythms of the earth. Such naïveté not only destroys the assumption that Cranford is a place uniquely connected to the cyclical rhythms of nature, but also suggests that it is a place that operates according to the rationalized time of the clock: as Mary Smith retrospectively observes, a quarter of an hour passes between each rearrangement of the newspapers.[20] Using the newspapers as a prophylactic against the sun, the women dramatize their appropriation of competing temporalities to suit the demands of their immediate environment.

Through their use of old newspapers, the women of Cranford convert what modernity considers obsolete into a valuable means of stimulating their community. By doing so, they provide a new model for old age in the nineteenth century – not as a time of life excessive to that of youthful maturity, but as an age that takes on significance precisely by its ability to discover meaning in what has been cast away by the society at large. Indeed, the newspaper becomes most significant when it becomes old. For the Cranfordians, the newspaper's obsolescence marks the beginning of a multiplicity of uses that exceed its intended purpose. This challenge to the hegemony of usefulness feeds back into the novel's treatment of the women themselves, who have been left behind by one of the most important structures for determining significance in a woman's life: the marriage plot. As aging slowly disqualifies the women of Cranford from this plot, they find ways of turning their own superannuation into a meaningful alternative to the joint imperatives of marriage and modernity of the nineteenth century.

The Economics of Redundancy

Cranford's construction of a temporal alternative to marriage and modernity implies vast transformations to the economic and political life of the nineteenth century. In the 1850s what women did or did not do with their time became a political issue that was channeled through public debates about the "redundant woman." Following in the wake of the 1851 census, which revealed a statistical surplus of women in England, the "problem" of the redundant woman (and what to do with her) became a major concern.[21] As Mary Poovey observes in *Uneven Developments*, responses to this problem took the form of scathing public outcry and plans to facilitate the emigration of women to the colonies (4–5). Another response, supported by writers like Barbara Bodichon and Florence Nightingale, addressed this concern by making the case for the training of women for work outside the home. In *Cassandra* (1852), Nightingale writes that "Women often long to enter some man's profession where they would find direction, competition (or rather opportunity of measuring the intellect with others), and, above all, time" (210). The problem of redundant women is solved when women have something to do; however, opening the sphere of work to women requires radical changes in the way temporality is qualified according to gender. According to Nightingale, women have no choice but to "play through life":

> Yet time is the most valuable of all things. If they had come every morning and afternoon and robbed us of half-a-crown we should have had redress from the police. But it is laid down, that our time is of no value. If you offer a morning visit to a professional man, and say, "I will just stay an hour with you, if you will allow me, till so and so comes back to fetch me"; it costs him the earnings of an hour, and therefore he has a right to complain. But women have no right, because it is "*only* their time." (214)

Lamenting the inability of women to cultivate a profession, Nightingale singles out compulsory idleness as the primary cause of women's inferiority to men. By ceding ownership of time back to women – by giving them the opportunity of using their time for purposes other than polite conversation – Nightingale argues that the redundancy of idle spinsters might be mitigated.

While Nightingale suggests that women should convert idle time into useful action, the spinsters and widows of Cranford demonstrate the utility of idleness itself.[22] Even when the failure of a joint stock bank ruins Miss Matty and she opens a tea shop, she spends her time in much the same way as before entering into business: "Miss Matty sate behind her counter, knitting an elaborate pair of garters: elaborate they seemed to me, but the difficult stitch was not weight upon her mind, for she was singing in a low voice to herself as her needles went rapidly in and out" (*Cranford*, 145). Instead of showing how temporal proprietorship allows women to excel at masculine professions, Gaskell makes the stronger argument that the sphere of work can be fashioned around the temporality of domestic practices and communality. When Miss Matty first opens her shop, she solicits her competition to "inquire if it was likely to injure his business" (*Cranford*, 142); the narrator's father reacts to Miss Matty's un-capitalist behavior by wondering "how tradespeople were to get on if there was to be a continual consulting on each others' interests, which would put a stop to all competition directly" (*Cranford*, 142). Through the way that Miss Matty runs her shop, Gaskell not only shows how control over one's time facilitates a woman's entry into business, but also how she can make business function according to her own time. Gaskell's response to the problem of the redundant woman is not that women need to be offered an opportunity to excel in the realm of men, but that women can interlace work with the structure of domestic experience. As an emblem of this combination of public and private, Miss Matty open her business in the small dining-parlour of her home, where a "very small 'Matilda Jenkyns, licensed to sell tea' was hidden under the lintel of the new door" (*Cranford*, 142).

While Nightingale suggests that women must conquer idleness, for Gaskell it is the slow, hypnotic pace of everyday life that underwrites the success of Miss Matty's business venture. Far from being meaningless, the idleness of the women of Cranford enables the success of their community. Nightingale's scathing portrait of an idle woman serves as an ironic endorsement of Gaskell's project in *Cranford*:

> But, in general, a "lady" has too many sketches on hand. She has a sketch of society, a sketch of her children's education, sketches of her "charities," sketches of her reading. She is like a painter who should have five pictures in his studio at once, and giving now a stroke to one, and now a stroke to another, till he had made the whole round, should continue this routine to the end. (*Cassandra*, 222)

Like Miss Matty, Miss Pole, and Mrs. Forrester, who spend most of their time telling stories, Gaskell structures *Cranford* around the surprising productivity of idleness: her novel works *because* it is composed of a series of vignettes that draw attention to the time of the telling rather than the anticipation of the end. By rerouting desire through the process of narrative production instead of cultivating anticipation of the end, Gaskell formally reproduces Miss Matty's success in the business world, which has less to do with the value of her commodity than with the way she goes about selling it.

For the redundant women of Cranford, marriage is not likely and, for some, not wanted. Yet this does not render them superfluous in the way W. R. Greg imagined in *Why are Women Redundant* (1869): "old maids, with just enough income to live upon, but wretched and deteriorating, their minds narrowing, and their hearts withering, because they have nothing to do, and none to love, cherish, and obey" (6). Instead, by replacing capitalist competition with an economics of contentment – exemplified by Miss Matty's business practices – Cranford illustrates how the linked discourses of old age and femininity can be used to challenge the exploitive aspects of the nineteenth-century market. In Gaskell's account, redundancy should not result in either exclusion or retraining – to make the redundant women more in line with the status quo. Rather, she imagines a society based upon the principles of redundancy – a place where the temporality of senescence sinks into the very transactions of everyday life.

Conclusion

Cranford's community of older women provides an alternative to the masculine temporality of nineteenth-century modernity by replacing the competition of the marriage market – and, by extension, capitalism – with the duration of contentment. Yet the very aspects of femininity and age that allow Cranford to critique the fashionable world also give rise to painful incongruities between one's youthful and older selves. In an intimate conversation with the narrator, Miss Matty reveals:

> "My father once made us," she began, "keep a diary in two columns; on one side we were to put down in the morning what we thought would be the course and events of the coming day, and at night we were to put down on the other side what really had happened. It would be to some people rather a sad way of telling their lives" – (a tear dropped upon my hand at these words) – "I don't mean that mine has been sad, only so very different to what I expected. I remember, one winter's evening, sitting over our bed-room fire with Deborah – I remember it as if it were yesterday – and we were planning our future lives – both of us were planning, though only she talked about it. She said she should like to marry an archdeacon, and write his charges; and you know, my dear, she never was married, and, for aught I know, she never spoke to an unmarried archdeacon in her life." (*Cranford*, 106)

While the women of Cranford find a socially and economically meaningful life beyond the marriage plot, it was also not the future that they envisioned for themselves as young women. The double-entry bookkeeping of the soul that Miss Matty describes – weighing one's expectation of the future with the reality of what occurred – illustrates the centrality of marriage for the youthful imagination. Yet Miss Matty's affirmation that her life has not "been sad, only so very different to what I expected" allows the youthful desire of marriage to exist alongside the acceptance in old age that this did not come to pass. In the next chapter, on Thomas Hardy's *The Well-Beloved*, I argue that this style of counterfactual thinking provides an ambivalent way of expanding the possibilities for old age by confronting the ever-expanding contingencies of the past.

Excluded from the marriage plot, the women of Cranford find meaning in other forms. Through the role that the newspaper and the story play in shaping Cranford's community, Gaskell suggests that the women establish an alternative temporal zone to the temporalities of modernization, displacing the desire for ends with an interminable desire for more stories. The success of this experiment is in some ways impossible: the story *must* end just as the community of Cranford will eventually pass out of existence. But *Cranford* draws attention to the fact that any conclusion is arbitrary, a construction that does not fulfill the reader's desire so much as reroute it. Registering Cranford's transience even as it celebrates the persistence of the community in the wake of inexorable modernization, Mary Smith's narrative registers both the contingency and the inevitability of an ending. The novel does not reject the teleology of the marriage plot outright, but experiments with ways of thinking alongside it and after it. Thus, Gaskell's novel decenters marriage, revealing the social and cultural assumptions that privilege certain portions of the woman's lifespan over others.

Outside the gravity of the marriage plot, *Cranford* posits forms of desire enriched by feminine and senescent values that are not projected exclusively to the end of narrative, but rather inherent to storytelling or the recycling of old newspapers. By publishing her writing irregularly in *Household Words*, Gaskell repeatedly deferred the ending of her novel, continuing the narrative far beyond its initial double installment and even publishing a new episode, "The Cage at Cranford," ten years after the final installment in Dickens's periodical. *Cranford* really has no end – it could go on forever – and that seems to be precisely the point. In both its form and its content, Gaskell's *Cranford* suggests that the narrative of human life is defined not only by the youthful eventfulness of the marriage plot but also by the durable contentment of late life. This contentment remains open to possibility – of adventure, of more narrative – precisely because it does not slot into the developmental plot structures of the nineteenth century.

CHAPTER 4

A Wrinkle in Time

In Thomas Hardy's short story "Fellow-Townsmen" (1880), Mr. Barnet makes the mistake of marrying for station instead of love. Alienated from his haughty wife, he imagines counterfactual scenarios that suggest what his life could have been if he had married the right woman. As he observes the happy domesticity of his friend's wife, Barnet imagines "what might have been in my case" and later reflects "on what might have been his lot if he had only shown wisdom enough to claim Lucy Savile when . . . she was to be had for the taking" (FT, 94, 116). In a stroke of bad luck, Barnet receives news of his wife's death at the same moment that he learns of Lucy's engagement to his friend. The shock causes Barnet to age, and the narrative registers a wrinkle in the process of developing: "The sun blazing into his face would have shown a close watcher that a horizontal line, which had never been seen before, but which was never to be gone thereafter, was somehow gradually forming itself in the smooth of his forehead" (FT, 122). Barnet's wrinkle asserts the stubborn reality of time passing against the ever-expanding archive of counterfactual possibilities that unfold along a biological lifespan. In Hardy's work, the longer one lives, the more raw material one has in the past to reimagine and regret. But as the years pass, the protagonists often attempt to turn what could have been into a present reality. Twenty-one years after the death of his wife, the aged Barnet makes his first and final proposal to the widowed Lucy. She refuses.

Hardy embodies the difficult task of representing aging through the peculiar way that Barnet's wrinkle materializes, "somehow gradually forming itself." While it is easy to imagine a youthful or elderly person, it is much more difficult to imagine a person in the *process* of aging. The temporal continuity of an individual life resists representation, and aging is usually registered narratively only after it has already occurred. In Chapter 1 of this book I argued against a view of duration as a temporal background that can be extracted from the depths of experience. Barnet's wrinkling, for example, does not occur at a deep, structural level but on the surface of its representation. Hardy wants the reader to see his description move, and he draws on aging as a way of challenging the temporal limits of narrative representation.

Many critics note the importance of time in Thomas Hardy's prose and poetry. J. Hillis Miller identifies the play between "distance and desire" as the central theme running through Hardy's oeuvre: the temporal gap that separates the poet from his melancholy reflection on the past or the narrator's retrospective account of the characters' lives. Gillian Beer extends this notion of temporal distance to an evolutionary scale of "diverse time-codes" that are "unable to cohere."[1] Tess O'Toole and Sophie Gilmartin draw attention to the time scale of heredity and genealogy and suggest that the inevitable speculations involved in reconstructing a pedigree activate the same imaginative impulse that animates narrative.[2] The passage of generations, like the deep time of geologic epochs, produces a foundation upon which Hardy's narratives slowly build.[3] For these critics, the gaps between past, present, and future are writ large in Hardy's imagination, emphasizing temporal discontinuities that his fiction imaginatively, though unsuccessfully, struggles to bridge.

Yet by privileging the long view of geology, evolution, and genealogy, these critics overlook Hardy's interest in representing continuity at the level of the individual lifespan and his experimentation with writing the imperceptibly slow changes that occur before our eyes. Barnet does not just wake up one morning and notice a new wrinkle in the mirror; the wrinkle is represented in the process of its appearance. The bodily transformation of aging is not interpolated from two fixed points – the time before the wrinkle and after it – but is granted temporal depth as the reader witnesses Barnet's flesh fold in narrative time. Hardy begins one of his famous poems, "I look into my glass / And view my wasting skin," using the present participle "wasting" instead of the past tense "wasted."[4] He perceives the effects of aging as a process rather than a completed state. Such marking of time suggests that the past is not a static point distanced from the present moment by an interval of transformation, but that the past is itself a dynamic part of the continuity of process: as a point of departure that remains open to change. The process of geologic epochs or the evolutionary gaps between species might require the imagination in order fill in the blanks, but aging takes place right before us, constantly; the difficulty of perceiving it as such testifies to the phenomenological and psychological repression of aging that, I will argue, is tied to the pervasiveness of the plot of decline.

Scholars of literary naturalism use the term "plot of decline" to describe a pattern in late nineteenth- and early twentieth-century texts where the narrative trajectory of the novel follows the arc of social and biological deterioration. In contrast to realism's interest in questions of moral value, the plot of decline revolves "around strength and weakness . . . youth and age, freshness and exhaustion." This plot has social and biological aspects: the plot can be interpreted through the lens of economic social power, so that one reaches his peak at "the age sixty" after which follows a quick and precipitous decline. Or, the decline can be interpreted from a Darwinian perspective as "a rapid rise peaking at twenty and a long continuous decline that takes up the longest section of personal history."[5] Hardy's *The Mayor of Casterbridge* (1886), for example, follows a parabolic arc that indexes economic status with stages of the human lifespan: Henchard begins life as a lowly hay-trusser, becomes a powerful and wealthy businessman by middle age, and ends his life engaging in the same labor of his early years. The discourse of the novel does not give equal weight to each stage of Henchard's life; instead, it spends most of its time representing the progress of the wealthy, middle-aged Henchard into an elderly laborer.[6] The decline that marks the end of so many of Hardy's novels writes large the normative account of a human lifespan that begins with youthful possibility, reaches its apex in adulthood, and deteriorates into senescence and death.[7]

In the last published novel of his career, *The Well-Beloved* (1897), Hardy confronts the hegemony of the plot of decline by calling into question the temporal assumptions that underwrite the representation of duration. Narratavized through Jocelyn Pierston's aging, *The Well-Beloved* explores the biocultural antimony between the past tense of one's accumulated life and the restless linearity of life itself. The first two sections of this chapter analyze this antimony through the discourses of evolutionary biology and geology. Both sciences enrich Hardy's repertoire of images and metaphors to describe aging and provide conceptual models of time that – far from supporting the plot of decline, as many scholars have argued – problematize the teleology of late-life decrepitude. In the third section, I illustrate how these alternative models of temporality affect the narrative form of *The Well-Beloved.* I show how the counterfactual – at the level of both the character and the plot – serves as a narrative means of working through the impasse of representing the process of aging. On the one hand, the counterfactual offers Jocelyn a more fluid and continuous relation between youth and age, where the representation of the past is not distanced by time but grafted onto the present moment. On the other, the counterfactual prevents Jocelyn from moving forward, and his obsession with the past is matched with his physical and emotional inability to mature. Both Jocelyn and the narrative clash against the ageist compulsion to view growing older as a linear process that consumes time. Though the novel does not ultimately transcend the powerful narrative of decline, it retards its force and pace, thus serving as a reminder that aging's movement toward a certain end is coupled with a lateral expansion of counterfactual possibilities as time progresses.

Art and the Evolutionary Biology of Aging

The Well-Beloved tells the story of a sculptor who searches for an ideal beauty – the eponymous Well-Beloved – that capriciously moves from the body of one woman to another. As he explains to his friend Somers, "Each shape, or embodiment, has been a temporary residence only, which she has entered, lived in a while, and made her exit from, leaving the substance so far as I have been concerned, a corpse" (*WB*, 200). The novel contains three volumes that represent Jocelyn's love affairs at the age of twenty, forty, and sixty. In the first volume, Jocelyn proposes to Avice Caro, his childhood sweetheart, but breaks off the engagement to elope with the daughter of his father's business rival, Marcia Bencomb. After the failure of his relationship with Marcia, Jocelyn devotes himself to his art and becomes a successful sculptor. The second and third sections of the book relate Jocelyn's failed romances with the daughter and granddaughter of Avice Caro, a generational conceit that is made possible through the unique setting of the novel. Much of the action takes place on "The Isle of Slingers," where intermarriage among the natives is the norm; thus, certain phenotypes are as common as the names that pass between generations, "there being but half-a-dozen christian and surnames in the whole island" (*WB*, 180). Over the forty-year span of the novel's plot, Jocelyn does not age – biologically or emotionally – at the chronological rate one would expect (the sections of the novel are titled "A Young Man of Twenty," "A Young Man of Forty," "A Young Man of Sixty"). It is only at the end of the novel, when the sixty-two-year-old Jocelyn marries his estranged lover Marcia Bencomb, that time has its revenge on his body.

J. Hillis Miller suggests that Hardy developed the idea for the intergenerational plot of *The Well-Beloved* from reading August Weismann's *Essays Upon Heredity* (1889), in which the scientist outlines his theory of the germ plasm. Weismann argues against the Lamarkian idea that changes in the organism occur in response to external conditions and can be transmitted directly to that organism's progeny. Instead, the germ plasm – what we now call genetic information – passes from one organism to the next and does not modify in relation to the environment. In *Fiction and Repetition* Miller connects the idea of the germ plasm to Jocelyn's compulsion to repeat and the naturalist's sorrow that whatever "he does echoes something those forebears have already done" (169). Analyzing *The Well-Beloved* in the context of Weismann's germ plasm theory underlines the novel's message about heredity and repetition. Yet Miller's application of Weismann ignores the temporal extension of Jocelyn's life and renders the character's aging a passive interval where fate shapes his character. According to this view, growing older does not provide more possibilities for transformation but merely more time to repeat what has come before. Contrary to Miller's influential reading, I argue that the novel represents such repetitiveness as a way of illustrating the difficulty – but not the impossibility – of thinking outside the teleology of the human lifespan. By representing Jocelyn's aging across the cyclicality of generations, the novel suggests that aging is a dynamic process that opens a horizon of personal and aesthetic possibilities.

In the first of his *Essays Upon Heredity*, "The Duration of Life," Weismann argues that the length of life for an organism is not determined solely by physiological considerations such as "the size of the animal, the complexity of its structure, and the rate of its metabolism," but has roots in "the needs of the species" and its ability to adapt to external conditions (9). While it is the prerogative of the individual organism to live as long as possible, the interests of the species determine that an organism's life should extend long enough to produce offspring and rear them. Life beyond the parameters of reproduction and care is "a luxury without any corresponding advantage" (25). Nature, Weismann argues, "does not tend to secure the longest possible life to the adult individual, but, on the contrary, tends to shorten the period of reproductive activity as far as possible, and with this the duration of life" (11). The duration of life has Malthusian implications. In the first Darwinian explanation of aging, the naturalist Alfred Russel Wallace writes that, "if individuals did not die they would soon multiply inordinately and would interfere with each other's healthy existence."[8] Competition for resources between the parent organism and its offspring gives rise to "the origin of *old age*, *decay*, and *death*" as a way of preserving the younger generation and ensuring the survival of the species.[9] For Wallace, old age is the result of natural selection tilting the game in favor of the younger generation and the species, trading potential immortality for increased reproduction and favorable conditions for the successors.

While the life of the individual organism develops along a linear arc that results inevitably in death, the temporality of the species does not proceed through a series of teleological stages. The German physiologist Johannes Müller writes,

> While life is continued, with an appearance of immortality, from one individual to another, the individuals themselves perish: but if *all* the individuals of a species are destroyed, the species itself, whether of animals or plants, becomes extinct, as the history of the earth proves. The *vital* or *organic force* flows, as it were, in a stream from the producing parts into those ever newly produced, while the old parts perish. (Elements of Physiology, 40)

At the level of the species, the continual generation of new parts and the passing away of the old does not create the appearance of transformation but of "immortality." Weismann addresses Müller's provocative phrasing in "The Duration of Life": "That which remains over, that which persists, is not the individual itself – not the complex aggregate of cells which is conscious of itself – but an individuality which is outside its consciousness, and of a low order – an individuality which is made up of a single cell, which arises from the conscious individual" (34). This low order, single cell – what Weismann elsewhere calls the germ plasm – serves as a constant across time, creating the "appearance of immortality" by passing on traits to successors while the organisms themselves grow old and pass away. Nineteenth-century accounts of the evolutionary biology of aging articulate a dual temporality: for the species, continuity across time; and for the individual, the finitude of the lifespan.

Hardy's *The Well-Beloved* represents the macro-temporality of species and the micro-temporality of the individual as a romance, where the duration of Jocelyn's aging over a forty-year span crosses the generational plane of three women. Though Jocelyn ages throughout the novel, each iteration of Avice looks precisely the same: "She seemed not a year older, not a digit less slender, not a line more angular than when he had parted from her twenty years earlier" (*WB*, 235). The appearance of immortality that characterizes the species is brought down to the genealogical level, where each successive generation sustains the illusion of similarity across time: "The three Avices, the second something like the first, the third a glorification of the first, at all events externally, were the outcome of the immemorial island customs of intermarriage and of prenuptial union, under which conditions the type of feature was almost uniform from parent to child through generations" (*WB*, 294). In contrast to the image of Avice that persists across generations, Jocelyn's "record moved on with the years": "forty years had passed . . . till a secondly renewed copy of his sweetheart had arisen to fill her place. But he, alas, was not renewed" (*WB*, 245, 298). The relationship between Jocelyn and the three Avices requires the narrative to negotiate between its diachronic and synchronic axes.[10] The passage of time crucially affects the appearance of Jocelyn, but such duration is of less visual significance in the timescale of generations, where a new Avice eventually replaces the previous one.

The disparity between Jocelyn's aging and the Avices' renewed youth infuses Jocelyn's art with mixed temporal imperatives, as the impetuosity of his desires clash with the durability of his artistic creations. When Jocelyn proposes to Avice the first he is filled with "misgiving" and regret at "what he had said to her in a moment of impulse" (*WB*, 184). When he leaves the island to transact some business in London, he encounters Marcia Bencomb, the daughter of his father's business rival. The Well-Beloved migrates to Marcia's form, with its classical features, causing Jocelyn to transfer his affections and break his engagement with Avice. Gazing at Marcia's clothes as they dry before a fireplace, "In the course of ten minutes he adored her" (*WB*, 196). With respect to both affairs in Jocelyn's twenties, his affections move too fast. When an administrative blunder postpones the marriage between Jocelyn and Marcia, the passion between them cools, and she returns to her father on the island. Such feeling is intense but transient, like the "flash-telegraph" and "Too like the lightning" (*WB*, 197, 208). The very speed with which the Well-Beloved invests a woman with ideal beauty is matched by the quickness of its departure; as Jocelyn complains to Somers, as "flesh she dies daily, like the Apostle's corporeal self; because when I grapple with the reality she's no longer in it, so that I cannot stick to one incarnation if I would" (*WB*, 213). The Well-Beloved, like the present moment, rushes relentlessly forward – both slip away before they can be isolated and fixed.

After the failure of the "too rash, too unadvised, too sudden" relationship between Jocelyn and Marcia, the sculptor throws "into his plastic creations that ever-bubbling spring of emotion" (*WB*, 208, 211). He becomes "successful by a seemingly sudden spurt, which carried him at one bound over the hindrances of years" (*WB*, 211). Jocelyn's success as an artist, like his love affairs, elides the arduous passage of years and arrives all at once. The irony is that his artistic creations attempt to capture the very ephemerality that characterizes the beautiful: "The study of beauty was his only joy for years onward. In the streets he would observe a face . . . which seemed to express to a hair's-breadth in mutable flesh what he was at that moment wishing to express in durable shape" (*WB*, 211). Jocelyn's aesthetic ambition lies in conceptualizing ways to temporally extend moments of beauty. His work appeals to the "public taste," and the narrator warns that he was "in danger of drifting away from a solid artistic reputation to a popularity which might possibly be as brief as it would be brilliant and exciting" (*WB*, 212). The final sentence of the novel confirms that his sculptures are not aesthetically durable enough to stand the test of time: "his productions are alluded to as those of a man not without genius, whose powers were insufficiently recognized in his lifetime" (*WB*, 356). As the Well-Beloved moves lightsomely from one woman to the next, so too Jocelyn achieves artistic renown without grueling years of toil and obscurity. But such success does not last long, and Jocelyn's lament about the ephemerality of beauty is met with Somers's advice: "Wait till you are older" (*WB*, 213).

The contrast between the bodies of women who are temporarily imbued with the Well-Beloved and the unchanging essence of the Well-Beloved itself stages the evolutionary drama between aging individuals and the continuity of the species. Jocelyn's attempt to preserve his momentary aesthetic experiences through sculpture further reinforces this connection, as the models for his art pass away while his durable creations remain unchanged. Even at a young age, Jocelyn shows sensitivity to the effect of age on the viability of his aesthetic ideal. As a boy, Jocelyn falls in love with a young woman many years older than himself; when he narrates the experience to Somers he recalls "a sense of disparity in our ages disturbing my mind" (*WB*, 201). Not yet through puberty, Jocelyn is too young to sexually engage the nineteen-year-old woman who intrigues him. Later, when he is seventeen, Jocelyn complains when the Well-Beloved migrates to a married woman with a child: a "tantalizing situation of an inaccessible matron's form" (*WB*, 202). In both cases, the Well-Beloved's inaccessibility pivots on the years that separate Jocelyn from his beloved, between his own sexual impotence and the alluring sexuality of the woman that he pursues. Later in the novel, a similar disparity in years characterizes the romance between the older Jocelyn – now in his forties and sixties – and the twenty-year-old daughter and granddaughter of Avice Caro. The asynchrony of ages provides the most consistent rationale for Jocelyn's inability to consummate his relationships and finally capture the beauty that eludes him.

In his agonizing pursuit of the Well-Beloved, Jocelyn confuses the dual temporalities of aging. The embodiment of the Well-Beloved in a woman's form cannot be reconciled with that of ideal beauty because the two exist on different temporal planes: the biological aging of the human lifespan and the "appearance of immortality" that characterizes the species. As biologists such as Wallace and Weismann suggest, these two planes overlap without being reducible to one another; that is, the species contains members of different age groups even as it maintains the appearance of similarity across generations. Because they infuse his desire for another individual with the supratemporal imperatives of the species, Jocelyn's love affairs result in a sexual impasse that is rooted in the asynchrony of attempting to locate the ideal in the real. This ambition is a common mistake of Hardy's male characters, a fault that Kathleen Blake identifies in "Pure Tess," as attempting to "regard the particular . . . as an expression of the universal" (699). Yet the disturbance of Jocelyn's fantasy is unique insofar as the depredations of time erode its ideality: "during the slow and colourless days he had to sit and behold the mournful departure of his Well-Beloved from the form he had lately cherished, till she had almost vanished away. The exact moment of her complete withdrawal Pierston knew not, but not many lines of her were longer discernible in Marcia's recalled accents" (*WB*, 209). The slow exit of the Well-Beloved from Marcia's form, the difficulty of marking the exact moment of her withdrawal, aestheticizes the role of aging and time. The moment that Marcia loses the ideal and becomes mere flesh falls out of the narrator's account, though we know that such a transfer has occurred. By turning the boundary between particular and universal, real and ideal, individual and species into the subject matter for art, Hardy renders the scientific distinction between the categories into a temporal one. Such boundary-crossings are narratable but inherently ambiguous, as difficult to pinpoint as the moment when the youth attains maturity or the adult becomes old. The lack of definition between these categories breaks down the normative stages of a human life, opening artistic possibilities through the transgression of culturally bounded intervals of time.

Geologic Features

The second section of the novel chronicles Jocelyn's changed attitude toward the Well-Beloved. Now in his forties, Jocelyn begins a relationship with the widowed Nichola Pine-Avon, which is cut short when he receives a letter notifying him that the woman he jilted long ago, Avice Caro, has died. The Well-Beloved immediately exits from Nichola and takes up permanent residence in the form of "an Inaccessible Ghost" – Jocelyn's memory of the deceased Avice (*WB*, 229). His reception of the news of Avice's death is marked by the irruption of the past into the present moment of a dinner party: "By imperceptible and slow degrees the scene at the dinner-table receded into the background, behind the vivid presentment of Avice Caro, and the old, old scenes on Isle Vindilia which were inseparable from her personality. The dining-room was real no more" (*WB*, 229). The dining room becomes a palimpsest written over by the powerful memories of the past: "The crannied features of the old society lady . . . shaped themselves to the dusty quarries of his and Avice's parents, down which he had clambered with Avice hundreds of times" (*WB*, 229). As the wrinkles of the elderly woman transform into the geologic features of Jocelyn's rocky home, they illustrate the complex layering of past and present shared by the material stratification of the earth and the aging of the human face.

The face plays an important role in connecting the discourse of geology to that of aging. William Cohen argues in *Embodied: Victorian Literature and the Senses* that in Hardy's work the "face can serve as both record and screen on which layers of conflicting meaning might variously arise" (93). The ethereality of thought and feeling is written into the material of the individual's face, confusing the semantic boundaries that usually separate binaries such as subject and object, interior and exterior. Cohen goes on to suggest that "the features of Hardy's facial lexicon" include "an inseparability of face from environment, a fluid shift between roles of object and subject, and an inscribed record of the encounter between external phenomena and subjective emotion" (106–7). The earth gains the features of subjective agency by linking the interiority of the individual to the materiality of the face, and the human body with landscape description (98). For Cohen, the earth and the face do not form a material substance that the mind writes upon, but serve as "mutually inscribing surfaces" (92). Cohen's argument provides a materialist account for understanding Hardy's naturalist ethos, as agency is no longer the sole prerogative of the thinking individual but categorically linked to the body and the natural world.

As the face develops wrinkles and loses the appearance of being an unbroken surface, it gains a corresponding temporal depth that is associated in *The Well-Beloved* with geological time. When Avice the third flees from her engagement to the aged Jocelyn, she elopes with her lover, Henri Leverre, in a small boat. As the lovers are caught in the dangerous current called the Race, the landscape takes on the threatening aspects of age that Avice is attempting to escape: "they beheld the gray rocks near them, and the grim wrinkled forehead of the isle above" (*WB*, 323). Unable to control the boat, the two lovers look away from the landscape and gaze "helplessly at each other" (*WB*, 323). The young couple form a microcosm against the menacing backdrop of the aged landscape, taking solace in each other's presence even as their agency is taken from them and placed in the hands of the natural world. The fact that Avice and Henri turn toward each other at this crucial moment, rather than outward toward the world that threatens to engulf them, underlines the novel's configuration of age and power. Though Jocelyn's wealth and fame as an artist give him considerable social power, his age makes him an outsider. In the mind of Avice he is "a strange fossilized relic in human form," a curiosity that belongs in the background like that of the landscape that frames the two youths: powerful, fearsome, and ignored (*WB*, 306). The temporal gap that separates the sixty-year-old Jocelyn from the twenty-year-old Avice takes on the incomprehensibility of remote geological epochs.

For Geri Berg and Sally Gadow, wrinkles not only testify to passing time but also serve as a phenomenological event:

> It is as though, through these changes, body and mind express the greater intricacies, the finer articulations that are possible in the person for whom reality has become many-layered, folded upon itself, woven and richly textured, a reality no longer ordered in the more familiar linear fashion, but now a world filled with leaps, windings, countless crossings, immeasurably more intricate and perhaps also more true than the world of one-dimensional thought and self-evident distinctions. ("Toward More Human Meanings of Aging," 86)

The wrinkle does not merely bear witness to old age, but also serves as a metaphor for the temporal complexity – with its leaps, windings, and crossings – that constitutes the tortuous process of a human life. Hardy was particularly sensitive to the wrinkle's potential to destabilize linear models of time. The first sentence of *Far from the Madding Crowd* (1874) describes the transformation of Gabriel Oak's face as he smiles: "his eyes were reduced to chinks, and diverging wrinkles appeared round them, extending upon his countenance like the rays in a rudimentary sketch of the rising sun" (9). Just entering the adult stage of his life, Oak's wrinkles do not signify old age but mirth and good humor – the narrator remarks that in the "remoter crannies" of his face remained "some relics of the boy" (10).

In Hardy's poetry wrinkles also destabilize culturally defined stages of life. In "In the Night She Came," the speaker promises his lover that time's depredations will not change his feeling of adoration. However, that very night he has a dream in which his lover appears

> Toothless, and wan, and old
> With leaden concaves round her eyes,
> And wrinkles manifold.
>
> (lines 6–8)

The apparition shocks the speaker and causes him to think twice about his pledge, and the next day he feels "Divided by some shade" from his beloved (line 24).[11] The premature arrival of old age, even in the form of a dream, illustrates how an imaginative reordering of normative life stages can have a profound impact on the decisions made in the present moment. A similar crossing of the present and future occurs in "At the Dinner Table" when a man tricks his young wife by replacing a normal mirror with a distorting one. She remarks that

> Wrenched wrinkled features met my sight,
> Grinning back to me as my own;
> I well-nigh fainted with affright
> At finding me a haggard crone.
>
> (lines 5–8)

The speaker picks up the narrative fifty years later after the death of her husband, as she looks again into the non-distorted sideboard mirror:

> from this mirror looked the lean
> Thing I'd become, each wrinkle and score
> The image of me that I had seen
> In jest there fifty years before.
>
> (lines 21–4)[12]

Wrinkles are written on the youthful face just as they appear on the aged – through laughter, dreams, and distorting mirrors traces of what will be in the future appear in the present moment.

Though they result from the passage of linear time, wrinkles provide a key to imagining what the body looked like in the past and what it will look like in the future. The signifying potential of wrinkles relies upon the belief that the present record – the face – is a reliable index to bodily states far removed from its current state. Scientists engaged in similar imaginative work through close observation of the geological record. The theory of uniformitarianism, popularized by Charles Lyell in his *Principles of*

Geology, held that the processes occurring to the earth at the present held true in the past and would continue into the future. Uniformitarianism enabled the geologist to reconstruct scenes from the remote past, crafting a connection between the observable present to an astonishingly foreign landscape populated by alien and terrifying beasts.[13] When Jocelyn's former lover Marcia Bencomb nurses him during an illness late in the novel, she is described as "the image and superscription of Age – an old woman, pale and shrivelled, her forehead ploughed, her cheek hollow, her hair white as snow. To this the face he once kissed had been brought by the raspings, chisellings, scourgings, bakings, freezings of forty invidious years" (*WB*, 332). The narrator describes Marcia's face as a landscape affected by the ravages of geological processes. In fact, her face almost disappears from the description, as the long list of abrading forces destroy the integrity of her once youthful body. Such forces recall not only natural processes, but also the work of Jocelyn's sculpting, which creates art by rasping and chiseling pieces out of raw stone.

The narrator consistently describes Jocelyn's rocky island by referencing the interminable forces of geologic decay. He describes the waves "rising and falling against the pebble dyke" and the "regular intervals" of the sea washing "among the boulders" (*WB*, 186, 277). The continual effect of the water, however, produces no visible outcome: "The canine gnawing audible on the Pebble-bank had been repeated ever since at each tide, but the pebbles remained undevoured" (*WB*, 283). The natural process of the waves matches human attempts to quarry pieces of rock from the earth: "eternal saws . . . going to and fro upon eternal blocks of stone – the very same saws and the very same blocks that he had seen there when last in the island, so it seemed to him" (*WB*, 181). Observing the constant splashing of waves and the chiseling of picks, Jocelyn expects that the "vast cubes" of limestone "would be nibbled all away" (*WB*, 211). But these processes of deterioration produce surprisingly little result unless accounted in the span of "unreckonable geologic years" (*WB*, 233). For most of *The Well-Beloved*, Jocelyn's body registers the effects of passing time as little as the landscape. The narrator claims that Jocelyn "was always regarded as a young man, though he was now about forty" (*WB*, 218). Even at the age of sixty, Avice the second describes him as "just the same!" (*WB*, 287). The lack of perceptible change in Jocelyn's appearance takes on geologic overtones, as his "inability to ossify with the rest of his generation threw him out of proportion with the time" (*WB*, 287).

Geology's spatialization of time provides a potent metaphor for understanding the effects of duration on the human body. Using George Eliot's

Silas Marner as a test case, Andrea Charise and Pascale Manning argue that many Victorian authors struggled to "capture the immensity of the earth's antiquity by mapping planetary old age onto the human soma."[14] Temporality's imprint becomes legible only after long spans of time, as its effects are slowly written in the flesh of the human body or the crust of the earth. Noting the odd plantation of elms on the otherwise treeless island, the narrator of *The Well-Beloved* claims that other kinds of trees once existed during an ancient geologic epoch. To perceive them, "it was necessary to recede a little in time – to dig down to a loose stratum of the underlying stone-beds, where a forest of conifers lay as petrifactions" (*WB*, 241). The conflation of depth with time, digging with retrospection, aligns the imaginative work of geology with the physical labor of excavation. Businesses like that of Jocelyn's father – slowly quarrying the limestone from the island – serve as the metronomic backdrop by which the events of the novel are paced: "the chisels clinked in the quarries; file after file of whitey-brown horses, in strings of eight or ten, painfully dragged down the hill the square blocks of stone on the antediluvian wooden wheels just as usual" (*WB*, 283). The constant rhythm of work belies the change in the landscape; indeed, like the effect of aging on the human body, its regularity camouflages the ravages of passing time behind the veil of the everyday.

The narrator specifies that the limestone Jocelyn's father carves from the earth is oolite or "eggstone." One of the novel's first descriptions of the island brings geologic discourse together with that of human reproduction, as the narrator transitions from the "infinitely stratified walls of oolite" to the "melancholy ruins / Of cancelled cycles" of Shelley's *Prometheus Unbound* (*WB*, 179). As J. Hillis Miller points out, the eggs embedded into the oolite may seem to suggest a kind of fertility but are in fact "dead remnants" of a fossilized past. Yet the stone contains a germinative energy that exceeds even death: "what dies does not disappear but has the power, even in its cancellation, to initiate new cycles of the life-generating exchange of energy."[15] The dead organisms in the stones form the foundations of houses on the island and compose the material basis of Jocelyn's art as he sculpts "his ephemeral fancies into . . . the crude original matter" (*WB*, 217). The stratified layers of stone, Miller writes, "are one above the other like the stone houses on the island, each the bones of a generation of tiny sea creatures, crossed out like a mistaken passage in a piece of writing." For Sophie Gilmartin the geological layers of the earth serve as a metaphor for both the genealogical timescale – the "gradual layering or silting process by which human lives are with time forgotten" – and the novel form itself, which she describes as "stratified with geological and genealogical layers."[16] In drawing out Hardy's analogy between geology and temporally extended processes such as the construction of houses or the passage of generations, Miller and Gilmartin suggest that the process of sedimentation serves as the best way to understand the aesthetics of Hardy's slowly building narratives.

However, aging problematizes this view by suggesting that the slow, linear buildup of Hardy's narrative also contains asynchronies. Adelene Buckland writes in *Novel Science* that geology faced an interpretive problem because "local disturbances may have knocked individual exposures of rocks out of their original sequence" (7). She describes the experience of the geologist who, moving from east to west along a formation, might encounter "the lowest and oldest layer of rocks first and progressing through a series to the newest rocks, positioned on the inside" (7). In addition, continuities between rocks might be interrupted by a geologic event, thus "disguis[ing] their true features" from the geologist (9).[17] Age often plays similar tricks on the observer, playing off the discrepancy between one's physical appearance, chronological age, and feeling. When the sixty-year-old Jocelyn looks at himself in a mirror,

> The recognition startled him. The person he appeared was too grievously far, chronologically, in advance of the person he felt himself to be. Pierston did not care to regard the figure confronting him so mockingly. Its voice seemed to say, "There's tragedy hanging on to this!" But the question of age being pertinent he could not give the spectre up, and ultimately got out of bed under the weird fascination of the reflection. Whether he had overwalked himself lately, or what he had done, he knew not; but never had he seemed so aged by a score of years as he was represented in the glass in that cold grey morning light. (*WB*, 305)

Jocelyn's shock arises from the asynchrony between his appearance and feeling, prompting his fascinated disgust with his image in the mirror.[18] Jocelyn's face represents time out of joint, where the surface record of his existence does not synchronize with the depths of his feeling.[19]

A further disparity appears between Jocelyn's chronological age and his appearance: though he looks "considerably younger than he was," "there was *history* in his face – distinct *chapters* of it; his brow was not that *blank page* it once had been. He knew the origin of that *line* in his forehead" (*WB*, 300; emphasis added). The aging of Jocelyn's face transforms it into a narrative. History, chapters, blank pages, and lines – aging makes the body legible as a surface. The wrinkle's fold of skin, like the folds of earth that require the geologist's careful parsing, not only provide a material version of the temporal asynchronies of narrative, but also require careful reading and interpretation to become legible. The aged body registers the accumulation of time but tends to conceal or diminish the role of duration at the present moment: perceiving age as the product of years, we tend to ignore the imperceptible, slow processes at work right before our eyes. The geologic context of Jocelyn's aging enables Hardy to foreground the repressed duration of narrative, which disappears behind the stony inertness of the word. As with aging, the duration of narrative goes into hiding, an aspect of our temporal experience that fades into the background as the lines become more distinct.

Counterfactuals and the Queer Temporality of Aging

While evolutionary biology and geology provide Hardy with discourses that enrich the representation of aging, the duration of growing older also constitutes a formal problem that *The Well-Beloved* resolves through narrative means. The novel locks characters into static positions that clash with the progression of the story. Avice and her incarnations always remain at the age of twenty. Though Jocelyn ages forty years through the novel, his body does not mark the usual signs of passing time. He retains the emotional immaturity of his twenty-year-old self, which the narrator describes as "this curse of his heart not ageing while his frame moved naturally onward" (*WB*, 276). Jocelyn's aesthetic of extending transient beauty through sculpture is matched with his physiological and emotional ability to pass through time unchanged. By treating the three Avices as an embodiment of the Well-Beloved, Jocelyn transforms the linear movement of time – from Avice the first, to second, to third – into a planar field where distinctions such as past, present, and future are fluid. And yet something essential falls out of the relationship: Jocelyn achieves his counterfactual dream of "putting things right which had been wrong through many years" at the cost of time's passage (*WB*, 265).

Articulating the counterfactual tension between representing aging as a process and as a completed state requires a different methodological approach to time. In Eve Sedgwick's analysis of the paranoid and reparative epistemologies of criticism in *Touching Feeling*, she argues that the overwhelming emphasis placed on the hermeneutics of suspicion makes it seem not one among many interpretive modes but the only valid option. She describes the "dogged, defensive narrative stiffness of a paranoid temporality" as "anticipatory and retroactive," "in which yesterday can't be allowed to have differed from today and tomorrow must be even more so" (146–7). This attempt to curtail surprise and negative affect in the future follows an Oedipal pattern of generational succession: "it happened to my father, it is happening to me, it will happen to my son, and it will happen to my son's son" (147). The epistemology that supports paranoia – the need to expose or validate the truth behind appearances or surfaces – tends to crowd out other modes of interpretation, "blotting out any sense of the possibility of alternative ways of understanding *or* things to understand" (131).

Paranoia has become such a cornerstone of literary criticism because it is structured around the powerfully explanatory temporalities of revelation and development. In contrast, the reparative mode is "additive and accretive," not teleologically oriented toward the exposure of truth (149). Rather than making transhistorical or definitional claims, reparation is attuned "exquisitely to a heartbeat of contingency" (147). Instead of the Oedipal model of generational necessity, reparation finds queer possibility in synchronic relations: "No one is . . . passing on the family name . . . [our life narratives] slide up more intimately alongside one another than can any lives that are moving forward according to the regular schedule of the generations. It is one another immediately" (149). The reparative impulse models a horizontal field where a relation of *beside* takes the place of *above* and *below*. Sedgwick's epistemological and hermeneutic reorientation destabilizes the lockstep of linear temporality, stressing that "the future may be different from the present" and opening "such profoundly painful, profoundly relieving, ethically crucial possibilities as that the past, in turn, could've happened differently from the way it actually did" (146). The shift from a paranoid to reparative hermeneutics implies a shift from temporal necessity to contingency: from an understanding of the past as given and determinate, to one that emphasizes the counterfactual possibilities of the past.

The generational narrative of *The Well-Beloved* provides a test case for the repetitive, linear temporality of paranoia: each iteration of Avice Caro looks similar to her parent, and each woman is pursued unsuccessfully by Jocelyn. Such repetition is a way of preparing for the negative affect that will necessarily arrive. Brandon Bennett argues that Hardy's characters "transform the pain they feel over the loss of another by absorbing the full force of that pain all at once and in advance. Knowing that death or rupture is coming, they rush to have that separation now." Like Bennett, most critics read the repetitiveness of *The Well-Beloved* as a means of either preparing for the worst or foolishly extending passionate feeling.[20] Much of the scholarship on Hardy reveals the insensibility of the natural world as it overwhelms individual agency. David Lodge's claim about *Jude the Obscure* (1895) – that "life is a closed system of disappointment from which only death offers an escape" – can be taken as representative.[21]

But against the grain of *The Well-Beloved*'s narrative of generational repetition is Jocelyn's counterfactual turn away from linearity into the myriad possibilities of what could have happened in his past but did not. The first Avice Caro's death gives Jocelyn's recollection of his early relationship a counterfactual urgency. While she is alive, he merely thinks about Avice as "somebody he could have wedded"; but when she is gone, "the times of youthful friendship with her . . . flamed up into yearning and passionate attachment, embittered by regret beyond words" (*WB*, 231). When he returns for Avice's funeral, Jocelyn observes her daughter, almost identical in feature and the same age as when Jocelyn and her mother were engaged. Suddenly, Jocelyn's counterfactual imagination gains a material possibility of realization. This new Avice – the "rejuvenated Spirit of the past" – provides him with the opportunity of playing out the counterfactual in real time (*WB*, 252). She brings to life a past possibility – what if Jocelyn had followed through with his intention to marry Avice the first? – in the present moment. Though this possibility is foreclosed when Jocelyn learns that the second Avice is already married, the layering of the past and present enhances the eroticism of the relationship, driving him to ignore the impropriety of a marriage between "an uneducated laundress" and a sculptor "with a fortune and a reputation" (*WB*, 238).

For Andrew Miller, in *The Burdens of Perfection*, the counterfactual imagination underwrites the mode of self-formation that he calls the optative, a way of conceiving "of one's singularity – the sense that one has this particular life to live and no other – by contrasting it with lives one is not living" (191–2). Like Sedgwick, Miller identifies the counterfactual with the opening of possibility: it "relies on the thought that my present self is contingent, that there are alternatives to what I am now" (193). Such optative thinking is a crucial component of realism, as the attempt to represent how things really are implies relating how things could have been (196–7). Miller argues that children hold a privileged place in optative thinking: "The presence of a child encourages the thought that the future might be different; the presence of a dead child forces the thought that the past could have been different. This is the prize and punishment of contingency" (214). Just beginning life, the child serves as a powerful figure of possibility that can be projected both forward and backward in time. In contrast to childhood, old age is often classified by the closing down of possibilities – given the necessity of biological death, the longer one lives the less opportunity can be projected into the future. This hasty characterization, however, overlooks the way longer lives necessarily contain more contingencies in the past. The number of lives that one could have lived increases exponentially the longer one lives. Old age might be considered the master trope of the optative mode, and functions as a more positive figure than the dead child that Miller proposes. For Hardy, old age takes the optative out of the realm of pain and sacrifice and makes it a mechanism for producing new possibilities for self-formation.

The sixty-year-old Jocelyn reflects that his life has been shaped by a single decision made forty years previously, when the first Avice refused to engage in the island custom of premarital sex: "It was in this very spot that he was to have met the grandmother of the girl at his side, and in which he would have met her had she chosen to keep the appointment, a meeting which might – nay, must – have changed the whole current of his life" (*WB*, 298). In *Darwin's Plots*, Gillian Beer describes the painful sense of contingency in Hardy's work as the "persistently almost-attained happy alternatives [that] are never quite obliterated by the actual terrible events. The reader is pained by the sense of multiple possibilities, only one of which can occur and be thus verified in time, space, and actuality" (223). But this contingency inspires a counterfactual agency, as Jocelyn attempts to marry Avice the third and "set right something in [his] mind that has been wrong for forty years" (*WB*, 296). Drawing out the contingency of the past activates a counterfactual imagination that transgresses the naturalization of the past – the belief that things had to happen the way they did – and the conventionality of social norms regarding romance and age.

The overlapping and counterfactual possibility of the three Avices models a complex and multi-temporal understanding of the *now*. For Carolyn Dinshaw in *How Soon is Now?* the *now* is not only the present moment of a linear sequence, but also an arena where multiple temporalities overlap. Asynchrony and multi-temporality characterize what she calls the queerness of time: "forms of desirous, embodied being that are out of sync with the ordinary linear measurements of everyday life, that engage heterogeneous temporalities or that precipitate out of time altogether" (4). Though Jocelyn's desire in *The Well-Beloved* is heterosexual, an analysis of age highlights the queer temporality of his pursuit, which combines a teleological movement toward consummation with a lateral expansion of possibilities as time progresses. Jocelyn's pursuit reveals that opportunity is located not only in the hope of a better or different future, but also in a past that is enriched and, sometimes, embittered by the thought of what could have been. According to this model, old age emerges as more than the endpoint of linear and developmental models of the human lifespan, but as the nexus where the collision of multiple temporalities becomes most legible, where the counterfactual play of past and present becomes most fully realized.

Aging not only brings the latent queerness of time into focus, it also provides a means of understanding Jocelyn's sexuality as he grows older. Like John Marcher in Henry James's "The Beast in the Jungle," Jocelyn pursues an elusive idea that ultimately escapes him. In her influential reading of James's story in *Epistemology of the Closet*, Sedgwick argues that the secret of John Marcher's life is not merely the one implied by the conclusion of the text – that he should have married his friend, May Bartram – but that his character lacks the heterosexual desire to do so in the first place. Sedgwick references the culture of male bohemia as "the *temporal* space where the young, male bourgeois literary subject was required to navigate his way through his 'homosexual panic' – seen here as a *developmental* stage – toward the more repressive, self-ignorant, and apparently consolidated status of the mature bourgeois paterfamilias" (193). The end of the novella, marked by Marcher's counterfactual imagining of what his life could have been like if he had married Bartram, signifies his character's shift into the "irredeemably self-ignorant man who embodies and enforces heterosexual compulsion" (210). The development of the normative male subject follows a trajectory that closes down one's possibilities as time progresses.

Like Marcher's secret, Jocelyn's obsession with the ideal beauty of the Well-Beloved prevents him from falling in love with a real human being throughout the novel. Without the aura of the Well-Beloved, a woman is nothing more than a "corpse," "vehicle," "tenement," or "edition" (*WB*, 200–1). The misogyny of such objectifying language culminates in Jocelyn's conversion at the end of the novel, as he trades the aesthetic mediation of his sexuality for the social imperative of patriarchy. Hardy represents Jocelyn's conversion as a capitulation to cultural pressure: "It is extraordinary what an interest our neighbours take in our affairs . . . They say 'those old folk ought to marry; better late than never.' That's how people are – wanting to round off other people's histories in the best machine-made conventional manner" (*WB*, 334). As newly minted patriarch, Jocelyn replaces his interest in art with improving the infrastructure of the town and policing the relationship between the newly wed Avice and Henri Leverre. Jocelyn's marriage gives ideological symmetry or "geometrical shape" to his life (*WB*, 335). It also marks the loss of his aesthetic sense and the rapid degeneration of his body. He develops sciatica and dresses himself in clothes that were in fashion thirty years before. He becomes bald and allows his beard to grow wild, so that "numbering in years but two-and-sixty, he might have passed for seventy-five" (*WB*, 334). When the possibility of the Well-Beloved no longer ignites Jocelyn's imagination, he falls into the well-worn track of heteronormativity that is as predictable as it is biologically enervating.

The fact that Jocelyn and John Marcher make these revelations late in life – indeed, that they could be made at no other time than as an old man – is not included in Sedgwick's account of the lapse into cultural normativity. Her interpretation gains in explanatory force because of the assumption that the end of life is marked by the closing down of possibilities. The teleological narrative of a man whose sexual possibilities are foreclosed in old age must also contend with social and cultural expectations regarding normative behavior at the end of life. By this account, Marcher and Jocelyn are as much victims of ageist stereotypes as they are heterosexual compulsion, drawn into the powerful current of twinned ideological narratives. The experience of both men draws attention to the submerged role that temporality plays in configuring dominant and subversive sexualities.

For all of Jocelyn's interest in pursuing the three Avices, the foundation of his desire is not heterosexual but aesthetic. The lack of heterosexual desire masquerades as an aesthetic compulsion. Similarly, given that the novel's tripartite structure foregrounds the importance of Jocelyn's age, there is a peculiar lack of aging on the part of Jocelyn himself throughout most of the narrative. Aging, along with sexuality, has become aestheticized. Such aestheticization emphasizes the visibility of aging and sexuality while emptying them of content. As the narrator observes of Jocelyn's art: "How futilely he had laboured to express the character of that face in clay, and, while catching it in substance, had yet lost something that was essential!" (*WB*, 268). In its representation of heterosexual desire and aging, *The Well-Beloved* constructs bold outlines that have been hollowed out of meaning, that lack the "essential." Jocelyn ages without seeming to grow older in much the same way as art attempts to preserve the ephemerality of the aesthetic moment; indeed, the very duration that is essential to aging as such vanishes behind the announcement of its occurrence. Aging becomes an open secret in the novel, and its repression obscures the field of counterfactual possibility that emerges as Jocelyn ages. As *The Well-Beloved* nears its end, the novel becomes more conventional – its structure ossifies along with the body and ideology of its protagonist.

In a letter to Edmund Gosse, Hardy writes, "I, too, am getting old like Pierston!" Ten days later, Hardy sent another letter to Gosse that referenced his first sketch for the tale: "when I was virtually a young man . . . I afterwards developed & modified it to what you now see."[22] Though Hardy contrasts his elderly, writing self with the young man who sketches out the idea for the story, such a dichotomy belies the imaginative connection between the two aged subjectivities. Hardy might lament his aging body, but it provides him with the perspective to look back upon his youthful ideas and formulate them into a creative work. Even *The Well-Beloved*'s publication history attests to the negotiation between the work of past and present selves. Serialized in 1892 as *The Pursuit of the Well-Beloved*, the novel was substantially revised into a single volume by Hardy in 1897. In the 1892 version Jocelyn marries Marcia Bencomb during their youthful affair, while in 1897 he does not marry Marcia until they are both quite old. In the early version Jocelyn attempts to commit suicide by setting himself adrift in the Race; in the later version Avice and Henri elope by the very same route. The 1897 version materializes the kind of counterfactual possibility that motivates Jocelyn throughout much of the novel: "what if I had done things differently?" *The Pursuit of the Well-Beloved* and *The Well-Beloved* function as the material emblem for the story's counterfactual resistance to the teleology of linear time. It maps out old age as a zone of counterfactual possibility, where the contingency of the past can emerge from the straightjacket of history.

Conclusion

Much of *The Well-Beloved* attests to the powerful allure of time that stands still, where linearity folds back upon itself like a wrinkle in time. Jocelyn's desire to possess the deceased Avice Caro through her daughter and granddaughter trebles the affect of the relationship, and as Jocelyn attempts to bring the "what if. . .?" of his past into a present reality, the forward press of time stalls. Jocelyn's lack of physical and emotional development mark out the limits of narrative's diachronicity, which is unable to account for change that moves too slowly for the narrator to register. Jocelyn's arrested development thus comes to stand in for the narrative difficulty of making descriptions move: of witnessing a wrinkle appear on a forehead or a hair turn gray. Such change lingers at the margins of a human's perceptual range: it happens, imperceptibly, right before us. Hardy urges the reader's attention to this repressed duration, which returns at the end of *The Well-Beloved* with a vengeance. After Avice the third jilts Jocelyn he becomes ill and ages rapidly, and as the appearance of Jocelyn's body quickly outpaces his chronological age, the reader is presented with a powerful reminder of time's passage – not in the form of extraordinary events (such as the novel's partitioning into sections that reflect Jocelyn's twenties, forties, and sixties) but time as process, change, and duration.

The discourses of evolutionary biology and geology provide Hardy with an arsenal of metaphors to describe the process of aging in new and surprising ways. Both sciences illustrate that the visual record cannot serve as a reliable index for explaining processes across long spans of time. Rather, appearances must be subject to intense scrutiny and related to the environment that contextualizes it. For Weismann, the individual organism's duration of life becomes intelligible when contextualized against the immortality of the species. For nineteenth-century geologists the earth's crust records a chaotic record of geologic developments, requiring careful parsing by the scientist in order to reconstruct the true sequence of events. While aging is a key term in evolutionary biology's analysis of the human lifespan, it is also a potent metaphor for the geologist's understanding of the earth. In Hardy's novel, these scientific discourses expand the possibilities for representing aging, resulting in a powerful, non-linear model that requires rethinking expectations about how the human body – particularly the face – indexes chronological time.

By unhinging the body's aging from linear models of time, evolutionary biology and geology provide the ground for Hardy's reassessment of an influential and culturally embedded narrative structure: the plot of decline. Most of *The Well-Beloved* experiments with a view of aging that is based upon counterfactual possibility rather than inevitable diminishment and loss in the future. However, Jocelyn's rapid decline at the end of the novel reveals the resilience and power of this narrative structure. His shocking capitulation to decrepit old age is both biological and cultural, enforced on Jocelyn from a society that demands he fulfill the function of an aged patriarch of the community.

Though evolutionary biology and geology provide the tools to describe aging in increasingly fine detail, such discourses do not help us to understand aging as a process. Such description allows for a thorough analysis into aging's *effects* but freezes the very duration that is essential to aging as such. The texture of this passing time is the duration of life itself, something that Hardy's characters never fully confront. The structure used to make sense of this elusive temporality – the narrative of decline – is both a byproduct and a way of capturing the experience of aging that is pervasive and imperceptible. By placing emphasis upon the cultural and narratological stakes of aging, *The Well-Beloved* draws attention to the repressed temporality of all novels, the extended length of which often stands in for the reality of process and duration. Representing the long life of Jocelyn as one surprisingly bereft of biological depredations, *The Well-Beloved* underlines the way narrative – especially the plots that account for development over a human lifespan – construct an image of reality that is strangely devoid of temporality as change, a world where aging occurs but we never see it happen.

CHAPTER 5

The Technology Age

In H. G. Wells's "The Story of the Late Mr. Elvesham" (1896), Edward Eden comes to the horrifying realization that he is old. Waking up in a strange room, he asks himself aloud "How the devil did I get here?" and shudders at the fact that "*the voice was not my own*" (Elvesham, 131). "It was not my own," he repeats, "it was thin, the articulation was slurred ... I ran one hand over the other, and felt loose folds of skin, the bony laxity of age" (Elvesham, 131). Eden slowly comes to terms with the "ghastly change" of his body: "I was indeed, suddenly and abruptly, an old man. I had in some unaccountable manner fallen through my life and come to old age, in some way I had been cheated of all the best of my life, of love, of struggle, of strength and hope" (Elvesham, 131). Eden's bewilderment testifies to the jarring asynchrony between the process of aging and the shattering awareness of one's old age. For Wells, this asynchrony takes the form of a disorienting identification with one's younger self in the past and the sense of physical entrapment in one's elderly body. Wells probably sympathized with Eden's premature senescence. After sustaining injuries to his kidney and lungs during a football match in 1887, Wells endured violent bouts of coughing followed by intervals of fatigue throughout much of his early adulthood. He writes in his autobiography that "As late as 1900, I was building a house at Sandgate specially facing towards the sun, with bedrooms, living rooms, loggia and study all on one floor, because I believed I should presently have to live in a bath-chair and be wheeled from room to room."[1] While Wells was writing his major scientific romances in the 1890s, he could share in Eden's lament: "To be young and full of the desire and energy of youth, and to be caught, and presently to be crushed in this tottering ruin of a body" (Elvesham, 132).

The eponymous Elvesham is a philosopher and chemist who concocts a potion that transfers the consciousness of one individual to another, enabling him to exchange his old body for Eden's youthful one. Rather than confer an aura of plausibility onto Eden's premature senescence, the alchemical transfer of consciousness highlights the unreality of aging's mundane process: its very banality confers upon it the power to surprise and shock. When Eden realizes his great age, he must come to terms with this shocking loss of duration – how his arrival at old age omits the time it takes to get there. Many of Wells's scientific romances bear witness to this estranging loss of duration: *The Time Machine* (1895), for example, enables the Time Traveller to bypass thousands of years while he catapults into the future. Istvan Csicsery-Ronay writes in *The Seven Beauties of Science Fiction* that this is true of time travel narratives in general: "The journey is nearly always extremely rapid or instantaneous, without a mediating experience of passage and duration. Bracketing out problems of duration can turn the relation of the future to the past into one purely of logic, the geometrization of time" (100). Yet the elided duration of time travelling results in more than logical paradoxes.[2] For David Wittenberg, "time travel fiction [is] already, and inherently, a fiction explicitly about the temporality of literary form." Both can "manipulate the order, duration, and significance of events in time," and thus time travelling emerges "as a literalization of structuring conditions of storytelling."[3] Whereas most critics underline the novelty of time travel – its ability to spatialize time or narrative – I argue here that it is rooted in the mundane temporality of growing older. Aging is, after all, time travelling at a constant rate.

Aging as time travel confers a revelatory aspect on the quotidian temporality of everyday life. In the popular biology textbook *The Science of Life* (1929) that Wells co-authored with Julian Huxley and G. P. Wells, the authors write about the body as a simple machine that is capable of the most extraordinary transformations. They imagine an individual who "realizes a slow rusting up of this strange machine with which he is identified, and neither he nor any help he can call in seem able to arrest that inevitable march towards cessation" (140). The necessity of the process of bodily decay does not detract from the individual's surprise when it occurs, which takes the form of micro-revelations that puncture the routine of the everyday: "Perhaps as he dresses he is reminded of that slow, relentless change that no man can stay – he may drop his comb and note that he cannot stoop as swiftly and supplely as he used to do; he may look carefully in the glass and pluck a white sheep out of his flock of hair" (25). The morning routine gives rise to a moment of critical age awareness that strips away the uneventfulness that defines everyday duration, revealing the extraordinary transformations that occur to the body over stretches of unreflective time.

Science fiction narrativizes the duration of the everyday into fantastic forms: time that has been unreflectively passed through rises to the level of shocking narrative content. In *The War in the Air* Wells represents modernity as creating "a world of obstinate and incessant change ... Vicissitude was in the very soil" (2). The accelerated pace of modernity stimulates spectacular events that marginalize intervals of wasted or empty time. However, in an ironic turn, the churn of modernity becomes normalized while duration becomes exceptional and, paradoxically, eventful. *The Time Machine* provides an example of this occurrence. Near the end of the novel, as the Time Traveller's machine hurtles ever faster through time, when seconds mark the passage of thousands of years, change does not become more pronounced, but rather indistinct and homogeneous: "The alternations of night and day grew slower and slower, and so did the passage of the sun across the sky, until they seemed to stretch through centuries. At last a steady twilight brooded over the earth" (*TM*, 157–8).

While most accounts of *The Time Machine* celebrate the machine's spectacular ability to conquer the linearity of time's passage, the next section of this chapter draws attention to the timescale of the Traveller's body, which continues to age despite his position on a chronological timeline. The unhinging of the body from the lockstep of linear time destabilizes the view that the human lifespan is one of inexorable decay, as the machine offers the possibility of aging at a much slower rate than is normally possible (in a few minutes the Time Traveller might pass through thousands of years) or aging backwards in time (the Time Traveller could be older many years in the past). The body's temporal mobility responds to the difficult necessity of imagining a socialist future, a future that remains unattainable if the young, whose possibilities give urgency to the project, have difficulty sympathizing with the elderly person they might one day become. The section that follows argues that the dialectic of young and old takes the form of a generational struggle. Through readings of three of Wells's scientific romances – *The War of the Worlds* (1897), *The Food of the Gods* (1904), and *In the Days of the Comet* (1906) – I show how the confrontation between generations figures the incessant change of modernity and, by extension, the estranged duration of the novel itself. In his attempt to imagine the future, Wells draws on the multi-temporality of aging to capture the obscure, radically alien experience of passing time.

The Riddle of Socialist Provision

For the Time Traveller, the "real body must have extension in *four* directions: it must have Length, Breadth, Thickness, and – Duration" (*TM*, 27). While the body can move about in the first three dimensions with some degree of freedom, human consciousness can only navigate duration one way: by growing older. The Time Traveller explains this view of time as a series of snapshots taken at different ages: "here is a portrait of a man at eight years old, another at fifteen, another at seventeen, another at twenty-three, and so on. All these are evidently sections, as it were, Three-Dimensional representations of his Four-Dimensioned being, which is a fixed and unalterable thing" (*TM*, 30). The very continuity that defines aging as a process falls out of the attempt to represent it through a sequence of images. The representation of life parcels it out into stages, repressing the interval of duration that connects them. The Traveller wants his companions to see the temporal through-line of lived experience that, phenomenologically speaking, appears limited to the narrow confines of the present moment. The Time Machine is a technology of representation that makes the duration of a human life legible.

The representation of aging forms one of the riddles of *The Time Machine*. When the Traveller arrives in the year 802, 701, he sees a massive sculpture of a sphinx:

> It was of white marble in shape something like a winged sphinx, but the wings, instead of being carried vertically at the sides, were spread so that it seemed to hover. The pedestal, it appeared to me, was of bronze, and was thick with verdigris. It chanced that the face was towards me; the sightless eyes seemed to watch me; there was the faint shadow of a smile on the lips. It was greatly weather-worn, and that imparted an unpleasant suggestion of disease. (*TM*, 59–60)

Leon Stover connects the sphinx to Thomas Carlyle's *Past and Present* and the question of organizing the working classes, a point that Matthew Beaumont expands by arguing that the "secret content of future history [the triumph of the proletariat] is enclosed in the present."[4] Most critics reference the form of the Oedipus myth, emphasizing the life or death stakes of a socially intractable problem. The actual content of the riddle becomes a mere footnote: "On earth there is a two-footed creature, whose voice is one. / It is also three-footed. It alone changes its nature of all the creatures."[5] While Oedipus correctly answers "man," the existence of the time machine places a different stress on the question, bringing into relief the temporality of change that the riddle encloses. The content of the riddle is age, insofar as it defines humanity primarily in terms of the bodily transformations that occur as one grows older. And like the Traveller's critique of representing life as a series of points – at eight, fifteen, seventeen, and twenty-three – the sphinx's riddle plots the human life as three discrete stages. *The Time Machine* provides a solution to the riddle of duration at the heart of the sphinx's question. One man cannot be an infant, an adult, and an old man all at once – unless he has a time machine.

By disrupting the link between linear time and the body, the time machine allows for new ways of representing the relationship between subjective experience and objective reality. Veronica Hollinger writes in "Deconstructing the Time Machine" that by separating "the subjective time of [the] Traveller from the objective time by which his temporal perceptions are supposedly determined ... the concept of 'now' becomes displaced from its privileged point on the time-line" (210). By travelling so quickly, the machine uncouples the relationship between perception and the reality of time: "If it is travelling through time fifty times or a hundred times faster than we are, if it gets through a minute while we get through a second, the impression it creates will of course be only one-fiftieth or one-hundredth of what it would make if it were not travelling in time" (*TM*, 43). Wells's short story "The New Accelerator" explores a similar idea through the lens of chemistry. The inventor Professor Gibberne develops a solution that quickens the mind and body many thousands of times beyond the normal pace of life: "a man repeatedly dosed with such a preparation ... would live an active and record life indeed, but he would be an adult at eleven, middle-aged at twenty-five, and by thirty well on the road to senile decay."[6] Like the Time Traveller, the accelerated human being moves too fast for the human eye to perceive and ages at an unprecedented rate. When the frame narrator Hillyer sees the Time Traveller after his adventure, he remarks that the Traveller's "hair seemed to me greyer – either with dust and dirt or because its colour had actually faded" (*TM*, 48). Over the span of approximately four hours the Traveller has "lived eight days ... as no human being ever lived before!" (*TM*, 53). Both *The Time Machine* and "The New Accelerator" make legible temporalities that exist in an asynchronous relationship to the hegemony of linear chronology. The incredulity expressed by the Traveller's dinner companions – indeed, by the dubious reader of science fiction itself – attests to the difficulty of legitimizing these alternative temporalities. What is more, this resistance illustrates the poverty of imagining aging outside culturally regulated temporal norms. The time machine and the accelerator potion provide the creative stimulus to imagine a senile thirty-year-old or, as Wells would go on to write in *The Sleeper Awakes*, a middle-aged man who is over two hundred years old.

The Time Traveller's exemplary Victorian exclamation – "with a kind of madness growing upon me, I flung myself into futurity" – contrasts with the decadent Eloi of the future, who care little for time as progress (*TM*, 57). The vestiges of a wealthy capitalist class, the Eloi devolve over the course of 800,000 years into a race of tubercular hedonists. As the Time Traveller marvels at how a race of pleasure-seeking consumers could produce the shoes and garments to clothe themselves, he remarks "that aged and infirm among this people there were none" (*TM*, 41). He learns that the labor of production has gone underground. The Morlocks – nocturnal, ape-like creatures descended from the proletariat – turn upon their ancestral employers and farm the Eloi like "fatted cattle" (*TM*, 130). The removal of old age from society comes with a high cost: the Morlocks merely slaughter the Eloi when they are no longer useful for reproduction. The Morlocks' cannibalism, hidden deep within the earth, serves as the nightmarish counterpart to the Eloi's conspicuous consumption.[7] The many analyses of the economic allegory in *The Time Machine* have yet to identify the role of age in enabling Wells's vision of the dystopian society.[8] A community composed entirely of individuals at the prime of life seems to realize what many economists dream of: a youthful workforce, unburdened by the drag of an aging population. In Andrea Charise's analysis of the language used to describe the elderly demographic, she writes of "a modern and interdisciplinary habit of conceiving agedness as a damaging and destructive excess."[9] Though they are all reproductive adults, the Eloi are coded economically as this so-called elderly excess – their ageless society represents a species that has evolved into a perpetual retirement, the second childhood of the race, where play replaces the rigors of work and duty.

All of this is very disconcerting to a Victorian culture infused with the gospel of work bequeathed by Thomas Carlyle. And yet, the economic problem in the late nineteenth century was not a lack of production, but overproduction. Michael Sayeau writes in *Against the Event*, "Rather than an outbreak of *scarcity*, during this period and for the first time the world economy was threatened by its own increasing productivity, by an overwhelming *abundance* . . . Instead the agent of collapse was the very efficiency of the system of production itself" (115). The second half of the nineteenth century witnessed a shift in economic theory from production to consumption, as William Jevons theorized the idea of marginal utility to account for consumer behavior. While the limitless consumption of the Eloi provides an imaginative solution to the problem of consumer demand, it conflicts with the deeply embedded masculine ideology of production; thus, the Traveller has difficulty distinguishing the gender of the Eloi, who have evolved more effete characteristics. Solving the problem of consumer demand takes the unacceptable form of emasculating the species.

In addition to feminine characteristics, the Eloi's diminutive size and stunted intelligence prompt the Traveller to compare them to children.[10] In response to the Traveller's attempts to explain his arrival, "one of them suddenly asked me a question that showed him to be on the intellectual level of one of our five-year-old children" (*TM*, 65). Events delight them easily, but they soon lose interest and "wander away after some other toy" (*TM*, 70). Though the mature Eloi do not progress beyond the mental capability of a child, the Eloi children are "extremely precocious, physically at least" (*TM*, 74). In her analysis of age inversion in Victorian literature, *Precocious Children and Childish Adults*, Claudia Nelson suggests that the "arrested child man" serves as a figure for degeneration anxieties about the diminution of male sexual potency. She shows how this anxiety takes an economic form, for though the arrested child men "produce nothing, their approach to life is typified by excess" (58). One of the mysteries that puzzles the Traveller relates to the economic life of the Eloi. He observes, "I saw mankind housed in splendid shelters, gloriously clothed, and yet I found them engaged in no toil. There were no signs of struggle, neither social nor economical struggle" (*TM*, 79). Consisting entirely of childish adults and sexually precocious children, the Eloi do not engage in any means of economic production. Instead, their age inversion and exclusive consumption of pleasures exhibit symptoms of a degenerate society that "takes to art and to eroticism, and then . . . languor and decay" (*TM*, 80).

The degenerated Eloi exemplify the kind of evolutionary backsliding that Wells summarizes in "Zoological Retrogression" (1891), where he dispels the optimistic belief in biological progress: "The zoologist demonstrates that advance has been fitful and uncertain; rapid progress has often been followed by rapid extinction or degeneration, while, on the other hand, a form lowly and degraded has in its degradation often happened upon some fortunate discovery" (167). As William Greenslade argues in *Degeneration, Culture and the Novel 1800–1940*, the fin-de-siècle intensified degeneration anxieties about the "decline of the age," "that the world was getting old and was running out of time" (30). Max Nordau popularized the idea of evolutionary retrogression in his *Degeneration* (1892) by expanding the concept's reach to culture and aesthetics.[11] Nordau often uses old age as a figure for the exhaustion and decrepitude of the human race, reserving some of his harshest criticism for the degenerate who upsets conventional assumptions about life stages. He warns the reader about youthful appearances obscuring the true state of enervation: "the outbursts of gushing, youthful vigour and turbulent constructive impulses are really nothing but the convulsions and spasms of exhaustion" (43). In a degenerate society, the signifier of youth becomes unhinged from its semiotic anchoring in chronological age. A similar misconception occurs when "Decrepit graybeards" are "filled with a ridiculous dread of betraying their real age ... because they hope to be thought young when seen in an assembly in which young persons predominate" (33). Because most critics focus on Nordau's anxiety about gender inversion and demasculinization, the role of aging in shaping the narrative of degeneration has been largely ignored.[12] Degeneration's cultural threat denaturalizes the normative lifespan – from youth, to maturity, to old age – and results in a world of temporal confusion, where, according to Nordau, "youth-simulating" "degenerates are not only not young, but ... they are weirdly senile" (553–4).

The weird senility of the degenerate provides a way of understanding the age confusion of the Eloi, who are youthful and yet coded economically as non-productive and excessive. The decade Wells was writing *The Time Machine* witnessed the first major political discussions about pensions for the aged poor. Pat Thane writes that Joseph Chamberlain's proposal for a 5s per week pension in 1892 was "the first time pensions were a major election issue." Although the issue of pensions was debated consistently during the 1890s, politicians were not able to resolve it because of the tremendous cost and lingering moral questions about merit. The Old Age Pensions Act was finally passed in 1908, giving a pension of 5s a week "to the very old, the very poor, and the very respectable, provided that they were also British subjects."[13] One of the most influential proponents of a pension in the 1890s was the activist Charles Booth, whose survey of the population of England and Wales provided a statistical basis for the political arguments in favor of universal relief. In *Pauperism and the Endowment of Old Age* (1892), Booth writes that,

> Old age fares hardly in our times. Life runs more intensely than it did, and the old tend to be thrown out. Not only does work on the whole go faster and require more perfect nerve, but it changes its character more frequently,

> and new men – young men – are needed to take hold of the new machines or new methods employed. The community gains by this, but the old suffer. They suffer beyond any measure of actual incapacity, for the fact that a man is old is often in itself enough to debar him from obtaining work, and it is in vain he makes pretence by dyeing his hair or wearing false teeth. (167–8)

While Nordau condemns the old degenerate who apes youthful fashion, Booth highlights the pathos of the elderly jobseeker who attempts to disguise his age to compete in the modern job market. Booth suggests that the pension is not only a way of providing succor to the elderly, but also an investment in the nation's future: a "security of position which will stimulate rather than weaken the play of individuality on which progress and prosperity depend" (*Pauperism*, 241). Unlike the Poor Law, which alienated the elderly through the humiliation of the workhouse or the stigma of out-relief, Booth viewed the compulsory pension for old age as a way of unleashing the youthful energies of social and economic development.

Of the many solutions to the problem of old-age pauperism – such as friendly societies, employer contributions, or voluntary provision – Booth argues that the only successful relief will be universal and compulsory, eliminating the shame attached to state aid. The state would finance this scheme through progressive taxation: "We have seen that, on the plan proposed, year by year the young and middle-aged lose to the advantage of the old, and the rich to the advantage of the poor, and it is the same with regard to men and women. Throughout it is those who are weakest who profit" (*Pauperism*, 201). In *Life and Labour of the People in London* (1889), Booth argues that social welfare benefits not only the recipient of aid, but also the more affluent contributors. The poor "hang as a heavy weight" on the upper classes, and, Booth suggests, "ill-paid and half-starved as they are, they [the poor] consume or waste or have expended on them more wealth than they create" (162, 165). Poverty costs the state more than welfare because an entire class of society engages in wasteful consumption instead of beneficial production. Booth's characterization of the abject poor applies to the impoverished elderly, who exist outside the realm of production and yet still require resources to survive.

George Turner draws upon Booth's ideas in a tract for the Fabian Society titled "Case for State Pensions in Old Age" (1897). Turner's impassioned rhetoric reveals some of the assumptions about old age that stimulated support for pensions. For Turner, "the aged members are handicapping the societies. Turn how or where they will, the claims and necessities of their aged brethren are forced upon them" (9). One of the difficulties in encouraging the young to invest for old age relates to a failure of the imagination: "To young people in the full flush and energy of early life, old age appears so far off that it is not easy to induce them to provide for it in any class" (3). Both Booth and Turner show how the failure to imagine the future of old age corresponds to the failure to imagine the socialist society of the future.

Wells's definition of the spirit of socialism was precisely this forward-looking imagination of a better future: as he writes in *New Worlds for Old* (1908), socialism is a "project for the reshaping of human society upon new and better lines" (3). Wells became an official member of the Fabian society in 1903, but he participated in open meetings of the Fabians between 1886 and 1887 and espoused socialist principles for the entirety of his adult life.[14] His central belief , expressed in *New Worlds*, was that socialism could replace the casualty of life with an "orderly plan for the half-conceived wilderness of human effort" (26). Yet old age constitutes a symbolic impasse for the socialist imagination. Looking forward to a "new society full of life, full of youth, full of the spirit of creation" involves looking backward to ameliorate the lives of those older workers the competitive market economy has left behind (21). However, the young – at such a great temporal distance from their older selves – seem least prepared for imagining a future world as one simultaneously defined by youthful opportunity and elderly provision. Near the end of *The Time Machine*, Wells provides a resonant image of what happens when the two poles of this dialectic become disconnected, as the Traveller apprehends an enervated and dying planet bereft of possibilities for development.

The Time Machine serves as a warning for the socialist imagination. The future-oriented arguments that underwrite Booth's pension scheme in particular and Fabian reform more generally require a temporal leap of the imagination from the present moment to a possible future. For many, this leap constitutes an impassable gulf of time. As the Traveller relates the story of the future to his guests, he is met with derision and incredulity. The Editor condescendingly tells the Traveller, "What a pity it is you're not a writer of stories!" and the Medical Man diagnoses him with "over-work" (*TM*, 167, 169).[15] This lack of forward thinking condemns the world to an uninhabitable wasteland at the end of time: without concerted anticipation and planning, the collapse of society – and the natural world – is more probable than its durability. The twinned discourses of excessive consumption and old age attest to the difficulty of imagining a future beyond present conditions and the disaster that awaits when this challenge is not met. However, the Traveller also exemplifies the dangers of excessive extrapolation when he mistakenly identifies the society of the Eloi as the triumph of communist principles, while it actually represents the nightmare of capitalist class division. The novel thus reveals that looking forward to the socialist utopia of the future is not merely a linear process, but one that requires the temporal diversity enabled by the time machine: an imagination capable of negotiating between present experience and future possibility, the energies of youth and old age, and the processes of production and consumption.[16]

The dialectical negotiation necessary for the socialist imagination requires literary representation to be more temporally dynamic than what the conventions of realism support. Elana Gomel writes in "Shapes of the Past and the Future" that "time travel is not a technology but a formalized ideology, which is to say, a technology of subjectivity. But this is a technology that only produces defective merchandise" (347). But far from the "deterioration of subjectivity" that Gomel diagnoses, *The Time Machine* provides a powerful image of temporal indeterminacy that subverts the chronological relationship between the body and aging, opening the possibility of subject positions outside of the linear and inevitable decline of youth to old age. The novel's representation of age enables Wells to imagine new economic subjectivities: the absolute dominance of the capitalist class results in a perennially youthful population that, far from forming a utopia, serve only as meat in the hellish world they created. By destabilizing the engrained narrative of progress and decline – the trajectory of a human life from youth to old age, or the amelioration of society under capitalism – *The Time Machine* demonstrates the need to look beyond the conventions of temporal realism to imagine a different future.[17]

War of the Generations

The majority of Wells's scientific romances emphasize the tension that arises between the recalcitrant present and the imminent future.[18] In *The War of the Worlds*, technologically advanced aliens invade an unprepared earth; in *Food of the Gods,* forty-foot tall giants supersede average-sized humans; and *In the Days of the Comet*, an enlightened society struggles to understand the vicissitudes of life before a vast change. In this section I argue that Wells represents the conflict between old and new orders through a generational dynamic. This "war of generations" underwrites the Darwinian thesis of evolutionary development and the colonial discourse of Western patronage, illustrating how modernity demands new configurations of youth and old age. In his piece of scientific journalism titled "Death" (1895), Wells uses the rhetoric of war to describe the relation between generations and echoes the language of August Weismann analyzed in Chapter 4 of this book: "In order that each regiment of animals and plants may be kept full of creatures resplendent with young and vigorous life, an age is fixed at which the battered veterans must retire" (136). The conflicting interests of generations results in a volatile binary logic that cuts off the channel of sympathy between youth and old age.

Not surprisingly, the genre of science fiction tends to privilege the youthful side of this generational rivalry. Darko Suvin writes in *Metamorphoses of Science Fiction* that an appreciation for the new is at the heart of the genre. He argues that the novum – some aspect of novelty or innovation such as a gadget (time machine) or setting (alien planet) – "entails a change of the whole universe of the tale" (64). The novum provokes a displacement of reality, within both the narrative and the empirical world of the reader; for as readers process the differences between their world and the novum in the text, they return to the actual world with a new perspective (71). Suvin describes the oscillation between the real world and the novum of science fiction as an enlightening estrangement "from constrictive old norms into a different and alternative timestream" (84). According to this model, the novum functions very much like the triumphant passage of one generation to the next: from the old, conventional way of looking at things to the demystified perspective offered by the new. Even horrific novums – such as the alien invasions and animal hybrids of Wells – result in knowledge that allows the reader to challenge the naturalization of a given social context.

However, Wells's novels are also troubled by a violence at the heart of the novum. To illuminate the present, empirical world of the reader, science fiction posits an imagined novelty or newness. And yet, by doing so, it makes the temporal distance between present and future – the very gap that Wells argues that we must work to close – integral to the form. The violence of Wells's texts between old and new generations represents this conflict between a present and a future that can be mutually illuminating only by being at odds with one another. Mary Mullen's theorization of anachronism provides a framework for understanding this intergenerational dynamic. Mullen argues in her article "Anachronistic Aesthetics" that "anachronistic pasts emphasize the political value of discordance, contingency, and historical misuse to undercut imperial circuits of meaning within the novel. These pasts refuse the assumed futurity that useful history naturalizes, allowing history's heterogeneity – the way it resists generalization and ordered chronologies – to imagine political possibilities" (235). The anachronism opens new, non-determined ways of imagining the future. In Wells's work, the present moment of narration serves as an arena where the values of the past and the future collide. The resulting text does not illustrate an anachronism so much as dramatize anachronization, a process of temporal uncertainty in which past and future battle for dominance. This conflict not only takes the form of a generational war, but also offers the possibility of continuity as the old and new merge into a chaotic, overdetermined present.

The War of the Worlds begins by famously destabilizing human preeminence over earth. The narrator reflects:

> No one would have believed, in the last years of the nineteenth century, that this world was being watched keenly and closely by intelligences greater than man's and yet as mortal as his own; that as men busied themselves about their various concerns they were scrutinized and studied, perhaps almost as narrowly as a man with a microscope might scrutinize the transient creatures that swarm and multiply in a drop of water. With infinite complacency men went to and fro over this globe about their little affairs, serene in their assurance of their empire over matter. It is possible that the infusoria under the microscope do the same. No one gave a thought to the older worlds of space as sources of human danger, or thought of them only to dismiss the idea of life upon them as impossible or improbable. (*WW*, 7)

The gap between Martian and human yawns as wide as that between the human and the infusoria that form the object of his scientific research. Wells scales this gap to the evolutionary timescale, as the "older worlds of space" surpass human development to make mutual understanding between the two species impossible. Most importantly, sympathy fails to cross the developmental gap between species. The appearance of the Martians – all tentacles and dripping saliva – immediately produces "disgust and dread" in the narrator, while another spectator merely exclaims "'Good God! What ugly brutes!' . . . over and over again" (*WW*, 22, 24). The Martians are similarly unable to sympathize with humans, treating them as nothing more than an irritating obstacle to be destroyed: "the Martian machine took no more notice for the moment of the people running this way and that than a man would of the confusion of ants in a nest against which his foot has kicked" (*WW*, 63).

Though Wells highlights anthropological differences such as appearance and eating habits, the functional difference between species relates to age.

Since "Mars is older than our earth," the planet "is far gone in its cooling" and is quickly becoming uninhabitable for the native population (*WW*, 8). For the survival of the species, the Martians look sunward to colonize more fertile planets. Echoing the degeneration rhetoric that he used in *The Time Machine*, Wells describes the inhabitants of Mars as "more distant from life's beginning but nearer its end" and suffering from that "last stage of exhaustion" (*WW*, 8). The long process of evolution leaves the Martians with "intellects vast and cool and unsympathetic" (*WW*, 7). Mechanism replaces the work of the body, which has atrophied to the point where the Martians appear as "heads – merely heads" (*WW*, 125). As the narrator observes the Martians at work, the machines appear more alive than the masters operating them, further emphasizing their alienation from the heartbeat of organic life (*WW*, 135). In contrast to the over-evolved Martians, humanity represents a youthful stage of development "incredibly remote" from the degenerative exhaustion that afflicts their invaders (*WW*, 8). Whatever sympathy the Martians might have for less developed organisms does not bridge the gap between the two species: to them, the narrator asserts with increasingly dehumanizing imagery as the novel progresses, humans appear as "monkeys," "rabbits," and "ants" (*WW*, 8, 144, 153).

Through the process of invasion, the different timescales of the planets are brought into anachronistic coexistence. However, the elder race, though unsympathetic to their developmentally inferior antagonists, represents a possible future for humankind. Given enough time, Earth will experience the same cooling as Mars. If the population continues to evolve and develop new technologies, humans will eventually (many millions of years in the future) experience the same colonial urgency as the Martians. Of course, at the time Wells was writing *The War of the Worlds* Western nations were already seasoned imperialists: the narrator reminds us that the "Tasmanians, in spite of their human likeness, were entirely swept out of existence in a war of extermination waged by European immigrants in the space of fifty years" (*WW*, 9). For John Rieder, in *Colonialism and the Emergence of Science Fiction*, *The War of the Worlds* illustrates "that the indigenous, primitive other's present is the colonizer's own past" (5). This "anachronistic structure of anthropological difference is one of the key features that links emergent science fiction to colonialism" (6). The anachronism at the heart of science fiction's representation of colonialism takes on a comprehensible narrative form by mapping onto the uneven power relations between the young and the old: instead of providing resources to enable the younger generation (or subaltern) to flourish, the more mature generation, Cronus-like, cannibalizes the energies of youth. To emphasize this point, the Martians use humans as a food source, injecting the blood of the victim directly into their veins to bypass the wasteful work of digestion.

Thus, while it appears that *The War of the Worlds* encourages the reader to think of Mars and Earth as fundamentally different, the novel undermines this opposition as merely temporally contingent. Given enough time, the gap between the two species diminishes. The end of the novel underlines this point, as the leftover alien technology plays a key role in discovering the secret of flight (*WW*, 174). Martian technology enables a developmental leap for humans that makes them a little bit more like their alien antagonists. The static poles of binary oppositions such as Martian and human, older generation and young, collapses upon the constantly shifting grounds of biological and cultural development where, given enough time, difference converts into similarity. According to this view, the linear model of progress as improvement retains surprising vestiges from the past. Depicted as an ancient and exhausted race, the Martians nevertheless represent the future for mankind, and by doing so underline the process of decay that attends even the most triumphant developmental narrative. Indeed, *The War of the Worlds* begins and ends with discourse about progress. Blissfully unaware of the impending invasion, the narrator begins the novel "busy upon a series of papers discussing the probable developments of moral ideas as civilization progressed" (*WW*, 12). The events that follow render the narrator's extrapolation of moral progress ridiculous. One of the final scenes represents him surveying his "abandoned arguments": "It was a paper on the probable development of Moral Ideas with the development of the civilizing process; and the last sentence was the opening of a prophecy: 'In about two hundred years,' I had written, 'we may expect – '" (*WW*, 176). Written before the tragic events of the narrative, the narrator's ellipsis remains open to the future at the end of the novel, and contrasts with Victorian certainty about the narrative of progress.[19]

Wells's *In the Days of the Comet* inverts the structure of *The War of the Worlds*: in this novel, the arrival of a comet from outer space heralds a new era in which the rapacity of the human spirit gives way to understanding and enlightenment. The narrator, Willie Leadford, describes his life before the change as one plagued by class conflict and fierce passions. When his lover, Nettie, absconds with the wealthy Edward Verall, Leadford buys a revolver, steals money from a neighbor, and sets out to murder the two lovers. Just before he commits this act, the comet enters the earth's atmosphere and changes the chemical composition of the air, amplifying the beneficial function of oxygen on the human body. When the gas enters the atmosphere, every person on the planet falls asleep and awakens detached "from the tumid passions and entanglements of the personal life" (*DC*, 232). Bodily senses are "quickened" – the narrator perceives more vividly and remembers more detail – and altruistic feeling replaces gross self-interest (*DC*, 225). Upon awakening, Leadford disavows his revenge and works with politicians to bring a unified, World State into existence. The novel ends with Leadford's reconciliation with Nettie and Verall, and the beginning of a sexually progressive ménage-à-trois between the three characters.

In the Days of the Comet pivots on the contrast between an old and a new world, which the narrator filters through the rhetoric of youthful passions and mature rationality. Wells uses an unabashedly implausible frame narrative, where the now elderly Leadford writes his memoir and a mysterious visitor – a placeholder for a normative Victorian – inexplicably arrives to read his work. In this opening scene, the elderly Leadford says to his visitor that the "passage of years brings a man at last to retrospection; at seventy-two one's youth is far more important than it was at forty. And I am out of touch with my youth. The old life seems so cut off from the new, so alien and so unreasonable, that at times I find it bordering upon the incredible" (*DC*, 10). The difference between the elderly man of Wells's novel and that of Dickens's that I analyzed in Chapter 1 rests in a changed attitude toward modernity: where for Dickens the disappearance of an old way of life corresponds to a lack of place for the elderly, in Wells's utopia the emergence of the modern has no trouble expanding to include the senescent Leadford. Indeed, Leadford's importance is underlined by the fact that he can recall the vanished past and thus bring out, through contrast, the significance of the present moment: "I think too that those who are now growing up to take our places in the great enterprise of mankind, will need many such narratives as mine for even the most partial conception of the old world of shadows that came before our day" (*DC*, 10). In many of Wells's works, the present moment threatens to detach itself from the continuum of history and break ties with a past that it no longer recognizes as its own. Old age provides a privileged position for illustrating generational continuity that the modernity of the present either obscures or ignores.

For Leadford, youth carries an ambivalent charge: "the only effort against that universal tendency in all human institutions to thicken and clog, to work loosely and badly, to rust and weaken towards catastrophes, came from the young – the crude unmerciful young" (*DC*, 49–50). Youth acts as an institutional lubricant that enables social change, but it also contains a revolutionary, unsympathetic violence. Leadford's own passionate youth serves as a model for the "old" world before the comet: "In this story of my bitter, restricted youth that I have been telling you, I have sought constantly to convey the narrowness, the intensity, the confusion, muddle, and dusty heat of the old world" (*DC*, 232–3). The restriction of youthful energy, like water boiling in a tea kettle, eventually produces an explosive force. The seamless transition of Leadford's love into murderous rage takes place against the backdrop of a society composed of antagonistic classes. The chemical changes wrought by the comet's gasses merely enable the imagination of a world where society's hierarchical structure has been abolished in favor of a classless society. In his *Experiment in Autobiography*, Wells writes that his ideal society was "of an expanded middle-class which has incorporated both the aristocrat and plutocrat above and the peasant, proletarian and pauper below" (69). The comet essentially contains an ideological virus that converts the population of earth into the bustling, reforming bourgeoisie.

Yet the appeal of youth's brazen contradictions spills over into the cool maturity of the new age. The word "youth" exhibits a semiotic suppleness throughout *In the Days of the Comet*, taking on multiple and irreconcilable meanings. Leadford remarks: "there is something harsh in the earnest intensity of youth"; "the positiveness, the rationalism of youth"; "the disorder of passionate youth" (*DC*, 24, 62, 116). At the beginning of the novel, the elderly Leadford laments that the affective intensity of the old world has passed out of existence with the change, and that the homogenization of society has diluted the vivid contrast between extreme states of being. But he continues to question if such a loss inheres in the new social structure or if it is rooted in his own physiological development: "Is it the Change, I wonder, that has robbed life of its extremes, or is it perhaps only this, that youth has left me . . . and taken its despairs and raptures, leaving me judgment, perhaps, sympathy, memories?" (*DC*, 20). By configuring the old world with youth and the new world with old age, Wells deploys a chiastic structure that highlights both similarity and difference: the old world is unimaginably remote and yet also causally linked to the new one.

The frame narrative's Victorian visitor completes the chiasmus by embodying the youthful "old" world from which Leadford originated. The visitor's moral disgust upon hearing about Leadford's ménage with Nettie and Verall marks the end of the story, as the social and sexual differences of this new society make understanding difficult:

> I became a little inattentive ... He and these transfigured people – they were beautiful and noble people, like the people one sees in great pictures, like the gods of noble sculpture, but they had no nearer fellowship than these to men. As the change was realized, with every stage of realization the gulf widened and it was harder to follow his words. (*DC*, 376)

For the visitor, confronted with such drastic changes, the story begins to lose its human interest, and his attention wanders. *In the Days of the Comet*, like *The War of the Worlds*, emphasizes the radical difference between the old and new world and the difficulty of conceptualizing alien ways of life. The discourse of age provides a conceptual means of crossing the epistemological gap between "us" and "them" by mapping difference onto the structure of generations, where radical otherness offsets the temporal assurance of similarity across time. Fredric Jameson writes in *Archaeologies of the Future* that "in imagining ourselves to be attempting contact with the radically Other, we are in reality merely looking in a mirror and 'searching for an ideal image of our own world'" (111). Wells makes the radically new intelligible through an ironic mapping onto the biological and cultural coordinates of old age, in which we see reflected the shocking and obscure possibilities of our own future.

The play of extremes formed an important part of Wells's early socialist education, via Henry George, about the broadening of the class divide under the guise of the nineteenth-century progress.[20] George's influential *Progress and Poverty* (1879) critiques the popular belief that the development of new technologies, expansion of industry, and proliferation of railways will create wealth and improve the living conditions of all members of society. Wealth, however, is not distributed evenly, and grows exponentially only for those who happen to own land (for George, the basis of all value). The unequal distribution of wealth reveals the illusory nature of progress: "Where the conditions to which material progress everywhere tends are most fully realized – that is to say, where population is densest, wealth greatest, and the machinery of production and exchange most highly developed – we find the deepest poverty, the sharpest struggle for existence, and the most enforced idleness" (6). As wealth increases for the privileged class, the workers increasingly struggle for survival, wasting energy on subsistence rather than useful modes of production. This disequilibrium, originating in the speculative outpacing of land values in relation to the stagnating wages of the laboring class, gives rise to the "recurring paroxysms of industrial depression" that define the temporality of modern capitalism (252). For George, progress does not proceed in a linear fashion but in "perturbations or wave-like movements" and "bursts, and starts, and halts" (253, 455).

The impression that progress creates of an ever-upward thrust toward newer and better things is built upon the volatile temporality of boom and bust cycles. George's analysis reveals that such economic lurching does not tend toward progress (defined by the amelioration of society as a whole) but toward stasis or degeneration. Wells addresses the temporality of progress in *The Food of the Gods* by embodying it in physiological growth. In this novel, two scientists develop a chemical – dubbed Herakleophorbia by the scientists and "Boomfood" by the popular press – that unlocks extraordinary growth in whatever plant, animal, or human consumes it. The impetus for the discovery begins with Professor Redwood's measurements. He observes that growth does not occur at a regular pace but "with bursts and intermissions": "that apparently nothing grew regularly and steadily . . . it was as if every living thing had just to accumulate force to grow, grew with vigour only for a time, and then had to wait for a space before it could go on growing again" (*Food*, 12). In *The Food of the Gods*, the organic growth of Boomfood and the boom and bust economy share the same model of development, in which intervals of expansion are punctuated by periods of dormancy. The process of bodily development provides another way of understanding the illusory progress of society: the rapid growth of an infant to maturity belies the long period of stagnation as an adult, when growth stops and eventually gives way to decline.

The novel begins with the amusing and dangerous possibilities of gigantism. Early experiments on poultry result in "rumours of [a] great chicken" when an escaped hen roams the countryside (*Food*, 48). Yet negligence about the chemical's use also results in colossal wasps that make a "noise like a sawmill" and rats large enough to kill a horse (*Food*, 38). When infants consume Boomfood they surpass forty feet in height at maturity. The novel becomes more serious in its representation of how gigantic humans destabilize the traditional social order. Caterham, a politician who rises to prominence by campaigning against Herakleophorbia, makes his case by appealing to the entrenched values of social class: "No one; he says, wishes to prevent the children of the lower classes obtaining an education suited to their condition, but to give them a food of this sort will be to destroy their sense of proportion utterly . . . What Good will it do, he asks, to make poor people six-and-thirty feet high?" (*Food*, 112–13). Caterham's fears materialize when young Caddles, son of an impoverished country family, is discovered growing at an alarming rate. The oversized working-class child consumes a great amount of food and taxes the charity of the parsimonious Lady Wondershoot. Caddles literally doesn't fit into the institutions of Victorian society, sitting outside the schoolhouse window during classes and listening to the church service from a nearby porch. The authorities teach Caddles that his great strength "was a misfortune that he had to make the best of. He had to mind what was told him, do what was set him, be careful never to break anything nor hurt anything" (*Food*, 189).

When Caddles's play becomes troublesome to the community – he creates unseemly boats made of newspaper to float down the river – Lady Wondershoot puts him to work in the chalk pits. This demoralizing, rote labor inspires Caddles to contrast his toil with the genteel life of the country aristocracy: "What's work *for*, mother? Why do I cut chalk and you wash clothes, day after day, while Lady Wondershoot goes about in her carriage. . .?" (*Food*, 201–2). He presses his mother: "if there wasn't any gentlefolks, wouldn't things belong to people like me and you?" (*Food*, 202). As proletariat and giant, Caddles becomes increasingly discontent with his double marginalization. His vast size underscores the fact that there is no place for him – or the working class that he represents – in the Victorian scheme of social power: "And all the world is theirs! *I* don't come in – nowhere" (*Food*, 278). As public opinion turns against the hypertrophied offspring of Herakleophorbia, Caddles unknowingly violates new laws meant to quarantine the giants, resulting in his death, caused by the police. Caddles serves as a giant-sized reminder of the way the upper classes contain and instrumentalize the labor power of the working class.

Yet the pathos of Caddles's character is limited by his stereotyped ignorance and inane discourse. Moreover, his death does not serve the purpose of working-class reform, but functions primarily as a narrative impetus to galvanize resistance on the part of the middle-class giants. Wells's sympathies clearly lie with this group of industrious titans, who war successfully against the many millions of average-sized humans. The conflict between old and new is at the heart of *The Food of the Gods*, represented through a battle between the average and the great. However, the conflict does not take the form of a Marxist upheaval, but of the amplification of the bourgeois values of industry, equity, and merit. Wells's socialism does not privilege rupture but the Fabian idea of gradualism. Thus, while Caddles highlights the social injustices of an unfair system, he does not represent the future society of the proletariat. As *In the Days of the Comet*, the new world bears a filial resemblance to the old one, a bourgeois world enlarged and more capacious, a generational evolution rather than the crisis of revolution.

As the war rages on, the average-sized parents of the giants – Redwood and Cossar – reflect on the inevitability of supersession: "It is a new generation . . . and new emotions and new needs . . . All this is Youth . . . It isn't *our* youth, Cossar. They are taking things over. They are beginning upon their own emotions, their own experiences, their own way. We have made a new world, and it isn't ours. It isn't even – sympathetic" (*Food*, 317–18). While Caterham and the rest of humanity attempt to exterminate the giants, the parents realize that the problem is not one of size but of time. Each novum discussed so far – the Martian invaders, the comet, and Boomfood – illustrate the unsympathetic backward glance of a dominant future. And each novum borrows from the generational logic of biological succession. Redwood's realization is exemplary in this regard: he "realised how much more a son may be to his father than a father can ever be to a son; he realised the full predominance of the future over the past" (*Food*, 316). The emergence of the new coincides with the redefinition of the status quo as old, initiating the process of anachronization that Wells dramatizes as a generational war of kinetically opposed subjectivities: past and future, old and young.

By scaling growth to a higher level of magnitude, Herakleophorbia makes the relationship between time and development an observable phenomenon: "You can see it grow while you watch it" (*Food*, 80). Against the backdrop of gigantism, the image of inexorable growth emerges as the true content of *The Food of the Gods*. The giants themselves acknowledge the importance of this shift away from the product toward the process, as Redwood's son preaches to his peers: "We fight not for ourselves but for growth – growth that goes on for ever": "And then – still greater. To grow, and again – to grow. To grow at last into the fellowship and understanding of God. Growing . . . Till the earth is no more than a footstool . . . Till the spirit shall have driven fear into nothingness, and spread" (*Food*, 328). Such all-encompassing and visible growth produces the mutually opposed extremes – small and large, human and alien, old and new – that inform so many of Wells's scientific romances. This shift toward movement and progress defines Wells's modernity, which does not exclude the elderly like so many early Victorian texts, but acknowledges the necessity for old and new to exist in a dialectical, if antagonistic, relation. Thus, the elderly do not represent an anachronism in the present moment of youthful aspiration, but rather a necessary component of anchronization – the process of modernity, ever churning toward new configurations of the old and new.

Conclusion

Where *The Time Machine* uses mandatory provision for the elderly as a way of arguing for the difficult, but necessary, imagination of a socialist future, Wells's romances of generational conflict reveal the violent results of this imagination, which produce the conditions of modern change by constituting the dialectical pole of the "old" – often represented through metaphors or rhetoric pertaining to old age – in relation to the "new." The volatile modernity that Wells represents relies upon the failure of sympathy and the violent action that arise between these two positions. Thus, though imagining the future is indeed a necessity for socialist provision, doing so gives rise to the deeply ambivalent conditions by which generational antagonism arises alongside modernity's technological and social progress.

The difficulty of representing this restless modernity requires Wells to shift the generic affiliation of his novels away from realism, which powerfully represents the dominant social milieu, to what we now call science fiction. The cognitive estrangement and novum of science fiction provide potent ways of conceptualizing the new that transgress realism's adherence to an empirical past or present. Yet Wells is less interested in newness as such than the process of getting there. As we have seen, it is not the anachronism that underwrites his fiction, but the process of anachronization: not the synchronic incompatibility between a "then" and a "now" – for example, an industrial society that retains agricultural traditions – but the process of becoming modern. Despite the best attempts to define and fix values to modernity, it does not stand still. The moving target of aging and the passage of generations provide a way of embodying this baffling temporality. Constantly changing and yet recognizably the same person, the aging individual serves as a way of representing the invisible forces of a modernizing society in constant flux and yet recognizably the same.

Wells does not abandon realism entirely: in a letter written to Wells, Joseph Conrad called him a "Realist of the Fantastic, whether you like it or not."[21] Formally speaking, Wells's novels continue to deploy realism's conventional way of representing time. Even when an invention like the time machine enables his characters to move back and forth along a temporal continuum, the narrative itself registers these changes within a realist framework. The linearity of everyday time keeps pace quietly in the background of the narrative and does not violate the reader's expectations about temporal verisimilitude. The same temporal rules that apply in the reader's experience apply in *The Time Machine*, except that the reader is asked to imagine an invention that allows reality to be navigated in a different way. This precedent was already set in the nineteenth century, as inventions such as the railway and the telegraph changed the individual's experience of space without fundamentally changing anything about the physics of space itself.

Adhering to the rules of temporal realism, Wells narrativizes the radical change of modernity through other means. The trope of generational conflict illustrates one of the major synchronic tensions at the heart of modernity: the anachronistic existence of new and old ways of life. However, the generational conflict also conjures the diachronic aspects of modernity: its incessant movement and pervasive change. The static relation of generational opposition becomes an ironic model for change itself. This allows Wells to sidestep one of the more difficult problems of representing process, growth, and movement: duration. Unlike the modernists, who, as I will go on to discuss in the next chapter, confronted the limitations of temporal realism through experimentation, Wells circumvents the formal problem of novelistic duration by turning it into the content of his scientific romances – time machines, growth serum, and hyperevolved alien races – capturing the affect of modernity and change that inspires his work.

CHAPTER 6

Gray Modernism

The previous chapters of this book explore how, throughout the nineteenth century, the social marginalization of older people exists in tension with the role they play in negotiating questions relating to identity. Often, the novel uses old age as a figure of release from the cultural codes that restrict youth and maturity. Whether the aged are othered by the *Bildungsroman* or internalized in the plot of decline, the presence of old age continually exceeds the margins in which it is placed, giving a glimpse of narrative possibilities outside the lockstep of temporal realism. Yet if the novel and aging are as closely intertwined as I have argued, the turn from realism at the beginning of the twentieth century raises some important questions. How and why does the configuration of age, narrative, and time change in the formal experimentation of the early twentieth century? What kind of possibilities does this new configuration open or close for older people?

This chapter answers these questions by analyzing the rise of gerontology and geriatrics at the beginning of the twentieth century. The development of medical discourse about age impacted narrative form by revising expectations about the human lifespan, countering some of the Victorian era's entrenched beliefs about aging, such as the view that one was morally responsible for the quality of one's aging or that late life implied irrevocable decline.[1] The new medical views of old age proposed contrasting models: on the one hand, Ignatz Nasher argued that old age was "a distinct period of life" that required the same type of disciplinary protocols as the field of pediatrics. Élie Metchnikoff, on the other hand, asserted that old age was a pathology that could be cured. As I will argue in the first section, though the rise of geriatrics did not directly cause modernist experimentation, it revised the trajectory of human life and provided novelists with new matrices to plot the development of character.

For modernist writers like Virginia Woolf, aging provides a powerful means of testing the temporal limits of identity. Her novel *The Years*

(1937) examines the effects of aging on multiple generations of the Pargiter family, ranging from the Colonel's mental decline in old age to Eleanor's late-life travels. Senescence, exemplified by Woolf's ambivalent attitude toward old age in her diary, walks a thin line between stripping the individual of his or her identity and opening new pathways for aesthetic fulfillment. Indeed, old age provides a vantage point for surveying one's self across time – but rather than revealing a unified self, it shows the many discontinuities that accumulate over the lifespan. While this temporal distance gives rise to many of the positive effects that Woolf associates with aging – the forging of unexpected connections, aesthetic creativity, patience – it also places the elderly individual in a vulnerable, outsider relationship to society.

The analysis of old age and social marginality enriches the context of Woolf's feminism, which privileges the critical insight of women who have been excluded from the dominant milieu. In Woolf's *Orlando* (1928), the eponymous character lives from the sixteenth century to the twentieth but ages only twenty years. The development of early geriatric thinking provides a context for understanding how Woolf unhinges the protagonist's aging from the time of history. Departing from temporal realism enables Woolf to imagine different textures of aging, as chronological age and objective time no longer correspond to one another. This shift in literary mode puts a stronger emphasis on the social construction of gendered identity, which is illustrated by Orlando's transformation from a man to a woman halfway through the novel. This abrupt change attests to the ephemerality of identity, which can be performed differently from one moment to the next. However, Orlando's long life problematizes this view by asserting the continuity of aging across time. In this temporal zone of indeterminacy – between the momentary performance and the duration of aging – Woolf posits a feminist, non-realist model of character development enabled by the geriatric revaluation of the human lifespan.

By drawing on the medicalization of age, this reading of Woolf theorizes an approach to social construction and performativity that intersects with the duration of the aging body. Judith Butler argues in *Gender Trouble* that gender identity does not arise merely from one's biological sex, but from contingent discursive practices that regulate the body. She displaces the primacy of a subject with the performance of certain traits within a matrix of power. Central to her argument is the concept of repetition, in which the dominant order reproduces itself but also gives rise to parodies that draw attention to the constructedness of so-called natural identities. The repetition implies a temporal gap between the repeated and its repetition, an interval that enables "the cultural emergence of those 'incoherent' or 'discontinuous' gendered beings who appear to be persons but who fail to conform to the gendered norms of cultural intelligibility by which persons are defined" (17). Without this interval, power would merely reproduce itself continually and parody would have no time to act. According to Butler, the performance of identity hinges on a temporal fissure in the homogeneous film of a unified, coherent, and continuous self: "gender is an identity tenuously constituted in time, instituted in an exterior space through a stylized repetition of acts" (140).

Butler articulates identity as a constellation of positions on a grid, upon which an individual may move from one position to another depending on the stylized performance of coded behaviors. Theoretically, one can perform the set of behaviors associated with heterosexual masculinity and then, moments later, parody these codes through a drag performance. The time that intervenes between these two performances does not play a major role in Butler's theory except as a hinge that pivots from one repetition to the next. In contrast, my analysis of Woolf and aging draws out the significance of this interval's duration, which connects the different performances of gender identity. The discontinuous performances of one's identity are inextricably linked to the continuity of the aging body. Woolf posits gender as arising in the irresolvable tension between these two configurations of the body and time, which prompts her to invent formal strategies – such as narrative fragmentation and non-linear temporality – to represent the complex, harrowing, and exhilarating experience of aging that the realist scaffolding of the human lifespan omits.

The Medical Subject of Aging

In Chapter 5, I showed how Charles Booth's work in the 1890s developed a new approach to the study of older populations. In *Pauperism and the Endowment of Old Age* and *Life and Labour of the People in London*, Booth demonstrated the importance of thinking about older people as a subject that required discrete analysis rather than treating late life with imported assumptions about adults. Drawing on Foucault, Stephen Katz suggests in *Disciplining Old Age* that this was an ambivalent development, at once allowing more specialized attention to the aged and casting "old age . . . as a social problem requiring governmental response" (24). Booth's analyses played an integral role in the passage of a compulsory pension for the aged in 1908. Yet Booth's work was so persuasive, in part, because it helped to institutionalize the boundaries distinguishing the elderly from everyone else, an important shift in thinking about the lifespan that informed the rise of gerontology and geriatrics.

Élie Metchnikoff, widely credited with developing the interdisciplinary field of gerontology, argued that science could ameliorate late life and reduce the economic burden of older people, effectively eliminating the need for Booth's universal pension.[2] Early in *The Prolongation of Life* (1907) he writes that it "has been thought the proper course to make such laws [universal pension], and to lay the burden on the general population, without inquiring if it may not be possible to retard the debility of old age to such an extent that very old people might still be able to earn their livelihood by work" (*Prolongation*, 4). Gerontology promises to improve the conditions of late life, transforming the elderly from a drain on the economy back into productive members of the society. While old age was an afterthought from the standpoint of early twentieth-century medicine – an outlier that did not interest ambitious physicians hungry to publish prestigious research – Metchnikoff argues that improving conditions of life for older people would feed back into the quality of life for both the young and the mature. By insisting that science can turn old age into an extension of the productive years of maturity, Metchnikoff creates a line of economic continuity that cuts across the later stages of life.

The continuity of Metchnikoff's theory has much to do with his theory of how aging afflicts the body. He received the Nobel Prize in Physiology or Medicine for his discovery of phagocytes, cells that play a crucial role in immunity by consuming harmful particles in the blood (the most well-known phagocyte is the white blood cell). According to Metchnikoff's now disproved theory, these phagocytes also play a role in aging the organism by cleaning up after the toxic microbes in the large intestine. Along with many physicians in the late nineteenth century, Metchnikoff believed that the large intestine contained poisons that slowly leaked into the organism. In *The Nature of Man* (1903) he writes that these poisons "produce the arterial sclerosis of old age" and the general ossification of the circulatory system (*Nature*, 252). In addition, these intestinal poisons "strengthen the phagocytes" (*Nature*, 253). Such strengthening of phagocytes does not bolster the immune system but produces the counter-intuitive effect of aging. Central to Metchnikoff's theory was the belief that phagocytes cause senile decay by clustering around organs and slowly consuming them, replacing healthy tissue with hard, connective matter (*Nature*, 240–1).

Metchnikoff identifies many ways of addressing the malignancy of the large intestine. He notes some attempts made to eliminate harmful microbes by ingesting purgatives and antiseptics, though he derides this option as resulting in more harm than good. He also considers mastication, as over-chewing and slow eating contribute to problems with digestion. Metchnikoff's most famous remedy for aging, however, was sour milk. Arguing against the view of longevity as an inherited characteristic, he draws attention instead to the hygienic practices of societies with long-lived people. Among the longest living, healthiest aged people in the world, he observes a pattern of consumption of cultured milk, which inhibits the introduction of harmful microbes and promotes the increase of beneficial ones: "these are the means by which the pathological symptoms may be removed from old age, and by which, in all probability, the duration of the life of man may be considerably increased" (*Nature*, 257).

Metchnikoff espoused a pathological view of old age: that, through the deployment of proper hygiene, the surface of old age would be rolled back to reveal a fully functional, productive adult. He continually underlines the pathology of senescence to cultivate a sense of urgency: "after maturity, greater or lesser abnormality begins, and ends in old age and death that are premature and pathological" (*Nature*, 287). For Metchnikoff, the difficulty of distinguishing senility from disease contributes to an innate "repugnance we all experience at the approach of old age . . . An instinctive feeling tells us that there is something abnormal in old age" (*Nature*, 244). By associating old age with terminal diseases such as cancer, Metchnikoff follows a long line of thought that views senescence as something other and alien to normal life. The continuity of old age with other stages of life makes sense only when the pathological aspects of late life have been removed. Senility, sclerosis, and dementia mark off the elderly from the rest of humanity.

Normal – as opposed to pathological – old age does not imply immortality, but rather a longer lifespan (past one hundred years) that is free from the mental and physical debilities commonly associated with late life. However, the prospect of this improved old age creates some additional problems. Will healthy years before death create an even stronger impulse to cling to life? Could debility be a natural way of preparing the individual to welcome death? Metchnikoff observes an ironic change in attitude toward death over the human lifespan. The young, with the prospect of a long life in front of them, "know that death is a terrible thing, but they have not the horror of it that comes to a mature man in whom the instinct of life has become fully developed" (*Prolongation*, 256). Where the "instinct of life is little developed in youth," just the opposite applies for the aged: the older one becomes, the more one clings to life

(*Prolongation*, 254). Yet Metchnikoff asserts that a long and healthy old age prepares the individual for a different attitude toward death, replacing the grasping desire for more life with satiety and "a wish for death" (*Prolongation*, 327). Though the instinct for death appears to contradict the evolutionary imperative toward life, Metchnikoff posits that a pleasurable sense of passing out of existence could be reconciled with the maintenance of the species. He mentions the biologist August Weismann multiple times as laying out the evolutionary rationale for death, allowing for the proliferation of reproductive young by eliminating competition with older members of the species.[3]

Yet Metchnikoff envisages much more than a mere evolutionary benefit to old age. When pathological old age has been replaced by its healthy counterpart, the very structure of society changes. Instead of a population burdened with aged dependents, he imagines a society full of vibrant elderly citizens, equipped with the perspective of their many years to act as civil servants. "Endowed with their long experience of life," old men are uniquely suited to play the "parts as advisers and judges," while "young men of twenty-one years of age will no longer be thought mature or ready to fulfil functions so difficult as taking a share in public affairs" (*Prolongation*, 135, 329). He writes in *The Nature of Man* that "Young people judge of their impressions by comparison with their ideals, and as the latter are very high, they are dissatisfied with things as they really are . . . those of advanced years are more easily satisfied because they have a clearer knowledge of the true value of things" (*Nature*, 263). Old age enables direct confrontation with reality that avoids the distortion of youthful ideals. Metchnikoff's optimistic philosophy pivots on this attitude toward reality, circumventing the disappointing asymmetry between one's experience of the world and one's belief about what it should be.

In a surprisingly emotional passage from *The Prolongation of Life*, Metchnikoff writes his own truncated biography in the third person to exemplify the changes that occur in old age. In his youth he was prone to depression, pained by loud noises, shocked by the death of his wife, and addicted to the only substance that offered him relief: morphine. Later in life, however, he discovers that many of his youthful cares have disappeared. He comes to the realization that,

> "It is old age which is come upon me," he cried; "I feel painful impressions much less acutely and pleasant impressions have less effect on me. The relative proportions of the two remain as before, that is to say, unpleasant things still impress me much more strongly than pleasant things." By analysing and comparing his emotions, he discovered something new, in

> fact that some impressions were, so to speak, neutral. As he was less sensitive to unharmonious sounds, and at the same time less affected by music itself, he found himself in a more tranquil condition. Awakening in the middle of the night, he experienced a kind of happiness which reminded him of that formerly produced by morphine, and which was characterised by his hearing no sound, either pleasant or unpleasant. (*Prolongation*, 253)

Separated from the pathological symptoms, the other effects of old age – for Metchnikoff, the mitigation of painful intensities – produce a harmonious, more reflective state of being. The sensitivity of youth arises from being out of joint with reality. Old age insulates his body against the piercing onslaught of everyday life.

The transformations of old age outlined by Metchnikoff inspire a shift in the center of reality and, by extension, the literary conventions used to convey this reality. In Metchnikoff's gerontological imagination, the everyday world is filled with painful stimuli that negatively affect the youthful sensorium. In pathological old age, many of these negative effects are heightened, as the senile individual retains the susceptibility of his or her younger self and yet lacks the resilience to deal with these pressures. Normal old age, on the other hand, mitigates these negative effects and enables a more direct appreciation of reality. It is as if, by using a shade to block the blinding rays of the sun, one can finally look at it directly. In Metchnikoff's early gerontological model, old age serves as a paradoxical figure for the representation of reality – a tentative mode of being that requires a bit of luck to achieve, enabling the difficult perception of reality by smoothing off the rough edges. Healthy old age becomes the privileged mode for managing this overpowering reality.

In contrast to Metchnikoff's influential view of old age, a very different approach emerged – spearheaded by the Austrian-born American doctor Ignatz Nascher – to redefine the treatment of the elderly. Nascher coined the term "geriatrics" in his short article of the same name in *The New York Medical Journal* in 1909. Contrary to Metchnikoff's pathological view of old age, Nascher argues that many of the symptoms of senescence should not be treated as diseases but rather as normal aspects of senility: "Physicians have come to look upon the features of senility . . . as pathological features of maturity instead of considering them normal features of senility, and they are treated as diseases" ("Geriatrics," 358). While Nascher acknowledges in his book *Geriatrics* (1914) that the "most prominent theory of ageing today is Metchnikoff's theory, or rather theories, of tissue phagocytosis," he argues against the science of this view, noting the lack of phagocytes in damaged tissue samples taken from aged patients (*Geriatrics*, 41). Ultimately, the lack of empirical evidence for Metchnikoff's theory undermined many of his more optimistic views about "curing" old age through hygiene and nutrition.

Nascher reframed the medical understanding of the elderly body, carefully setting aside diseases from the normal depredations of aging. Although conditions such as arteriosclerosis, bronchitis, and pneumonia require special treatment for the aged, other forms of bodily degeneration should be accepted as standard processes in late life. Nascher's picture of the "natural" state of old age, however, focuses primarily on the negative aspects of late life:

> The obvious characteristics of senility are evidenced in the appearance, attitude, gait, mentality and the tout ensemble of mental and physical decay. The appearance of the senile individual is repellent both to the esthetic sense and to the sense of independence ... The countenance is either expressionless, indicating mental weakness, or there is an apathetic moroseness indicative of helpless resignation, or else there is the anxious look associated with a haunting fear. The skin is dry, lusterless, darker than in maturity, often pigmented, loose and thin, showing varicosed veins and tortuous arteries underneath. (*Geriatrics*, 12–13)

Nascher's description of old age normalizes the most stigmatized aspects of aging: decrepitude, dependence, and disfigurement. This constitutes the natural condition of old age, upon which disease further debilitates the human body. As such, old age emerges as a separate category from the normative interval of the lifespan: maturity. He writes that "Senility is a state of physiological valetudinarianism. It requires special study, not as a pathological condition of maturity, but as an entity entirely apart from maturity" (*Geriatrics*, 496). Where Metchnikoff's theory underlines continuity across the lifespan, positing that the negative symptoms of old age exist as an aberration, Nascher's approach to the study of old age depends upon isolating it as a distinct stage in the human lifespan.

Nascher's creation of the discipline of geriatrics derives from the science behind his view of aging. As opposed to Metchnikoff's model of phagocytosis, Nascher proposes a theory of cell-tissue evolution. As old cells are replaced by new ones, the organism eventually attains a state "most perfectly adapted to their surroundings and their available nutrition" (*Geriatrics*, 43). After reaching a peak in adulthood, however, the new cells become increasingly less suited for sustaining the organism, resulting in the slow degeneration of tissue over time. This theory of aging also comes freighted with philosophical assumptions about the individual and identity: "in the constant waste and repair of tissue the newer cells differ from the earlier ones, that in advanced life none of the early cells are left (except brain cells), that the aged individual is in fact an entirely different individual from the one who was formed from the ancestors of the late cells" (*Geriatrics*, 2). In a rare metaphorical flourish, Nascher writes that "Like the old vessel which has been repeatedly repaired until not a splinter of the original timbers is left, the individuality and the name remain" (*Geriatrics*, 3). Though he suggests that brain cells do not decay in the same way as other cells, thus securely grounding one's identity across time, his rhetoric emphasizes the physiological discontinuity between one's younger and older self. Over time we become completely different bodies. This view supports the medical distinction between old age and maturity, because the body one ages into is no longer the body of one's adulthood.

Metchnikoff's gerontological and Nascher's geriatric approach to old age differ in fundamental ways: where Metchnikoff views the symptoms of old age as a pathology to be cured, Nascher normalizes the common symptoms of senility;[4] where Metchnikoff constructs an interdisciplinary and inclusive methodology, Nascher narrows his focus to medical research and argues for the creation of a discipline for the study of old age; where Metchnikoff's theory of phagocytosis emphasizes physiological continuity across time, Nascher's theory of cellular evolution underlines bodily difference. While these differences imply a stark division, when considered together the two men represent the beginning of a vibrant movement to understand old age at the beginning of the twentieth century. As Mark Clarfield writes in "Dr. Ignatz Nascher and the Birth of Geriatrics," "The study of aging has been going on for centuries, yet it is one of the youngest medical specialties" (944). Though the positions of Metchnikoff and Nascher result in very different perspectives on old age, privileging one over the other – suggesting that one of the men got it "right" about senescence – loses much of the richness of thinking about the two approaches together. Gerontology and geriatrics sidle alongside one another – even to the present day – capturing different elements of the complex process of growing older. When senescence becomes the object of new medical disciplines in the early twentieth century, it constructs the humble subject of old age into a frontier of knowledge contested by multiple and evolving theories.

Metchnikoff and Nascher shaped the discourse about age in America in the years between 1900 and 1920, setting the groundwork for new scientific models of the aging individual. While England did not produce the same kind of theoretical works on age during this period, the trend toward scientific scrutiny manifested in revolutionary solutions to the treatment of the elderly by institutions. In 1935, Marjory Warren took responsibility for the care of 714 chronically ill patients of the workhouse wards.[5] She was among the first to develop practical solutions to mitigate the suffering of the older patients by classifying the homogeneous population of the old, generating a five-tiered system that would enable many to return home while reserving hospital care for only the most demanding cases.[6] For Warren, improvement in the quality of life for older people reflects on the state of the nation as a whole. In "Care of the Chronic Aged Sick" she writes, "If we are to maintain the right to call ourselves a great nation and a cultured civilization we must make provision in our scheme for all members of the community, old and young, sick and well, poor and rich, helpless and independent" (841). Warren's work reveals how the principles outlined in America resonated across the Atlantic, manifesting in institutional changes to the lives of older people in English society.

While the developing discourse about old age was realized in Warren's reforms, the work of Nascher and Metchnikoff also influenced cultural attitudes toward growing old in less tangible ways. First, they drew attention to older people as more than just a homogeneous population, another social problem to be solved. Though not always described sympathetically, the older subject emerges with a wide spectrum of differences and needs. Warren's classification scheme, for example, attests to the proliferation of senescent identities in the early twentieth century. Moreover, this opening of the elderly demographic provokes an unsettling shift in the configuration of identity. Often thought as the interval of life where one's identity is most fixed or even fades away entirely through dementia, old age instead splits and transforms. Both Metchnikoff and Nascher provide scientific models for the way identity persists over time and into old age: for the former, one's body and mind remain the same, but the disease of old age obscures what is most essential about one's personality. For the latter, while the cells that sustain the mind remain the same, the body radically changes – so much so that it becomes an entirely different body. In the early twentieth century, the old body becomes an arena where identity was contested – both through medical research and, as I will show in the following section, through literary representation.

Woolf's Geriatric Style

> How terrible old age was, she thought; shearing off all one's faculties, one by one, but leaving something alive in the centre: leaving – she swept up the

> press cuttings – a game of chess, a drive in the park, and a visit from old General Arbuthnot in the evening. (*Years*, 153–4)

As Eleanor Pargiter gazes upon her elderly father, she posits that old age is a process of subtraction – a narrowing that results in the most essential and basic form of one's personality. Yet even this remainder of the self becomes displaced by his actions, as old age inverts the conventional relationship between subject and object. Instead of Colonel Pargiter playing chess, taking a drive, or paying a visit, these activities perform Colonel Pargiter. The man fades into the background of Eleanor's perception, and she sees instead the impersonal process of aging at work, an attenuation of the Colonel's agency to the point that his everyday actions do not merely provide conduits for the expression of his personality, but constitute its very pith.[7]

For Virginia Woolf, old age writes large a commonplace in literary criticism and theory: that no essential or natural self preexists culture, that one performs one's sexual, gender, and race identity within a social matrix of power. It is as if the Colonel's senescence lays bare the whole process for everyone to see – for him, the game of identity is up, as he has been reduced to what Giorgio Agamben calls "bare life." For Agamben, bare life refers to the individual who has been outcast by the sovereign power – a body stripped of political affiliations and vulnerable to violence from anyone in the community. In the example from *The Years*, as the Colonel loses the ability to manifest his identity in culturally meaningful ways he becomes increasingly identified with a "mere" body. While Agamben charts the rise of biopolitics in the twentieth century to fascist regimes and the concentration camp, gerontology and geriatrics responded to many of the same questions by probing the point "at which life ceases to be politically relevant." The medical treatment of the aged provided an institutional means of exploring the temporal limit at which the body transitioned into bare life, thus distinguishing the boundaries of "life that does not deserve to be lived . . . along with its implicit and more familiar correlate – life that deserves to be lived."[8] For example, Nascher developed the term "senile climacteric" to identify the frontier where normal maturity gives way to a rapid decline (*Geriatrics*, 18). During this stage, the qualities of life that defined the individual's position within society – intelligence, mobility, creativity – become replaced by the overwhelming needs of a degenerating body.

Reduced to bare life in his way, old age decontextualizes the body by stripping it of the most significant markers of one's social identity.

However, this takes place alongside a subtle recontextualization that gains in power insofar as it does not appear to be a context at all: the elderly individual is now "beyond" the vicissitudes of identity. Revealing the social construction of identity, old age nevertheless constructs a position that, imaginatively, exists outside the cultural system in which it is enmeshed. Yet as Agamben points out, the exclusion of bare life is also an inclusion, as it constitutes the sphere against which the normative biopolitical body defines itself. In other words, the production of the elderly subject as bare life produces the adult, reproductive body. While the attribution of socially maligned contexts to the individual (poor, woman, queer) can greatly affect one's existence, to age past the necessity of this politicization is to simply not matter at all.

In several of her diary entries, Woolf connects the politics of aging and identity to aesthetics. In some cases, she views growing older positively; for example, when she writes that "poetry [is] wholly an elderly taste" made possible through stronger concentration on language: "the words all glued together, fused, glowing: have no more time to waste any more on prose" (*Diary*, II, 310). Aging enables a different attitude toward language's inscrutable density, allowing for the patience to appreciate the unity of form rather than the impatience of drilling down into analysis. Later, she anticipates menopause as a "difficult and dangerous time," but rationalizes the climacteric as one of "these curious intervals in life – I've had many – are the most fruitful artistically – one becomes fertilized – think of my madness at Hogarth – and all the little illnesses – that before I wrote *To the Lighthouse* for instance" (*Diary*, III, 254). Pathologizing menopause by placing it alongside madness and illness, Woolf nevertheless represents it as an interval of creativity. Significantly, she sets off the term "fertilized" to militate against the view of menopause – and, by extension, of aging – as one of barrenness. Though still drawing on the view of old age as a pathology, Woolf suggests that it offers some aesthetic compensations.

But Woolf's ambivalence toward age often slides into more explicitly negative attitudes, especially when it comes to the ability of age to obliterate identity. This occurs to Woolf after a visit to the oculist, who tells her, "Perhaps you're not as young as you were" (*Diary*, III, 230). She writes that this "seemed to me an astonishing statement. It means that one now seems to a stranger not a woman, but an elderly woman. Yet, although I felt wrinkled and aged for an hour . . . I forget it soon; and become 'a woman' again" (*Diary*, III, 230). The oculist's statement about Woolf's age shocks her into an acute crisis of identity. Her brief interval as an "elderly woman," before returning to the category of "woman" an hour later, reveals the discontinuity that old age draws across identity over the lifespan. In Woolf's formulation, it is as if one cannot be a woman and an elderly woman at the same time.

Though she claims to retreat to the identity of "a woman," Woolf displaces her anxieties about age onto Leonard's elderly mother later in the same diary entry. She writes that "Nothing of life, as we see it, remains to her – [she] can't read or sleep . . . She . . . demands more life, more life, at seventy-eight. She quarrels; she can't walk; she is alone; she is looked after by nurses; lives in an hotel, but demands more life, more life" (*Diaries*, III, 230–1). Old age takes on a doubly vampiric quality: at once hungry for more life and yet lacking life itself. This notion confuses two different senses of life: the amount of time that one has remaining and the quality of one's existence. The problem, for Woolf, is that Leonard's mother desires more time of life even as the quality of her life declines. Metchnikoff diagnosed this as one of the pathological aspects of old age: "the longer a man has lived the more he wishes to live" (*Prolongation*, 127). On the drive to see Leonard's mother, Virginia and Leonard agree that in her condition "one should take poison" (*Diary*, III, 231). Able to recognize how aging into her own maturity opens new avenues for creative expression, Woolf stops short at senescence, which she often views as abolishing the differences that constitute identity. When Leonard's mother passes away, Woolf reflects that "age had taken everything that was real, I think: only age left the pathetic animal, the body that wanted to live. I know nothing of any interest about her now that I come to write, only little anecdotes; nothing that makes her a real person" (*Diary*, IV, 225). Like Colonel Pargiter, as the constitutive parts of one's identity flake away from the senile self, only the body remains – the "pathetic animal" – or bare life – instinctually clinging to the ever-diminishing habits that accrete into a life.

Old age thus serves as a figure for the limit of identity – a dusky interval that blurs the distinction between body and personality. This period of life, however, does not leech identity away from the elderly subject. Rather, it draws attention to the labyrinthine nature of identity as such, which Woolf reflects through the senescent architectonics of her prose. In *The Years*, after Eleanor Pargiter passes her critical gaze over her aging father, she also experiences shocking moments of age awareness that recall Woolf's own reaction to the words of her oculist. As a young person, sitting amidst a group of people who "looked settled, elderly, as if their minds were made up," Eleanor feels as though she is always the youngest person on the omnibus (*Years*, 101). Yet as she grows older her body and her perception change: "And I thought to myself, I'm the youngest person in this omnibus; now I'm the oldest . . . Millions of things came back to her. Atoms danced apart and massed themselves. But how did they compose what people called a life? . . . Perhaps there's 'I' at the middle of it, she thought; a knot; a centre" (*Years*, 366–7).[9] It is only from the perspective of old age that the survey of one's life can be made as a whole, and the narrative threads can be organized into a meaningful image of one's self. Thus, for Woolf, it is only from the perspective of old age that one can realize the futility of this project: the atoms of the self dance but never congeal; the center of identity does not hold.[10] This modernist conception of identity becomes most legible in old age, confirming the fragmentariness that underlies the youthful confidence in self-unity.

As *The Years* draws to a close, long after Colonel Pargiter's death, Eleanor ages into her seventies and becomes the subject of her niece's ageist gaze. As Peggy, a doctor, prods Eleanor for information about her grandmother, Peggy becomes "irritated by her aunt's habit of adding unnecessary details. It was age coming on, she supposed: age that loosened screws and made the whole apparatus of the mind rattle and jingle" (*Years*, 325). Peggy merely wants information in response to her questions – what did her grandmother look like? Was she pretty? – but Eleanor's mind refuses to work in a linear manner. She meanders from one thought to another over the course of the conversation: imagining her nephew and cousin dining together, suggesting a good man to clean paintings, reminding Sara about the party later that evening. Eleanor registers the frustration of her young interlocutor: "She gave up the attempt to account for the order in which her thoughts came to her. There was an order, doubtless; but it took so long to find it, and this rambling, she knew, annoyed Peggy, for young people's minds worked so quickly" (*Years*, 332–3). Eleanor reflexively acknowledges the difference between her own "senile" thought process and Peggy's younger one, and yet does not feel compelled to organize her mind according to the youthful paradigm. She accepts her thoughts without searching behind them for a unifying principle. Without this organization, each thought stands on its own – not infused with a special meaning beyond itself, but whole.

Peggy's initial irritation, however, gives way to deeper reflection about the possibilities of Eleanor's way of thinking: "Old age must have endless avenues, stretching away and away down its darkness, she supposed, and now one door opened and then another" (*Years*, 332). This departs from the linear, teleological path that Peggy's medical mind privileges (though she often departs from this model herself). The endless avenues of old age stretch into darkness, but the negative connotation of this image is offset by the opening of doors. These doors do not constitute endpoints but rather further opportunities, an interminable branching of possibility. This view contrasts with the stereotyped image of old age as a dead end, which Eleanor underlines when she thinks: "old age they say is like this; but it isn't. It's different; quite different" (*Years*, 382–3). Influenced by her medical background, Peggy initially projects pathologized aspects of senility onto Eleanor's rambling thought, but later realizes – along with Eleanor herself – that old age is "different." Such difference prompts a revaluation – not unlike that which occurred at the beginning of the twentieth century in medical discourse – of the very symptoms that Peggy once believed to be decline. Senescence grants the creative freedom that Woolf associated with aging in her diaries: "'How nice it is,' [Eleanor] said, 'not to be young! How nice not to mind what people think! Now one can live as one likes,' she added, '. . . now that one's seventy'" (*Years*, 421).

Both Woolf's diary and *The Years* raise a tension between aging and the loss of identity, tending, on the one hand, toward the pathetic animal that Woolf observed in her mother-in-law, and, on the other, toward the endless avenues unstructured by the expectations of youth. This theme emerges in many of Woolf's novels.[11] In *The Waves*, for example, Bernard reflects that "we are slipping away. Little bits of ourselves are crumbling" (*Waves*, 235). Yet this very crumbling over time enables one of the novel's central arguments about how individual identity disperses across the selves of others:

> How swift life runs from January to December! We are all swept on by the torrent of things grown so familiar that they cast no shade; we make no comparisons; think scarcely ever of I or of you; and in this unconsciousness attain the utmost freedom from friction and part the weeds that grow over the mouths of sunken channels. (*Waves*, 216)

Echoing *The Years*'s language of senile possibility, *The Waves* suggests that aging enables an intersubjective liberty that removes the "friction" between "I" and "you." Bernard asserts that old age lifts the veil that obscures "sunken channels" – a metaphor, reminiscent of Eleanor's endless avenues, that emphasizes the subterranean mingling of identity over time. This view of aging reflects the overall trajectory of *The Waves*, which tells the story of characters whose identities are inextricably linked to those of others. Aging's breakdown of identity, therefore, occurs alongside a compensatory intersubjectivity. As one ages, the unacknowledged lines of dependence become more legible: previously hidden pathways and channels of connection emerge.

Old age thus disavows conventionally linear thinking in favor of a network that disperses the self across many different nodes. This network not only applies to the characters in Woolf's novels, but also underwrites the most idiosyncratic aspects of her formal intervention. Departing from the propulsive plots of nineteenth-century realism, her narratives linger descriptively and abruptly lurch forward; connections are not logically necessary so much as affectively inspired. H. Porter Abbott writes in "Old Virginia and the Night Writer" that Woolf's prose meanders instead of driving forward, resembling a "stream or flood, going nowhere in particular, [and] realizing itself at any point in its movement" (243). A paradigmatic example of this style appears in *Jacob's Room*:

> Ah, but where are you going if instead of brushing past the old man with the white beard, the silver medal, and the cheap violin, you let him go on with his story, which ends in an invitation to step somewhere, to his room, presumably, off Queen's square, and there he shows you a collection of bird's eggs and a letter from the Prince of Wales's secretary, and this (skipping the intermediate stages) brings you one winter's day to the Essex coast, where the little boat makes off to the ship, and the ship sails and you behold on the skyline the Azores; and the flamingoes rise; and there you sit on the verge of the marsh drinking rum-punch, an outcast from civilization, for you have committed a crime, are infected with yellow fever as likely as not, and – fill in the sketch as you like. (82)

Woolf works against the reader's expectations by stripping away the connective tissue that causally links the events she describes. In this way the figure of the old man's rambling story provides the strongest logic for the ordering of events. The narrative follows the wandering mind of the elderly man, privileging contiguity over the rationalization of plot.[12]

This passage from *Jacob's Room* provides a concise example of what occurs in Woolf's novels more generally: her novelistic form draws inspiration from her ambivalent understanding of old age and its effect on consciousness. Consider, for example, what Woolf writes about a "shaky ramshackle old lady of seventy-six" in her diary: "Her talk never stops; never follows a line; is always about people; starts anywhere; at any moment" (*Diary*, III, 194). Without beginning or end, without predetermined direction, where every moment takes on significance despite its placement within a unified whole, the elderly woman's speech exemplifies much of what makes Woolf's style modernist, but also, I would argue, geriatric.

In *The Years*, Woolf shows how the position of old age on the human lifespan allows for the necessary distance to survey the span of one's life.

Yet far from revealing one's identity once and for all – the almost complete story of who one has been – it confirms the modernist suspicion that identity drifts without a center. In addition, the quality that defines the aging of Woolf's characters resonates at the level of narrative form. Woolf's geriatric style contests the paradigm of organic unity, where every part of the novel contains some aspect of the whole. The most characteristic aspects of her style reveal the temporal discontinuities that punctuate the narrative representation of events. The thread of narrative, like the thread of identity across the lifespan, constantly snaps. By privileging the logic of contiguity over that of continuity, Woolf reveals that the duration that binds linear narrative slips away like one's identity over time – that duration, like one's self, results from a projection rather than an innate essence. It is on the strength of this recognition that Woolf's geriatric style critiques the assumptions about identity made by temporal realism.

Feminism, Aging, and Realism

While aging plays a major – and critically unacknowledged – role in the development of Woolf's modernist style, it also shapes her understanding of the relation between feminism and the novel's representation of reality. By destabilizing the hegemony of male dominance, Woolf's novels shift from the view of subjectivity as a pre-given essence in favor of a more constructivist and intersubjective view. Yet Woolf's novel *Orlando* illustrates how this aspect of her characterization runs into a temporal impasse. On the one hand, Orlando's rapid change in gender from a man to a woman suggests that the performance of identity can change at any moment. On the other hand, Orlando's body remains the same as it ages across time. Woolf's novel negotiates the subjective possibilities for feminism by positioning her character within a temporal antinomy that offers two possible models for the development of a self.

The topic of aging has not formed a major component of contemporary feminist theory. While Simone de Beauvoir's *The Coming of Age* helped to set the groundwork for age studies, she repeatedly insists that aging is a problem for men and not for women. She writes that "When he loses his powers he takes on the appearance of *another*; he then becomes, and to a far more radical extent than a woman, a mere object. She is necessary to society whereas he is of no worth at all" (89). The nature of women's work allows them to retain value in old age, while men often feel unimportant when they retire. In a surprising statement from the author of *The Second Sex*, Beauvoir writes in *The Coming of Age* that "we live in a male world and . . . old age is primarily a male problem" (217). However, she continually contradicts this male bias in her own writing. She observes, for example, that in history and folklore "the old woman and the witch were often looked upon as one," whereas the older male could occupy the position as sage or wise man (150). Moreover, she notes that in the modern workplace elderly "women are particularly badly paid" (242). Such examples testify to Beauvoir's awareness about the unique difficulties for the aging female.

So why does Beauvoir assert that aging is "primarily a male problem"? In part, because she wants to emphasize the objectification that occurs over the course of the aging process. Since women are already objectified within the dominant milieu, it is the elderly male that most explicitly registers the negative effects of aging. An important facet of Beauvoir's argument relates to the outsider position of old age. She begins *The Coming of Age* by asserting that "either by their virtue or by their degradation they [the elderly] stand outside humanity" (4). The marginalization of age in a youth-obsessed culture drills down to the very process of subject formation, preventing identification of the subject with the older self he or she will become. She goes on to write that "for the outsider it is a dialectic relationship between my being as he defines it objectively and the awareness of myself that I acquire by means of him. Within me it is the Other – that is to say the person I am for the outsider – who is old: and that Other is myself" (284). Beauvoir suggests that one's sense of being old derives not from the self, but from outside. Others impose an age identity upon us, constructing an "Other within us who is old" (288). Old age thus confers a double outsider status: on the one hand, old age is something that arrives to us from the outside rather than from within. And on the other, one is an outsider in culture that privileges youth above all other ages. An outsider to oneself and to society.

The concept of the outsider also plays a significant role in Virginia Woolf's feminist writings. In *Three Guineas* she defines the differences between the two sexes in terms of their outsider and insider status: where men have access to political and economic power, women remain "outside," and "experiment not with public means in public but with private means in private. Those experiments will not be merely critical but creative" (113). For Woolf this outsider status confers upon women a special ability to create outside the stultifying expectations of the status quo. She writes that "the power to change and the power to grow, can only be preserved by obscurity" and that "making their absence felt their presence becomes desirable. What light this throws upon the power of outsiders to abolish or modify other institutions of which they disapprove" (114, 119). In *A Room of One's Own*, Woolf writes about the peculiar way women's subjectivity overflows the boundaries of the self: "Again if one is a woman one is often surprised by a sudden splitting off of consciousness, say in walking down Whitehall, when from being the natural inheritor of that civilization, she becomes, on the contrary, outside of it, alien and critical" (97). While being an outsider comes with crippling losses, Woolf highlights the creative benefits of this marginalization. In *Three Guineas*, for example, the aspects of femininity derided by the culture at large serve as the starting point for imagining a possible solution to the ongoing threat of war.

For Beauvoir, writing in *The Coming of Age*, old age has similar compensations to what Woolf associates with women's outsider status: "it is true that broadly speaking old age does have certain advantages. Being relegated to the fringe of humanity means escaping from the obligations and the alienations that are its portion" (487). Thus, although Beauvoir does not directly address aging women and Woolf does not explicitly discuss old age in her feminist literature, synthesizing the two views through the related discourse about the outsider provides a compelling account of the double othering of the older woman: a woman who, at extreme risk from the society around her, attains the distance to critique the world that excludes her. Woolf's *Orlando* illuminates some of the creative compensations of this outsider status by plotting the relationship between aging and feminism. Though the novel only represents the aging of its protagonist from sixteen to thirty-six, it spans over three hundred years of historical time from the Elizabethan era to the "present moment" in 1928. As such, it releases aging from its anchoring in an objective, shared temporality. The novel's representation of gender fluidity occurs alongside Orlando's freedom from the conventions of time, where one year of aging corresponds to one year of chronological time.

As the young Orlando enjoys himself at court early in the novel, he meets a young Russian woman whose ambiguous sexuality immediately attracts his attention. The Russian fashion disguises Sasha's sex, filling Orlando "with the highest curiosity": an "extraordinary seductiveness issued from the whole person" (*Orlando*, 37). "Booted like a man" and openly displaying her desire, Sasha greatly differs from the strictly defined femininity that characterizes Orlando's previous love interests; for example, the noble – and yet boring – Euphrosyne, with all of the accomplishments of a young lady and "never without a whippet or spaniel at her knee" (*Orlando*, 59, 33). Sasha's alluring androgyny was inspired by

Woolf's relationship with Vita Sackville West, a woman whom Woolf describes in her diary as "very opulent, in her brown velvet coat, pearl necklace, and slightly furred cheeks" (*Orlando*, 233). *Orlando* attests to the seductiveness of that which crosses the normative boundaries of sexuality, enhancing desire by drawing attention to the unexpectedness of what arises from outside the realm of gendered expectations.

While one would not readily associate the sexualized androgyny of the novel's major characters with old age, the very characteristics that make them desirable recall the senescent convergence of sexual traits. As Nascher writes, "This growth force is now mainly exerted toward the approximation of the sexes and in old age they approach a neutral type. This is more pronounced in the virilescence of the female. In the female there is usually a growth of hair upon the face, while the hair on the face of the male becomes thin. Her voice becomes lower, his becomes higher in pitch" (*Geriatrics*, 6). When Orlando ponders his relationship to Sasha he feeds into this association, imagining what will happen to her as she ages: "he fancied her at forty grown unwieldy though she was now slim as a reed, and lethargic, though she was now blithe as a lark" (*Orlando*, 52–3). Though youthful beauty attracts most of the attention in *Orlando*, the alluring androgyny of characters like Sasha and Orlando reminds the reader of the processes of aging that underlie and threaten their seductiveness.

Orlando transforms suddenly into a woman while serving as ambassador to Constantinople and finally recognizes the wider consequences of this change on a boat returning to England. She "tossed her foot impatiently, and showed an inch or two of calf," almost causing the death of a sailor who, upon seeing her leg, "started so violently that he missed his footing and only saved himself by the skin of his teeth" (*Orlando*, 157). As a novel split in half by the protagonist's masculine and feminine persona, *Orlando* provides many instances of how the treatment of individuals differs depending on gender. The unequal treatment of men and women, moreover, derives from what Susan Sontag calls the "double standard" of aging: "there is a double standard about aging that denounces women with special severity. Society is much more permissive about aging in men, as it is more tolerant of the sexual infidelities of husbands. Men are 'allowed' to age, without penalty, in several ways that women are not." Drawing out the discrepancy in the treatment of men and women as they age, Sontag also provides a rich account of what makes women's aging distinctive. For women, the double standard of aging makes the passage of time toxic. Sontag writes, "One of the greatest tragedies of each woman's life is simply getting older; it is certainly the *longest* tragedy." For Sontag, the very duration of the human lifespan looms threateningly to the woman: aging is a "movable doom" and a "crisis that never exhausts itself."[13] The stigma attached to women's aging turns the future into a dreaded time of obsolescence – something to be delayed through the aid of cosmetics or surgery. Near the end of *Orlando* time takes on a similarly foreboding quality, as Orlando exclaims that "it is a great shock to the nervous system, hearing a clock strike" (*Orlando*, 306).

The allusion to the nervous system and the clock emphasizes *Orlando*'s interest in the complex relationship between time and the body. While time passes with "amazing punctuality" in the natural world, for the "mind of man" it undergoes radical fluctuations: "An hour, once it lodges in the queer element of the human spirit, may be stretched to fifty or a hundred times its clock length; on the other hand, an hour may be accurately represented on the timepiece of the mind by one second" (*Orlando*, 98). *Orlando* extends this modernist formulation of the subjectivity of time to the bodies of its characters, which also span time in defiance of objective standards. Most prominently, Orlando ages twenty years over the course of about three hundred years. It is tempting to view Orlando's aging as a mere reflection of her development as a character – that the three hundred years of chronological time is only a metaphor for the difficult process of a mind grappling for its identity. However, this reading reduces Orlando's body to an epiphenomenon of her mind. For all the novel's attention to Orlando's body and the bodies of other characters, such an interpretation would surely be a mistake. Instead, we must take Orlando's aging at face value and examine what it means to grow older outside the strictures of objective time.

The novel describes Orlando's aging as a series of stops and starts, when his age serves as the sliding marker of his development as a human being:

> It would be no exaggeration to say that he would go out after breakfast a man of thirty and come home to dinner a man of fifty-five at least. Some weeks added a century to his age, others no more than three seconds at most. Altogether, the task of estimating the length of human life . . . is beyond our capacity, for directly we say it is ages long, we are reminded that it is briefer than the fall of a rose leaf to the ground. (*Orlando*, 99)

One's age, like the subjective experience of time, is highly fluid and dependent on circumstance. Weeks can write centuries or seconds onto the body as these units of shared time dilate or contract according to the unique experience of the individual: after what must have been a particularly stimulating breakfast, Orlando returns twenty-five years older. Such time-keeping, the narrator suggests, provides a more truthful insight into the development of character than temporal realism's adherence to a shared objective time.

Unhinging aging from chronological time opens further asynchronies for the individual's relationship to his or her self. As the mature Orlando reflects on her life, the narrator notes that she drifts "a little too far from the present moment," recalling memories of Persian mountains as she enters her motorcar in London (*Orlando*, 305). In contrast to Orlando's out-of-timeness, the narrator observes that there are "successful practitioners of the art of life" who "contrive to synchronise the sixty or seventy different times which beat simultaneously in every normal human system so that when eleven strikes, all the rest chime in unison, and the present is neither a violent disruption nor completely forgotten in the past" (*Orlando*, 305). The perfectly synchronized person does not live in a present compounded by memories of the past, lurching faster or slower into the future; instead, this ideal person proceeds in step with the "amazing punctuality" of the material world. The body occupies a liminal place in this formulation, as it is part of the material world and yet inextricably tied to the mental world of the subject. One's age serves as a nexus that binds the mind and the body through time – the tally of how long the two different systems have been working (or not working) together.

For the synchronized few, "we can justly say that they live precisely the sixty-eight or seventy-two years allotted them on the tombstone" (*Orlando*, 305). "Of the rest," the narrator writes, "some we know to be dead, though they walk among us; some are not yet born, though they go through the forms of life; others are hundreds of years old though they call themselves thirty-six" (*Orlando*, 305). Orlando's aging, the narrator implies, is the model that applies to most people. The number that we assign to the body – whether it is sixty-seven or thirty-six – provides only a dubiously useful tool of categorization, since the body's intersection with the mind complicates the equation, suggesting that true age has more to do with the richness or poverty of experience than the passage of chronological time. When it comes to the time-keeping of a person's life, "nothing more quickly disorders it than contact with any of the arts," a claim which is supported by Orlando's many reflections on art and the eventual publication of "The Oak Tree" (*Orlando*, 306).

Orlando's constant revision of "The Oak Tree" provides one of the threads that weaves the novel together. Very early, Orlando climbs an oak tree to survey the landscape and later flings himself on its roots. The tree serves both to provide perspective and as an anchor: "he felt the need of something which he could attach his floating heart . . . To the oak tree he tied it and as he lay there, gradually the flutter in and about him stilled itself" (*Orlando*, 19). This early experience at the oak tree explains why Orlando returns to this manuscript over the course of his and her life, providing a point of stability amidst the many physical and mental changes that the character experiences. Thus, while art encourages the temporal asynchrony that makes an individual out of step with objective time, it also provides a touchstone that allows for a degree of personal coherence. The tentative process of stitching together identity requires this return to the past, to memory: "Memory is the seamstress, and a capricious one at that. Memory runs her needle in and out, up and down, hither and thither. We know not what comes next, or what follows after" (*Orlando*, 78). Punctuated by aesthetically charged moments of return, Orlando's life lurches forward and slows down.

In her asynchronous relation to chronological time and gender, Orlando inhabits the double outsider status associated with both old age and femininity. Becoming unhinged from time occurs alongside a similar loosening of the restrictions related to gender: "Different though the sexes are, they intermix. In every human being a vacillation from one sex to the other takes place, and often it is only the clothes that keep the male or female likeness, while underneath the sex is the very opposite of what it is above" (*Orlando*, 189). *Orlando* not only shows how a three-hundred-year-old can inhabit the body of someone who is thirty-six, but also suggests that a man can have the body of a woman. These two facets of identity – age and gender – are not treated as separate processes but as inextricably linked. Orlando does not begin the novel as a woman because it requires time and experience for the revelation to occur. In other words, Orlando's realization about gender could not happen immediately, although the transformation itself occurs almost overnight: this foundation for the new, feminine Orlando can only be set over aging's duration.

The construction of Orlando's identity pivots on two different timescales: the scale of the momentary, exemplified by her rapid transformation from a man to a woman; and the duration of aging, which binds the larger and smaller transformations of her character over time. Despite the major changes that occur to Orlando over the course of the novel, the narrator asserts that she remains the same: "The change of sex, though it altered their future, did nothing whatever to alter their identity" (*Orlando*, 138).[14] Yet for Woolf, identity is not merely an essence that anchors the individual, but a much more tenuous construction across time: a long thread that strings together all the different selves that pile up over the course of one's lifetime: "these selves of which we are built up, one on top of another, as plates are piled on a waiter's hand" (*Orlando*, 308). While memory often serves this connecting function, in *Orlando* the continuity goes deeper – drilling down into duration itself, writing its passage into the fibers of the body as its ages.

The ability to immediately perform one's age or gender identity takes place alongside the duration of the body's aging, and results in what Lynne Segal in *Out of Time* terms one of the "temporal paradoxes of ageing": "As we age, changing year on year, we also retain, in one manifestation or another, traces of all the selves we have been, creating a type of temporal vertigo and rendering us psychically, in one sense, all ages and no age" (4). One reaction to this paradox, as Beauvoir argues in *Coming of Age*, is for the older person to assert "their solidary with their youth . . . each in his heart preserves the conviction of having remained unalterable . . . They set up a fixed, unchanging essence against the deteriorations of age, and tirelessly they tell stories of this being that they were, this being that lives on inside them" (362). Beauvoir critiques this excessive identification with one's youth as an unhealthy and tiresome obsession with the past. Segal, on the other hand, finds the paradox difficult and yet enabling: the "attempt to recognize ourselves as in some sense still the same person we always have been is certainly one of the challenges of old age. Nowhere is this task more fraught than in matters of sex and intimacy, where distinctly gendered apprehensions rise" (*Out of Time*, 75). The problem of aging runs both ways, as the temporal distance from one's young or middle-aged self can sometimes produce a bewildering sense of disconnection – for Segal, this sense of disconnection in old age becomes even more acute for women who have been judged by their appearance for much of their life.

Focusing on the relationship between gender and time, Woolf's *Orlando* holds up the duration of aging as an integral aspect of one's gendered identity. Orlando's transformation of sex – the brief interval where *his* performance of identity changes to *her* performance – takes place against the backdrop of three hundred years of growth and development. Instead of relying upon a pre-given essence to explain Orlando's identity, the novel suggests that the continuity of the aging body serves as a relay for the performance of different selves. While one's age is a construction – one can perform old age just as one can act conventionally young – the body serves as a physical and very public stage upon which one's sense of self intersects with the perception of others. In this sense, the body serves as a temporally porous membrane between private and public, recording one's passage through time and yet often at odds with the age identity intuited by one's self and perceived by others. Analyzing aging in *Orlando* reveals the temporal substrate of Woolf's feminism, an axis of development that provides a new set of coordinates for the plotting of gender beyond the inherited conventions of the Victorian era.

While *Orlando* illustrates the temporal dialectic that underpins the representation of gendered identity, Woolf also weaves her feminism into the very form of the novel. The temporal antimony between the momentary performance of identity and the duration of the aging body has a structural analogue in the way *Orlando* wavers between retaining the temporal norms of realism (linearity) and departing significantly from others (characters do not share the same objective time, a year passing in a human life does not correspond to chronology). While the passage of time still affects characters in the novel, it does not affect them in a consistent way; for example, Queen Elizabeth remains tied to the sixteenth century, while Orlando and the literary critic Nick Greene live across centuries. However, when Greene and Orlando meet again at the end of the novel, he has become a plump man "verging on seventy" while Orlando has aged to only thirty-six (*Orlando*, 279). Even the long-livers in the novel age at different rates. By multiplying the different timescales of the novel, *Orlando* challenges the shared temporality of realism, which further unsettles the social expansiveness of the realist project. Woolf posits duration as having multiple tracks rather than as a homogeneous medium that applies to everyone: her novel decenters the very idea of the social itself, which splinters into asynchronous slivers of time. This contributes to the sense of alienation and fragmentation that critics often associate with modernism, but it also reconfigures the position of those who remain outsiders to the society at large. When the temporal center of realism cannot hold, it is no longer possible to measure one's social power in relation to a normative standard: the position of the margins loses its meaning in a world that no longer has a shared time. The greatest irony of *Orlando* lies in the fact that the double outsider position of femininity and age enables the distance that reintegrates these positions within a temporally non-hierarchical system.

Conclusion

Though many of the novels I have analyzed in the first five chapters of this book take innovative approaches to old age and aging, they do so within a realist framework that functions according to specific expectations about how the human body passes through time: in a linear manner, declining after maturity, in step with the temporality that applies to the social world at large. But Woolf's feminism inspires a different attitude toward the relation between time and the body, provoking her to craft new modes of representation capable of containing non-normative aging processes. In her diary Woolf writes, "I don't believe in ageing. I believe in forever altering one's aspect to the sun" (*Diary*, IV, 125). Woolf's view decenters the individual's aging. Instead of tracking the subject's progress through time, Woolf locates the process of aging in the depersonalized relationship between one's bodily position and natural processes. Reflecting her modernist treatment of identity, she replaces the essence of aging with an ever-changing series of temporal coordinates.

In the early twentieth century, medical science was also demystifying the aging process. The work of gerontologists and geriatricians such as Metchnikoff and Nascher changed the medical culture that considered old age a mere afterthought and a less prestigious subject for research than the health of children and adults. By validating late life in this way, the work of these researchers redefined the limits of realism, which annexed regions of the human lifespan that were previously relegated to the social and cultural margins. Such work expanded the mimetic range for the representation of elderly. But rather than merely expanding the already capacious boundaries of realism to include more characters, modernists such as Woolf challenged the very nature of representation itself.

Woolf's work represents the process of aging in new ways: in *The Years*, old age provides the temporal vantage point from which the self's fragmentation can be confirmed; in *Orlando*, the process of aging splits from the passage of chronological time. In both cases, Woolf's critical attitude toward age enables her to propose relationships to the self and time that were not available to the Victorian authors I analyzed in the previous chapters. Indeed, Woolf demonstrates how reconceptualizing aging leads to the dissolution of the conventions of temporal realism that rely upon normative accounts of the human lifespan. When elderly subjectivity becomes a narratable phenomenon – when one year of chronological time no longer corresponds to one year of age – the novel departs from the mimetic assumptions about how characters develop over time. In the clearing that opens in the dispersal of temporal realism, Woolf's novels posit formal innovations designed to represent the aging of characters according to the new possibilities outlined by gerontology and geriatrics. This renewed attention to aging also provides Woolf with a temporal model for her feminism, which serves as a fulcrum point between the momentary performance of gendered identity and the duration of the aging body. Changes in medical and cultural attitudes toward age provided Woolf with a new lexicon for the representation of gender and further denaturalized the realist conventions that structure a human life through time.

Afterword

In her essay on cinema, Virginia Woolf reflects on the semiotic capabilities of the new artistic medium, asserting that its aesthetic potential cannot be realized while tied to the mimetic conventions of the novel. The most powerful moments in cinema, she argues, occur by accident – as when a "shadow shaped like a tadpole" appears on the screen of a showing of *Dr. Caligari* (Cinema, 174). For Woolf, this abstract image captures the essence of fear in a much more powerful way than the bodily tremors, widened eyes, and patina of sweat that actors use to signify terror. Rather than slavishly imitate the novel, the cinema requires an aesthetic repertoire to match its technical possibility. She writes that "The past could be unrolled, distances annihilated. And those terrible dislocations which are inevitable when Tolstoy has to pass from the story of Anna to the story of Levin could be bridged by some device of scenery. We should have the continuity of human life kept before us by the repetition of some object common to both lives" (Cinema, 175).[1] In contrast to the jarring transitions of the novel, cinema enables a formal smoothing away of the differences that jam the reader's sympathies, allowing for the representation of duration in a way that written narrative cannot. Though my book analyzes the many cultural and ideological implications that arise from the formal limitations inherent in the novel's representation of aging, the emergence of cinema's temporal possibility – through techniques such as the time lapse – expands the repertoire of representing aging as a process. This concluding gesture to cinema teases out the book's central arguments about duration and the novel through an illuminating contrast between the formal possibilities of the two mediums.[2]

For Henri Bergson, cinema exemplifies the mechanical way of thinking that privileges quantifiable intervals of time. He understands film as a series of sequential photographs – that is, as a series of static moments carefully arranged to produce the illusion of continuous movement. In *Creative Evolution* he writes that the movement of cinema is illusory because it relies upon a temporal paradox: "movement slips through the interval, because every attempt to reconstitute change out of states implies the absurd proposition, that movement is made of immobilities" (308). The film images placed side by side never truly embody the duration that they conjure on the screen. For Bergson, the "contrivance of the cinematograph" does not attach to "the inner becoming of things," but "recompose[s] their becoming artificially" (305–6). As he would go on to argue in *The Creative Mind*, "Succession thus understood . . . adds nothing; on the contrary, it takes something away; it marks a deficit; it reveals a weakness in our perception, which is forced by this weakness to divide up the film image by image instead of grasping it in the aggregate" (7–8). As Mary Ann Doane puts it in *The Emergence of Cinematic Time*, "No lack or loss of time is visible to the eye or accessible to the spectator. But this temporal continuity is in fact haunted by absence, by the lost time represented by the division between frames" (172). The duration of cinema, far from allowing the kind of continuity that written narrative lacks, makes duration more elusive by tricking the viewer into believing that he or she truly perceives becoming. Thus, cinema naturalizes the hegemony of mechanical thinking that divides time into useful intervals, training the viewer away from the consciousness of living duration.

While heavily indebted to Bergson's philosophy, Gilles Deleuze did not agree with his negative evaluation of cinema. Instead of lamenting the tendency to treat time abstractly, Deleuze argues that cinema produces innovative ways of organizing and perceiving time. He argues in *Cinema 1* that the cinematic shot "continuously divides duration into subdurations which are themselves heterogeneous, and reunites these into a duration which is immanent to the whole of the universe" (20). According to this view, cinema does not produce an artificial temporality but a new mode of relation to the living duration of the "whole." It does so through the technique of montage, or the assemblage of movement-images in cinema, revealing an "indirect image of time, of duration" (29).[3] The movement on the screen does not merely represent a false duration, but – through montage – allows the reader to deduce an image of time itself. The cinematic projection thus differs qualitatively from the discrete frames that form its material base, allowing for a new, modern means of representing temporality. André Bazin writes in "The Ontology of the Photographic Image" that "the cinema is objectivity in time . . . for the first time, the image of things is likewise the image of their duration, change mummified as it were" (14–15). For Deleuze and Bazin, cinema provides a means of accessing the temporality of becoming that written narrative elides.

Despite this technological possibility, early cinema remained tied to the textual representation of aging. Edwin Porter's *The Seven Ages* (1905), adapted from the famous speech in Shakespeare's *As You Like It*, represents short dramatizations of each stage of life. While following the basic structure that Shakespeare outlined, the film departs in its labeling of the life stages: beginning in "infancy," the film represents a male and female actor spanning the stages of "playmates," "schoolmates," "lovers," "the soldier," "the judge," and "second childhood." Porter briefly brings each stage to life: in "infancy," for example, a child coaxes a crying baby; or in "the soldier," a husband returns to comfort his anxious wife. The film attests to the significance of a stage-based taxonomy of the lifespan, which continues to structure thinking about age from Shakespeare to the early twentieth century. The interval of aging is omitted from Porter's film, replaced with a black screen and caption alerting the viewer about the next stage.

Though the becoming of aging falls between the cracks of each scene, *The Seven Ages* deploys cinematic techniques that establish continuity in other ways. Each stage represents kissing between the male and female actors – sometimes playful, bashful, or aggressive – that serves as a leitmotif across the entire film. Despite the vast changes in appearance from scene to scene, underscored by using different actors, the recurrent kissing provides a key to understanding the persistence of identity across time.[4] Since the characters of *The Seven Ages* lack names, the repetition of visual cues becomes the primary means of reconciling identity with the fact that the transformed bodies on the screen could, potentially, be anyone.

The final stage of life in *The Seven Ages* – "second childhood" – marks a departure from the film's Shakespearean source. In *As You Like It*, Jacques explains that the

> Last scene of all,
> That ends this strange eventful history,
> Is second childishness and mere oblivion,
> Sans teeth, sans eyes, sans taste, sans everything.
> (2.7.162–3)

In contrast to Jacques's image of old age as negation, *The Seven Ages* represents this time of life as play; as the elderly husband helps his wife spin yarn, he interrupts the action with a series of kisses that bring on smiles and laughter from the two characters. The difference in attitude between Porter's film and Jacques's speech arises in part from the mode of representation. Where Jacques *describes* the seven ages of man as a performance – "All the world's a stage, / And all the men and women merely players" – the film *The Seven Ages* actually *performs* these different aged identities (2.7.139–40). This distinction between description and the performance maps onto the gap between Jacques's cynicism and the film's more dynamic portrayal of age. Thus, even though early cinema channeled aging toward stages rather than a process of becoming, directors such as Porter used its formal possibilities to represent growing older.[5]

In his account of early cinema in "The Work of Art in the Age of Mechanical Reproduction," Walter Benjamin focuses on how the medium makes visible movements too fast for the eye to perceive. Analyzing Eadweard Muybridge's proto-cinematic "Horse in Motion" (1886), Benjamin argues that "the camera intervenes with the resources of its lowerings and liftings, its interruptions and isolations, its extensions and accelerations, its enlargements and reductions. The camera introduces us to unconscious optics as does psychoanalysis to unconscious impulses" (237). In the wake of Benjamin's influential argument, many critics have analyzed the perceptual possibilities of cinema through the medium's ability to retard movement, annexing the invisible actions of everyday life into the realm of the visible. As Friedrich Kittler suggests in *Gramophone, Film, Typewriter*, Muybridge's "serial photographs testified to the imaginary element in human perception" (116). "As phantasms of our deluded eyes," Kittler continues, cinema "reproduces the continuities and regularities of motion" (119). While early cinema's roots in serial photography place a great deal of stress on the medium's ability to slow down what was once too fast, the development of digital technologies allows for a perfection of speeding up movement that occurs below a human's perceptual threshold.[6]

From the mechanics of early cinema to more recent digital technologies, film provides powerful new ways of representing the duration of aging. It has the capability of holding aging before the viewer for an extended interval of time, texturing the duration of an experience that often recedes to the forgotten background of perception. However, cinema does not simply solve the representational problems of the novel that animate this book's analysis of the nineteenth and early twentieth centuries. Indeed, these problems remain productively unsolvable. One of the central tensions of the realist novel arises from the asynchrony between the biological lifespan of its characters and the artificiality of narrative conventions that warp the duration of their aging, whether through elision, acceleration, or retardation. Of course, the conventions of cinema are no less artificial than those of the novel, even as they enable glimpses of aging beyond the formal limitations of textual narrative. Instead of privileging one mode of representation over the other as capturing something "essential" about the process of aging, we can learn more by examining what forms such as the novel and cinema reveal or conceal about the value of age in specific historical contexts.

To borrow a term from Caroline Levine's *Forms: Whole, Rhythm, Hierarchy, Network*, the analysis of aging should attend to the "affordances" that its representational medium enables. For Levine, affordances "describe the potential uses or actions latent in materials and designs": "both the particular constraints and possibilities that different forms afford, and the fact that those patterns and arrangements carry their affordances with them as they move across time and space" (6). When it comes to the representation of aging, the novel and cinema afford very different possibilities. This brief analysis of cinema illustrates some of the affordances of the medium when it is no longer tethered to novelistic mimesis: of setting the continuous process of aging before the viewer, foregrounding a duration that he or she often ignores. Cinema's affordances allow the medium to respond to radical shifts in the understanding of aging throughout the twentieth century; for example, the medicalization of aging in the early decades of the century or the growing concern about increasing elderly populations in the later decades. Cinema captures this new visibility of aging in medicine and as a demographic, providing the formal means of confronting aging as a continuous, unescapable phenomenon.

Analyzing what cinema enables and disables regarding the representation of aging clarifies the novel's affordances on the subject in the nineteenth and early twentieth centuries. As this book has shown, the novel form tends to elide the aging of its characters by skipping ahead many years between chapters or through illnesses and traumatic events. In the novel, the characters have already arrived at an age – a stable, socially recognized state defined by chronology, appearance, or function. The novel's diachronicity serves a temporally restrictive function, reinforcing a view of aging as something that sneaks up on one rather than a process that happens continually. Yet the novel affords other possibilities. The chapters of this book illustrate how this formal restriction enables inventive approaches to the literary and cultural understanding of duration and the lifespan: how Charles Dickens empowers elderly men through their persistence beyond the teleology of plot; how Elizabeth Gaskell imagines a senescent version of the marriage plot; how Thomas Hardy queers the romances of old age; how H. G. Wells negotiates modernity between the positions of youth and age; how Virginia Woolf models modernist fragmentation on senility. The very limitations of the novel afford it a powerful means of capturing the persistence and transformation of identity across the lifespan, an increasingly important task as modernity reshaped the roles available to the elderly.

While cinema and the novel afford different possibilities for representation, age and aging function as forms with their own set of affordances. Age serves as a powerful tool for organizing human life – determining one's inclusion and exclusion from institutions such as education, suffrage, state sponsored healthcare (in the United States), and pensions. By indexing age to these milestones, the form of age sutures biological linearity to the narrative of social advancement and decline. The vicissitudes of nineteenth- century modernity – the maturation of a capitalist system in which one could rapidly rise or fall in the social hierarchy, or the discourse of imperialism that pegged empire to national vitality – relied upon the stability of age for its biopolitics. While age as a category affords the ability to make vast generalizations across society and informs the creation of policy, the becoming of aging does not help to make these calculations. As a process, aging remains excessive – something to be travelled through on the way to a meaningful age rather than lingered upon for its own sake. Yet the novels I examine in this book reveal the affordances of *aging*: an excessiveness that overspills the boundaries of modernity and capitalism's youthful ethos. Between the ages that mark out social milestones, the duration of aging provides an open form where meaning and identity are contested. The duration of aging cuts across the lifespan, serving as the interstitial temporality that binds together the diachronic events that give the novel – and the social life it represents – the feeling of passing time.

Notes

Introduction

1 For example, Gallagher writes that "The most prominent generic features of the novel have received remarkable little systematic attention in our criticism" ("Formalism and Time," 229). Levine claims that "the field has by and large inherited a dominant definition of literary form as spatially unifying, which has too often distracted us from the specificity of temporally unfolding forms" (*Forms*, 52).

2 See Teresa Mangum's "Little Women" for a discussion of how elderly women were "pushed to the margins of family groups" in Victorian era painting (60).

3 See especially Mary Poovey's *Making a Social Body*.

4 Kathleen Woodward's term "statistical panic" resembles what I am calling demographic dread: "Our bodies are figured as being in a perpetual state of risk. The statistics profiling the body are for the most part melancholy and grim" (*Statistical Panic*, 196). Though Woodward suggests that statistical panic is a particularly postmodern affect, an early form can be observed in the nineteenth-century response to its vulnerable elderly population.

5 See Corbet, "What Should England Do to be Saved?" 612.

6 See Gilleard, "Age and Aging Studies." See also Jan Baars's "Aging and the Exploration of Lived Ambivalence," especially his complaint that "As *time* is inherent in aging – which is, basically, living in time – it should be one of the dimensions that deserve more attention than it has been given." Also see Devoney Looser's "Age and Aging Studies, From Cradle to Grave."

7 Lars Tornstam's "Gero-Transcendence: A Theoretical and Empirical Exploration" serves as a useful introduction to this topic.

8 See Biggs, Estes, and Phillipson, *Social Theory, Social Policy, and Ageing*, 28–9, 35.

9 Some other important examples include Jan Baars's argument in "Concepts of Time" to unsettle gerontology's reliance on chronological time by asserting the temporality of narrative as a means of giving personal meaning to the aging process. Baars shows the necessity of multiple temporal frameworks for understanding the complex and deeply personal process of aging, the effects of which a mere number – despite its scientific exactitude – fails to encompass. See also Baars's "A Triple Temporality of Aging." In addition, through her

reading of William Godwin, Andrea Charise shows in "The Tyranny of Age" how the aging body serves as a figure for the "tyrannical authority of time, identical in effect to the insinuating influence of its political counterpart, government" (913).

10 In *The Mature Imagination*, Simon Biggs applies the notion of the mask to the process of aging: "it might be thought of as a signature of maturity that surface identities become malleable and can be used as needed, rather than being too firmly fixed in place or determined by social conformity" (6).

11 For an explication of "Bergson's synchronic explanation of duration," see David Hoy's *The Time of Our Lives* (139).

1 Aging Theory

1 Yahav, "Sonorous Duration," 896. See also Dames, *Physiology of the Novel*, 73–122.

2 Similarly, Ernst Bloch writes in *The Principle of Hope* that while depth usually relies upon metaphors of extraction to get "to the bottom of things," "there is also a depth upwards and forwards which takes up into itself profound material from below . . . Real depth always occurs in double-edged movement" (158). Instead of positing an insurmountable gap between the surface and the depth, Bloch's account links the "profound material from below" to critical vectors that bubble upwards toward the surface (158).

3 See Ricoeur, *Time and Narrative*, 76, 65.

4 Brian Massumi explains the relationship between position and duration at the beginning of his book *Parables of the Virtual*. Echoing the arguments of Bergson, Massumi illustrates how overemphasizing position reduces the ability to imagine possibilities outside the status quo: "The idea of positionality begins by subtracting movement from the picture. This catches the body in cultural freeze-frame" (3).

5 Grosz writes that "reduction of a continuity to step-by-step halts necessarily elides the dimension of duration," which denies "the dynamic and continuous nature of temporal change" (*The Nick of Time*, 54).

6 See Swann, "Déjà Vu: Déjà Lu," 46.

7 Lewes reproduces an anecdote from the *British Medical Journal* that further implicates the temporal gap between perceiving and understanding through the phenomenon of vision. The story relates to a murderer:

> The murderer, then unknown, had been dazzled by the reflection of the sun from a bucket of water, which another man was carrying before him: and soon afterwards, seeing in the air what he took for a bucketful of blood going before him, he was seized with such horror that he declared himself the murderer, and disclosed such facts as brought the crime home to him, so that he was convicted and executed. (Quoted in *Physiology of Common Life*, 284–5)

Dazzled by the light reflected off the bucket of water, the murderer turns away and sees a bucket of blood. Whereas the first bucket was an object in the world, the afterimage derives from his body. The murderer's afterimage and

Latimer's prevision illustrate how visual effects in the present are not determined solely by present stimuli. Through the temporal lag of the body, the past and future feed back (or forward) into the construction of duration, which becomes richly stereoscopic and temporally overdetermined. In the case of both the murderer and Latimer, the meaning extracted exceeds and transforms the original impression: while the murderer goes to the gallows because he cannot register the pastness of the afterimage, Latimer marries Bertha because he values the future based on his current desires. Both cases illustrate the risks involved with understanding duration exclusively from the standpoint of the present: "I trembled under a present glance, I hungered after a present joy, I was clogged and chilled by a present fear" (Eliot, *Lifted Veil*, 24).

8 These sentences echo the opening lines of Charles Dickens's *Sketches by Boz*: "How much is conveyed in those two short words – 'The Parish!' And with how many tales of distress and misery, of broken fortune and ruined hopes, too often of unrelieved wretchedness and successful knavery are the associated!" (17). For George Levine, Dickens's quote works as a thesis "for realism's effort to make the ordinary significant" (*The Realistic Imagination*, 13). Yet Eliot inverts the meaning – where for Dickens words have an explosive power of expression, for Eliot they reduce the temporal complexity of everyday life.

9 See Menke, *Telegraphic Realism*, Agathocleous, *Urban Realism and the Cosmopolitan Imagination in the Nineteenth Century*, and Greiner, *Sympathetic Realism in Nineteenth-Century British Fiction.*

10 Through her analysis of the role of suspense in scientific experiment in *The Serious Pleasures of Suspense*, Caroline Levine highlights the pleasurable aspects of waiting to verify one's hypothesis. However, in other contexts – such as the speculation in financial markets – the Victorians considered suspense to be morally dubious (see Jewusiak's "Suspenseful Speculation and the Pleasures of Waiting in *Little Dorrit*"). The development of character through suspenseful plots takes on this ambivalent charge.

11 This view has come under scrutiny by Ruth Leys, who criticizes affect theorists for drawing a distinction between the systems of non-cognitive affect and intentional consciousness. This dichotomy, she argues, is predicated upon the very mind–body dualism that these theorists want to deconstruct – the split between consciousness and affect is itself the product of a "highly intellectualist or rationalist concept of meaning" ('The Turn to Affect," 458).

12 Roland Barthes provides the most influential reading of the novel's descriptive excessiveness in his essay "The Reality Effect," in which he demonstrates how the inclusion of "insignificant" details connotes the real.

2 No Plots for Old Men

1 "No Plots for Old Men" was originally published in *Novel*, vol. 46, no. 2 (2013), 193–213.

2 In his account of the modernist *Bildungsroman*, *Unseasonable Youth*, Jed Esty argues that youth is suspended as a means of interrogating the contradictions of progress in a colonial and global context. In his preliminary reading of Rudyard Kipling's *Kim*, the eponymous hero's "antidevelopmental bildungsroman" "literalizes the problem of colonialism as failed or postponed modernization" (14). Esty's argument circumscribes adolescence as a discrete stage of life, downplaying the intervention of old age – in the form of the elderly Lama – on shaping the trajectory of Kim's youthful plot.

3 Quadagno, *Aging in an Early Industrial Society*, 21 and 63; Thane, *Old Age in English History*, 275. John Macnicol writes in *The Politics of Retirement* that "long-run labour market trends were bringing about an inexorable decrease in the labour force participation rates of older males, just as demographic trends were increasing both the number and proportion of old people in the population. Less and less able to earn a living through formal work, the growing numbers of old people formed an increasing population of 'dependants' at the top end of the population age structure. It was impossible not to provide state support for them" (6).

4 David Thomson suggests in "The Welfare of the Elderly in the Past" that "the majority of all elderly persons in England were maintained by the poor law" (202) while Thane asserts that relief was still distributed unevenly (*Old Age in English History*, 168–70, 175–6). Also, see Karen Chase's work on almshouses in chapter 2 of *The Victorians and Old Age.*

5 Woloch, *The One vs. the Many*, 13; Steinlight, "Dickens's 'Supernumeraries' and the Biopolitical Imagination of Victorian Fiction," 231 and 234.

6 See Dickens, *The Letters of Charles Dickens*, 563–4.

7 Patten, "'The Story-Weaver at His Loom," 63.

8 Stephen Katz notes that there was a growing trend toward pathologizing old age in the nineteenth century: "The medical impetus was to discover increasingly subtle distinctions and ailments that marked the aged body not simply as degenerative but also as different" (*Disciplining Old Age*, 44).

9 The condition of old age facilitates the kind of ambivalent imaginative transformation that Garrett Stewart identifies in Dickens's work. Writing on Dick Swiveller's "transfiguration" of gin and water into "rosy wine" through his poetic restyling, Stewart points out the "change that is wrought comes to symbolize the miracle worked by all imagination, both in art and in daydream, on the stuff of reality" (xiii). By the end of the novel, however, Swiveller has learned that "imagination begins to learn its surcharge" (*Dickens and the Trials of Imagination,* 113).

10 Katz suggests that it was not until the publication of Thomas Bailey's *Records of Longevity* in 1857 that "skepticism about the miraculous cases of long lifespans" was introduced along with an extensive list of long-livers (45).

11 Peter Stearns writes, "Men's growing dominance over work through most of the nineteenth century subjected them to many demanding challenges – for work was where industrialization created greatest flux and uncertainty – but it

served as a badge of masculinity and a source of real power that were carefully fostered" (*Be a Man!,* 52).

12 See Cole and Edwards, "The 19th Century," 254, Mangum, "Little Women," 76, and Hamilton, "New Women and 'Old' Men," 75.

13 As "muscularity" and athleticism became defining characteristics of masculinity at the mid-century, Kay Heath suggests that "the older man increasingly was pushed to the margins, and aging became more and more debilitating and effeminizing" (*Aging by the Book,* 30).

14 See Roget, "Age," 42 and Andrews, *A Cyclopedia of Domestic Medicine and Surgery*, 137–8.

15 In Barbara Hardy's reading, Old Martin's impersonation represents Dickens's "wasted opportunity" of generating some emotional identification on the part of the reader (112). He fails precisely because Old Martin is absent for so much of the novel: "Such scenes are frequent at the beginning, then thin out, and reappear in a conspicuous huddle towards the end when we have the revelation of Martin's trick . . . It is important at the beginning and end but stays more or less out of sight for a large part of the novel" (111). With my reading of Old Martin, however, his absence serves a specific purpose in diverting attention away from himself as the generator of plots.

16 Monod, *Martin Chuzzlewit*, 25.

17 Cole and Edwards, "The 19th Century," 224, Thane, *Old Age in English History*, 7, and Small, *Long Life*, 72.

18 The return to society is the most fundamental aspect of Georg Lukács's account of the *Bildungsroman*, where, through great difficulty, an isolated individuality is folded back into a social reality of similarly formed personalities: community "is achieved by personalities, previously lonely and confined within their own selves, adapting and accustoming themselves to one another; it is the fruit of a rich and enriching resignation, the crowning of a process of education, a maturity attained by struggle and effort" (*Theory of the Novel*, 133).

19 In Claudia Nelson's book-length study on age inversion in Victorian literature, she observes how categories like "child" and "adult" "could be turned inside out to interrogate pressing questions having to do with work and family life, responsibility and desire, faith and doubt, masculinity and femininity, the primitive and the civilized, and more" (*Precocious Children and Childish Adults*, 11).

20 As Nicholas Dames observes in "Untimely Contextualizations," there is a surplus of quantitative data about old age that makes it more "knowable" than other contexts such as race, class, or gender; however, the "numerical accuracy of our age" exists in tension with the fact that old age is "far less knowable, far more internal, private, and idiosyncratic, than these other categories" (114). According to Dames, "We can guess with some confidence what an annual income of, say, £300 in 1860 might mean, even how it would 'feel'; what it might 'feel' like to be 50 years old in 1860 is much more opaque" (115). As a result of this slippage, Dames suggests that "old age . . . is not fully

historicizable," and calls for scholarship that is sensitive to "the formal strategies by which old age eludes the contexts that inexorably pursue it" (116, 117).

21 In her reading of Dickens's elderly women of modest means, Karen Chase suggests that characters like Sarah Gamp and Betty Higden embody a resilience that is based on their ability to piece together a living from society's leftovers: "theirs is a resilience of the elderly bricoleuse, reduced to the most exiguous circumstances … who nevertheless discovers the tactics of persistence. Comic or sentimental, shrewd or innocent, these aging women retain a generative power that belongs to the composite image of the Victorian elderly and that should not be overlooked within simpler narratives, smoother trajectories" (*Victorians and Old Age*, 36).

3 Life After the Marriage Plot

1 Joseph Allen Boone suggests that the representation of memories "creates a sense of both circularity and stasis" that overwhelms "the logic of 'man-made' time" (*Tradition Counter Tradition*, 287). Jill Rappoport argues that Cranford is sustained by a "closed circuit" of sympathy that "draws imaginatively on cyclical time" in "contrast to the forward-pressing mentality of the mid-nineteenth-century" ("Conservation of Sympathy," 101, 105). Alyson Kiesel continues this trend by underlining the recursive movement of *Cranford*'s narrative: "It is exactly this 'simple movement forward' that eludes *Cranford* … The whole narrative consists of a series of these returns and repetitions" ("Meaning and Misinterpretation," 1013).

2 Stoneman, *Elizabeth Gaskell*, 61.

3 The reader's expectations are continually assaulted by *Cranford*'s narrative: Linda K. Hughes and Michael Lund point out how the narrator acknowledges her "irregular production of tales" by linking the time that passes within the narrative to the time that passes between the publication of *Cranford* (*Victorian Publishing and Mrs. Gaskell's Work*, 85). Andrew Miller also discusses the "dilatory manner" of Mary Smith's narration, especially with regard to the financial crisis: "Instead of immediately revealing this information [about the failure of the joint stock bank] – which would direct the narrative towards its crisis – Mary veers into a description of the postman and his relationship to various Cranford characters … we, as readers, must impatiently wait out exactly this delay ourselves" (*Novels Behind Plate Glass*, 107).

4 Schor, *Scheherezade in the Marketplace*, 86; Felski, *Doing Time*, 82.

5 According to Michal Peled Ginsburg, it is through Gaskell's reconfiguration of events in relation to each other, instead of a final end, that she is able to reinscribe the significance of domestic, everyday work: "the relative importance of events is not defined in terms of their contribution to a 'final' event. Ultimately, it is through her success in creating a compelling narrative, where events gain their importance in relation to each other rather than to a goal present from the beginning, that Gaskell defies our assumption that the

endless labor of reproduction that constitutes the everyday is excluded from novels because it is inherently uninteresting to read about" ("Narratives of Survival," 413).

6 Gaskell's interest in the story and storytelling was not simply relegated to her printed work, but formed a significant part in her personal and social life. See Uglow, *Elizabeth Gaskell*, 239–40.

7 Revising Benjamin's thesis, Ivan Krielkamp argues that the storyteller in Victorian fiction was an enabling fiction whereby the author might "idealize the speech community it has relegated to the past" (*Voice and the Victorian Storyteller*, 3).

8 See Nina Auerbach, *Communities of Women*, 81.

9 The wife's dependence on the husband was codified by the law of coverture, which absorbed the wife's legal identity into that of her husband. See, for example, Ablow, "'One Flesh,' One Person, and the 1870 Married Women's Property Act" and Rappoport, "Wives and Sons."

10 As both character in *Cranford* and narrator of it, Mary Smith begins the novel anonymous and almost disembodied, a mere reporter of the events that take place in the small town. As the novel progresses, her character develops a personality and agency: it is not until chapter 14, when she takes Miss Matty's financial crisis into her own hands and sends a letter to Peter in India, that Mary Smith is finally named. Her protean character and unique perspective of Cranford grounds Boris Knezevic's claim that Mary Smith is an "amateur reporter": "the crucial fact about Mary's position relative to Cranford is that, with her economic grounding in Drumble and her gendered place in the domestic circles of Cranford, she is equipped to assume the roles of both observer and participant in the visited culture" ("An Ethnography of the Provincial," 408, 411). As a sort of proto-anthropologist, Mary Smith is invested in her portrayal of Cranford life even as she represents it with an ironic distance that jars with the sincerity of her subjects.

11 Richard Altick observes in *The Presence of the Present* that Gaskell "deliberately blurred the time setting" of her novel for the sake of heightening the disparity between eighteenth-century values and encroaching modernization (136). Nonetheless, citing contemporary events represented in the text, Altick suggests that *Cranford* takes place in a "general sense of the late 1830s and early 1840s" (136).

12 According to Jennifer Wicke's article on Thomas Hardy and standardization, the years between 1881 and 1901 formed the time when "the notion of a standard is being crystallized in disparate cultural practices and concretized as a cultural concept" ("The Same and the Different," 575).

13 Schor, *Scheherezade in the Marketplace*, 85.

14 Felski, *Gender*, 16.

15 Gaskell deploys the same staggered delivery of the newspaper in her novel *Ruth* (composed while she was writing installments of *Cranford*). Mr. Benson, a poor minister, accepts Mr. Farquhar's charity, though it comes with a temporal differential that reproduces the socioeconomic inequality between

them: "Will you allow me to send you over my *Times*? I have generally done with it before twelve o'clock, and after that it is really waste-paper in my house" (*Ruth*, 304). Moreover, Farquhar's claim that after twelve o'clock the newspaper becomes "waste-paper" shows the same awareness that Miss Matty and Mary Smith have of the newspaper's transformation from timely information to a variety of domestic uses.

16 See Patricia Meyer Spacks on the socioeconomic causes of exclusion: "The problem of social gradation preoccupies Cranford gossips not only because it provides something to talk about . . . but because it helps them preserve a sense of their own importance. Cranford conversation emphasizes the exclusionary function of class distinctions. In order to be 'insiders,' the ladies must posit an outside" (*Gossip*, 185).

17 James Mulvihill further argues for a correspondence between "the local economy of Cranford/*Cranford* and the larger fictional economies directing Gaskell's narrative" (356). The same elegant economy that helps to structure the everyday life of Cranfordians also applies to the way that both the characters and the narrator manage their stories. Thus, Mulvihill argues, the women "ration their disclosures" and manage their "fictional store" according to the surplus or scarcity of stories available to them (351, 355).

18 Turner, "'Telling of my weekly doings': The Material Culture of the Victorian Novel," 125.

19 In Gaskell's short novel *Cousin Phillis* (1864), the newspaper also plays a central role in negotiating the confrontation between modernity and local communities. Whereas the representative of modernity and the railroad, Mr. Holdsworth, falls asleep when presented with an old edition of the newspaper, for the simple Holman family the newspaper's function is not tied exclusively to the timeliness of its information:

> Cousin Holman gave me the weekly county newspaper to read aloud to her, while she mended stockings out of a high piled-up basket . . . I read and read, unregardful of the words I was uttering, thinking of all manner of other things; of the bright color of Phillis' hair, as the afternoon sun fell on her bending head; of the silence of the house, which enabled me to hear the double tick of the old clock which stood halfway up the stairs . . . The tranquil monotony of that hour made me feel as if I had lived forever, and should live forever droning out paragraphs in that warm sunny room, with my two quiet hearers, and the curled-up pussy cat sleeping on the hearth-rug, and the clock on the house-stairs perpetually clicking out the passage of the moments. (58–9)

The tempo of the narrator's shared reading articulates the rhythm by which Phillis and her mother mend stockings. "Unregardful of the words," the content of the newspaper becomes secondary to a reading practice that is identified with time itself: "the double tick of the old clock," "the tranquil monotony of that hour," and the "clock . . . clicking out the passage of the moments." For the Holman family, as for the women in *Cranford*, the newspaper is not used for its timeliness but for its ability to mediate time, an appropriation of genre that is also a revision of modern – youthful, masculine – temporalities.

20 In addition to ignorance of the sun's passage, Miss Matty also lacks a more general sense of geologic time, expressing disbelief at the very rotation of the earth: "she had told me, she never could believe that the earth was moving constantly, and that she would not believe it if she could, it made her feel so tired and dizzy whenever she thought about it" (96).

21 See Dreher, "Redundancy and Emigration," 3.

22 For an account of the significance of the social category of the spinster and redundant woman in *Cranford,* see Lepine, "Strange and Rare Visitants" and Fenton-Hathaway, "Gaskell's Detours."

4 A Wrinkle in Time

1 Miller, *Thomas Hardy*, xii–xiii; Beer, *Darwin's Plots*, 235.

2 O'Toole, "Genealogy and Narrative Jamming," 5.

3 Gilmartin, *Ancestry and Narrative in Nineteenth-Century British Literature*, 198.

4 *Thomas Hardy: The Complete Poems*, 81, lines 1–2.

5 Fisher, *Hard Facts*, 170, 171.

6 June Howard uses the term "proletarianization" to refer to the way naturalism sequences "the progress of a character's deterioration" with his socioeconomic status (*Form and History in American Literary Naturalism*, 96).

7 Hardy's declining protagonists mostly fall into Jennifer Fleissner's gendering of naturalist plot, where it "is the older man's story that best fits prevailing views of naturalism as a 'plot of decline'; the young woman's plot, by contrast, moves in a nonlinear fashion epitomized by a language of 'drift'" (*Women, Compulsion, Modernity*, 163).

8 Quoted in Weismann, *Heredity*, 24. See also Rose, *Evolutionary Biology of Aging*, 4.

9 Quoted in Weismann, *Heredity*, 24.

10 According to Kevin Padian, such temporal dexterity is characteristic of Hardy's work: "Hardy slides easily among the scales of time from years to eons, accepting slow but relentless change through time – evolution – as the natural order of things" ("Evolution and Deep Time," 223).

11 "In the Night She Came," in *Thomas Hardy: The Complete Poems*, 228–9.

12 "At the Dinner Table," in *Thomas Hardy: The Complete Poems*, 654–5.

13 The immensity of these timescales threatens the human life with insignificance; see Gilmartin, *Ancestry and Narrative*, 220. Yet, as Virginia Zimmerman points out, deep time posed a liberating hermeneutic possibility alongside its existential threat: "Uniformitarianism insists on an expanded time scale which inevitably made humans feel very small, yet it also empowers people to imagine the tremendous potency of the small" (*Excavating Victorians*, 19). Surveying the bewildering expanse of the earth's history, the geologist does not become paralyzed by its scope but is empowered to interpret and narrate the story of the inert material that forms its record.

14 Charise and Manning, "Unexampled Eyes," 39–40.

15 Miller, *Fiction and Repetition*, 164.

16 Miller, *Fiction and Repetition*, 164; Gilmartin, *Ancestry and Narrative*, 224, 232.

17 Buckland further problematizes the relation between the geologist and his object of study by asserting the "hermeneutic instability" of the "geological material object" ("Thomas Hardy," 19). Arising from the disconnect between the local context in which a material object is found and the metropolitan center that recontextualizes it through institutions such as the museum, Buckland argues that geology activates "different interpretations by different social groups ... in different geographical settings" ("Thomas Hardy," 19). While the temporal scope of geology leads to some cynical conclusions about the significance of the individual, it also gives rise to a scientific subjectivity that is capable of organizing the material of the earth into a narrative structure. Such narrativization, however, is inherently unstable and dependent upon context. Rather than strive for the "single explanatory mechanism" of plot, Buckland shows how geologists offered a model of "narrative breakdown" that more accurately reflected the processes of the earth (*Novel Science*, 20, 27).

18 Drawing on Kathleen Woodward's concept of the mirror stage of old age – where one is "libidinally alienated from one's mirror image" (*Aging and its Discontents*, 67) – Kay Heath suggests that the disparity between appearance and feeling allows Jocelyn to retain his youthfulness: "Identifying with an aged body is . . . ultimately harmful to Pierston's emotional well-being and sets him on a downward trajectory" (*Aging by the Book*, 167).

19 The uneven temporal record presented by the science of geology inheres in Hardy's ambivalent position between ancient customs and modernity. As Andrew Radford shows, on the one hand Hardy enshrines tradition and regional practices passing out of existence, on the other he desires (in his personal life) to achieve social standing with the London elite and also represents many customs – such as the skimmity ride – in a negative light (*Thomas Hardy and the Survivals of Time*, 20–1).

20 Bennett, "Hardy's Noble Melancholics," 38–9. J. Hillis Miller argues that *The Well-Beloved* is about the inability to stop repeating – for to stop repeating would be to acknowledge the "emptiness of the beloved," a revelation that Jocelyn defers because it reflects the absence at the heart of his own creativity (*Fiction and Repetition*, 168). Ross DeAngelis writes that "Periodically disrupted, intersubjective, linear relationships generate patterns of action, reaction, and interaction amongst the players. The result of these momentary passionate interludes is a narrative in which the protagonist must continue the repetition if passion is to be sustained" ("Triangulated Passions," 404).

21 Lodge, "*Jude the Obscure*: Pessimism and Fictional Form," 196.

22 Hardy, *Collected Letters*, 153, 156–7.

5 The Technology Age

1 Wells, *Experiment in Autobiography*, 245.

2 For example, the grandfather paradox. In this paradox, a time traveller murders his grandfather, making it impossible for himself to be born. Yet by doing so, he makes it impossible for the murder to occur in the first place.

3 Wittenberg, *Time Travel*, 5, 1, 29.

4 See Stover's Introduction to his edition of *The Time Machine*, 3, and Beaumont, "Red Sphinx," 237. Frank Scafella claims that the sphinx poses the problem of the modern scientist who must "either exercise reason to gain control over paralyzing fear, or be devoured by the Sphinx" ("The White Sphinx," 257).

5 Mulroy, "Appendix 1: The Riddle of the Sphinx," 91.

6 "The New Accelerator," in *The Country of the Blind*, 299.

7 In their analysis of Wells's *Tono-Bungay*, Patrick Brantlinger and Richard Higgins write that production and consumption form two sides of the same worthless coin: "the concept of value at the heart of capitalist economics is hollow, a container waiting to be filled by whatever individual agents – producers or consumers – wish to put in it" ("Waste and Value," 469).

8 For a Marxist reading, see John S. Partington's "The Time Machine: A Polemic." For a psychoanalytic approach, see Beaumont's "The Red Sphinx."

9 Charise, "Let the Reader Think of the Burden," 2.

10 Paul Cantor and Peter Hufnagel make the point that the reference to children is a common trope of imperial literature, which also processed the relationship between colonizer and colonized in terms of consumption and production ("The Empire of the Future," 40, 64).

11 Nordau makes some unflattering appearances in Wells's novels. In *Food of the Gods* a bumbling parish doctor refers to Nordau as "a most gifted and celebrated philosopher" who "discovered that the abnormal is – abnormal, a most valuable discovery" (174). Nevertheless, Nordau's influential work brought together the discourse of aging with that of the decadent fin-de-siècle, and informed Wells's representation of the Eloi in *The Time Machine*, the monstrosities of *The Island of Dr. Moreau*, and the eugenicist policies of his socialist non-fiction.

12 With the exception of Claudia Nelson's book that I cite above. However, Nelson does not focus on old age so much as the relationship between adult men and children.

13 Thane, *Old Age in English History*, 198 and 225.

14 Partington, "H. G. Wells," 518, 522.

15 David Seed argues that this narrative frame – here represented by the Traveller discoursing with his dinner companions – provides Wells with a way of balancing verisimilitude with the fantastic: "framing functions as a convenience of reading, a means of gradually introducing the reader to the extraordinary" ("Framing the Reader in Early Science Fiction," 138).

16 Martin Middeke shows how the time machine figures a deconstructive openness to interpretation: "to keep going on their time-traveling hermeneutic spiral, moving to and fro between some lost past, some fleeting present, and some shapeless future" ("On Circles and Spirals,"123).

17 In Chapter 1 of this book, I define temporal realism as the conventions that solicit the reader's belief that the time represented in the story corresponds with how time passes in the real world. On the distinction between Wells's

realist fiction and science fiction, see Simon James's *Maps of Utopia*: "If Wells's realist writing exposes the insufficiencies of the 'real' world on which it draws, the scientific and utopian romances in turn allow the imagining of different, better, realities. Even if these visions are dystopian, as in *The Time Machine*, they still demonstrate the possibility of a reality alternate to the existing order of things" (134). Also, see Patrick Parrinder's "*News from Nowhere*, *The Time Machine*, and the Break-Up of Classical Realism," 273.

18 In *The Logic of Fantasy*, John Huntington argues that "opposition is the essential mechanism of Wells's imaginative strategy in all his early works" (8).

19 Wells writes in his autobiography that "Belief in the necessity of progress anyhow, was almost universal" (*Experiment in Autobiography*, 214).

20 Wells acknowledges in his autobiography that George "gave substance to a drift of dispositions and desires in my mind, that might otherwise have dispersed and left no trace" (*Experiment in Autobiography*, 140–1).

21 Conrad, *Selected Letters*, 106.

6 Gray Modernism

1 Andrew Achenbaum writes that by the early twentieth century, the "nineteenth-century images of old age being a period of natural decay were called into question" (*Crossing Frontiers*, 37). Pamela Gravagne emphasizes the legacy of these views, adding that the "dualism regarding old age instituted in Victorian times persists to this day, embodied in ideas such as intergenerational war, generational equity, the social redundancy of the elderly, and personal responsibility for the way we age" (*The Becoming of Age*, 19).

2 In his books *The Nature of Man* and *The Prolongation of Life*, he draws on sources from the east and west, including Buddha, the Bible, Nietzsche, Voltaire, and Schopenhauer. Religious and philosophical texts form important sources alongside empirical evidence from his own experiments and that which he cites from other scientists and medical practitioners. Laura Gillen and Diane Martin write that "Metchnikoff's assertion that aging processes extend beyond the boundaries set by medicine defines gerontology as the first interdisciplinary venture of the 20th century" ("Revisiting Gerontology's Scrapbook," 52).

3 See Chapter 4 in this book for a discussion of August Weismann.

4 The debate about aging and disease continues into contemporary scholarship, exemplified by Ruth Elaine Nieuwenhuis-Mark's argument against the trend to classify "normal aging as a disease, so that it can be 'manipulated, treated, and delayed'" ("Healthy Aging as Disease?").

5 Dale Matthews writes that Warren "created a successful geriatric unit, the first in the United Kingdom, based upon early rehabilitation of the patient by a multidisciplinary team" ("Dr. Marjory Warren and the Origin of British Geriatrics," 254). Ian Philp traces the legacy of Warren's work to the contemporary integrated approach to caring for the elderly in his article "The Contribution of Geriatric Medicine to Integrated Care for Older People."

6 As she writes in "Care of the Chronic Sick," "Many of the so-called 'incurable' cases only need the patience, tact, and quiet energy of a staff trained to work with this type of patient to show a considerable measure of improvement" (823).

7 Compare Karen Chase's observation in *The Victorians and Old Age*: "Especially at that moment of post-Darwinian bewilderment, the decrepit body is bound to seem like the body of someone else, a detached artifact in some unthinkable future. The aged are objects not subjects, and it seems painfully right to say that this is something they know about themselves. The worst losses of age include finally a loss of the power to constitute subjectivity – when the self surrenders and becomes a specimen" (253).

8 Agamben, *Homo Sacer*, 142, 137.

9 The double reference to aging and the omnibus in *The Years* draws from an observation that Woolf made in her diary. She wrote that "I shall be fifty on the 25th, Monday week that is; and sometimes feel that I have lived 250 years already, and sometimes that I am still the youngest person in the omnibus" (*Diaries*, IV, 63). Unlike Eleanor Pargiter, whose feeling of being the youngest and oldest person on the bus is separated by the span of decades, Woolf suggests that the aged positions are two interchangeable aspects of her current self.

10 Kathleen Woodward writes in "The Look and the Gaze" that Eleanor's old age allows her to accept "the variousness of experience at different stages in her life" (81). Because of this, Woodward claims, Eleanor does "not have a unified narrative of her life, or more accurately perhaps, does not need or desire such an intelligible account of her life. At several points in the evening her nieces – the middle-aged – ask her about her life. To *have* a life means to possess its narrative. But Eleanor cannot tell the story; nor does she wish to. She has only moments" (81).

11 In addition to the example from *The Waves* I consider below, one can also reference Lily Briscoe's revelation in *To the Lighthouse*: "Could it be, even for elderly people, that this was life? – startling, unexpected, unknown?" (180).

12 Woolf's novel *Between the Acts* addresses geriatric style in a reflexive manner, meeting the absence of a structured plot with an equally incoherent reflection upon its lack: "Did the plot matter? She shifted and looked over her right shoulder. The plot was only there to beget emotion. There were only two emotions: love, and hate. There was no need to puzzle out the plot. Perhaps Miss La Trobe meant that when she cut this knot in the centre? Don't bother about the plot: the plot's nothing" (90–1).

13 Sontag, "The Double Standard of Aging," 31, 33.

14 This contrasts with the state, which has a very difficult time adjudicating Orlando's identity. Her multiple identities confuse the system of classification: "Thus it was in a highly ambiguous condition, uncertain whether she was alive or dead, man or woman, Duke or nonentity, that she posted down

to her country seat, where, pending the legal judgment, she had the Law's permission to reside in a state of incognito or incognita as the case might turn out to be" (*Orlando*, 168).

Afterword

1 According to Jacques Rancière, "cinema has not lived up to the promise of a new anti-representational art." Without referencing Woolf directly, Rancière nonetheless addresses the failure of her ambition for the medium: "Cinema was being asked to fulfil the dream of a century of literature: to replace yesterday's stories and characters with the impersonal deployment of signs written on things, restoring the speeds and intensities of the real world. Literature had been able to carry that dream because its discourse on things and their intensities stayed written in the double game of words, which hide from the eye the palpable richness which shimmers in the mind. Cinema just shows what it shows" (*Intervals of Cinema*, 10).

2 For scholarship on representation of age in cinema see Chivers, *The Silvering Screen* and Gravagne, *The Becoming of Age*.

3 In *Cinema 2*, Deleuze analyzes films from the post-World War II era when the clearly demarcated realms of past, present, and future blur. Instead of merely flashing back to the past or forward to the future, these films – such as those from Italian neo-realism – demonstrate the way the past and future are interpenetrated with the present. For Deleuze, this destabilizes the priority between the actual and the virtual, presenting what he calls a "direct" image of time: "direct time-image, clearly goes beyond the purely empirical succession of time – past–present–future. It is, for example, a coexistence of distinct durations, or of levels of duration; a single event can belong to several levels: the sheets of past coexist in a non-chronological order" (*Cinema 2*, xii). Where the unnervingly still shots of directors like Yasujirō Ozu provide this kind of direct image of time, the representation of movement through montage – on which the examples I discuss below rely – provide an indirect image of time, or the linking of "one movement-image to another" (*Cinema 2*, 34–5).

4 For Doane, the representation of kissing plays a significant cultural and philosophical role in film. She writes that "For Zeno, the kiss never really takes place; its suggestion of union is only illusory, because movement can never be born from a series of immobilities. Infinitely halving the distance between them, the women never reach each other. In the classical cinema, the kiss is consistently returned to as the quite particular disproof of the paradox of Zeno's philosophy, as the guarantee of the cinema's ability to 'bridge the darkness.' The kiss here is the reassertion of the reigning doxa of family, race, nation, buttressed by a formal drive toward continuity" (*Emergence of Cinematic Time*, 204–5).

5 A similar case appears in William Dickson's 1903 *Rip Van Winkle*. Twenty years of Rip's life flash by, displaced by a placard that reads "Rip's Twenty

Year Sleep." When he awakens, the youthful man's clothes have deteriorated and his body has emaciated. His once full head of hair has been replaced by long white locks and he has a hoary beard. Rip has great difficulty picking up his cane, while only moments before in the film he easily hoisted a heavy keg.

6 See, for example, Anthony Cerniello's five-minute film, *Danielle* (2013), which represents the face of a woman growing older without cuts. Set against a clinically white background, the slow transformations allow the viewers to register movement, but they must constantly question the exact nature of the changes taking place. The direct gaze of Danielle displays confidence, yet the image trembles slightly throughout the performance, suffusing the production with an air of unreality. By doing so, the film renders the commonplace experience of aging strange. Instead of fading into the background of perception, growing older becomes an object of contemplation. The unsettling feeling that results – the journalist Ron Dicker referred to the film's "haunting effect" – attests to the unnerving effect of placing aging within the range of perception. Other examples include Noah Kalina's "Everyday" (2006), in which the artist compiles self-portraits taken daily over the course of six years into a five-and-a-half-minute video. Diego Goldberg's "The Arrow of Time," which is still ongoing, creates a genealogy of family photographs from 1976 to the present day, allowing the viewer to examine the individual transformations (and family additions) over the course of over forty years.

Bibliography

Abbott, H. Porter. "Old Virginia and the Night Writer: The Origins of Woolf's Narrative Meander." *Inscribing the Daily: Critical Essays on Women's Diaries*, edited by Suzanne Bunkers and Cynthia Huff. Amherst: University of Massachusetts Press, 1996, pp. 236–51.

Ablow, Rachel. *The Marriage of the Minds: Reading Sympathy in the Victorian Marriage Plot*. Stanford University Press, 2007.

"'One Flesh,' One Person, and the 1870 Married Women's Property Act." *BRANCH: Britain, Representation and Nineteenth-Century History*, edited by Dino Franco Felluga, www.branchcollective.org/?ps_articles=rachel-ablow-one-flesh-one-person-and-the-1870-married-womens-property-act. Accessed 12 April 2018.

Achenbaum, Andrew. *Crossing Frontiers: Gerontology Emerges as a Science*. Cambridge University Press, 1995.

Adam, Barbara. *Timewatch: The Social Analysis of Time*. Cambridge: Polity Press, 1995.

Adorno, Theodor. *Notes to Literature: Volume Two*, edited by Rolf Tiedemann. New York: Columbia University Press, 1992.

Agamben, Giorgio. *Homo Sacer: Sovereign Power and Bare Life*, translated by Daniel Heller-Roazen. Stanford University Press, 1998.

Agathocleous, Tanya. *Urban Realism and the Cosmopolitan Imagination in the Nineteenth Century: Visible City, Invisible World*. Cambridge University Press, 2011.

Altick, Richard D. *The Presence of the Present: Topics of the Day in the Victorian Novel*. Columbus: Ohio State University Press, 1991.

Anderson, Benedict. *Imagined Communities: Reflections on the Origin and Spread of Nationalism*. London: Verso, 2006.

Andrews, Thomas. *A Cyclopedia of Domestic Medicine and Surgery*. Glasgow and London: Blackie and Son, 1842.

Armstrong, Nancy. *Fiction in the Age of Photography: The Legacy of British Realism*. Cambridge, MA: Harvard University Press, 1999.

Auerbach, Erich. *Mimesis: The Representation of Reality in Western Literature*, translated by Willard Trask. Princeton University Press, 2003.

Auerbach, Nina. *Communities of Women: An Idea in Fiction*. Cambridge, MA: Harvard University Press, 1978.

Baars, Jan. "Aging and the Exploration of Lived Ambivalence." *Age, Culture, Humanities*, vol. 1, no. 1, 2014, www.ageculturehumanities.org/WP/aging-and-the-exploration-of-lived-ambivalence. Accessed 4 April 2018.

"Concepts of Time and Narrative Temporality in the Study of Aging." *Journal of Aging Studies*, vol. 11, no. 4, 1997, pp. 283–96.

"A Triple Temporality of Aging: Chronological Measurement, Personal Experience, and Narrative Articulation." *Aging and Time: Multidisciplinary Perspectives*, edited by Jan Baars and Henk Visser. Amityville, NY: Baywood, 2007, pp. 15–42.

Bailey, Thomas. *Records of Longevity*. London: Darton, 1857.

Barthes, Roland. "The Reality Effect." *The Rustle of Language*, translated by Richard Howard. Berkeley, CA: University of California Press, 1989, pp. 141–8.

Bazin, André. "The Ontology of the Photographic Image." *What is Cinema?*, translated by Hugh Gray, vol. 1. Berkeley, CA: University of California Press, 2005, pp. 9–16.

Beaumont, Matthew. "Red Sphinx: Mechanics of the Uncanny in 'The Time Machine.'" *Science Fiction Studies*, vol. 33, no. 2, 2006, pp. 230–50.

Beauvoir, Simone de. *The Coming of Age*, translated by Patrick O'Brian. New York: Putnam's Sons, 1972.

The Second Sex, translated by Constance Borde and Sheila Malovany-Chevallier. New York: Vintage, 2011.

Beer, Gillian. *Darwin's Plots: Evolutionary Narrative in Darwin, George Eliot and Nineteenth-Century Fiction*. Cambridge University Press, 1983.

Benjamin, Walter. "The Storyteller" and "The Work of Art in the Age of Mechanical Reproduction." *Illuminations*, translated by Harry Zohn. New York: Schocken, 1968, pp. 83–109 and 217–52.

Bennett, Brandon. "Hardy's Noble Melancholics." *NOVEL: A Forum on Fiction*, vol. 27, no. 1, 1993, pp. 24–39.

Berg, Geri and Sally Gadow. "Toward More Human Meanings of Aging: Ideals and Images from Philosophy and Art." *Aging and the Elderly: Humanistic Perspectives in Gerontology, Aging and Income*, edited by Stuart F. Spicker, Kathleen M. Woodward and David D. Van Tassel. Atlantic Highland, NJ: Humanities Press, 1978, pp. 83–92.

Bergson, Henri. *Creative Evolution*, translated by Arthur Mitchell. Mineola, NY: Dover, 1998.

The Creative Mind: An Introduction to Metaphysics, translated by Mabelle Andison. Mineola, NY: Dover, 2007.

Time and Free Will: An Essay on the Immediate Data of Consciousness, translated by F. L. Pogson. London and New York: Macmillan, 1913.

Best, Stephen and Sharon Marcus. "Surface Reading: An Introduction." *Representations*, vol. 108, no. 1, 2009, pp. 1–21.

Biggs, Simon. *The Mature Imagination: Dynamics of Identity in Midlife and Beyond*. Philadelphia: Open University Press, 1999.

Biggs, Simon, Carroll L. Estes, and Chris Phillipson. *Social Theory, Social Policy, and Ageing: A Critical Introduction*. Buckingham: Open University Press, 2003.

Blake, Kathleen. "Pure Tess: Hardy on Knowing a Woman." *SEL*, vol. 22, no. 4, 1982, pp. 689–705.

Bloch, Ernst. *The Principle of Hope*, translated by Neville Plaice, Stephen Plaice, and Paul Knight, vol. 1. Cambridge, MA: MIT Press, 1986.

Boone, Joseph Allen. *Tradition Counter Tradition: Love and the Form of Fiction*. University of Chicago Press, 1987.

Booth, Charles. *Life and Labour of the People in London*, vol. 1. London: Macmillan, [1889] 1902.

Pauperism and the Endowment of Old Age. London: Macmillan, 1892.

Bowen, John. *Other Dickens: Pickwick to Chuzzlewit*. Oxford University Press, 2000.

Brantlinger, Patrick and Richard Higgins. "Waste and Value: Thorstein Veblen and H. G. Wells." *Criticism*, vol. 48, no. 4, 2006, pp. 453–75.

Brooks, Peter. *Reading for the Plot: Design and Intention in Narrative*. Cambridge, MA: Harvard University Press, 1984.

Buckland, Adelene. "Thomas Hardy, Provincial Geology and the Material Imagination." *19: Interdisciplinary Studies in the Long Nineteenth Century*, vol. 6, 2008, www.19.bbk.ac.uk/articles/abstract/469. Accessed 7 April 2018.

Novel Science: Fiction and the Invention of Nineteenth-Century Geology. University of Chicago Press, 2013.

Buckley, Jerome. *Season of Youth: The Bildungsroman from Dickens to Golding*. Cambridge, MA: Harvard University Press, 1974.

Butler, Judith. *Gender Trouble: Feminism and the Subversion of Identity*. New York: Routledge, 1990.

Buzard, James. "Enumeration and Exhaustion: Taking Inventory in *The Old Curiosity Shop*." *Contemporary Dickens*, edited by Eileen Gillooly and Deirdre David. Columbus: Ohio State University Press, 2009, pp. 189–208.

Cerniello, Anthony. *Danielle*. anthonycerniello.com, 2013. Accessed 7 April 2018.

Cantor, Paul and Peter Hufnagel. "The Empire of the Future: Imperialism and Modernism in H. G. Wells," *Studies in the Novel*, vol. 38, no. 1, 2006, pp. 36–56.

Corbet, W. J. "What Should England Do to be Saved?" *Westminster Review*, vol. 155, no. 6, 1901, pp. 604–13.

Charise, Andrea. "'Let the Reader Think of the Burden': Old Age and the Crisis of Capacity." *Occasion: Interdisciplinary Studies in the Humanities*, vol. 4, 2012, pp. 1–16. http://occasion.stanford.edu/node/96. Accessed 7 April 2018.

"'The Tyranny of Age': Godwin's *St. Leon* and the Nineteenth-Century Longevity Narrative." *ELH*, vol. 79, no. 4, 2012, pp. 905–33.

Charise, Andrea and Pascale Manning. "'Unexampled eyes': Epochal Old Age and the Geological Imaginary." *Seachange*, vol. 4, 2013, www.seachangejournal.ca/PDF/2013_Age/Charise_Manning_Unexempled%20Eyes.pdf. Accessed 7 April 2018.

Chase, Karen. "'Senile' Sexuality." *Interdisciplinary Perspectives on Aging in Nineteenth-Century Culture*, edited by Katharina Boehm, Anna Farkas and Anne-Julia Zwierlien. New York: Routledge, 2014, pp. 132–46.

The Victorians and Old Age. Oxford University Press, 2009.

Chivers, Sally. *The Silvering Screen: Old Age and Disability in Cinema*. University of Toronto Press, 2011.

Chorley, Henry Fothergill. Review of Cranford. *Athenaeum*, vol. 1339, 1853, p. 765.

Clarfield, Mark. "Dr. Ignatz Nascher and the Birth of Geriatrics." *Canadian Medical Association Journal*, vol. 143, no. 9, 1990, pp. 944–48.

Cohen, William. *Embodied: Victorian Literature and the Senses*. Minneapolis: Minnesota University Press, 2009.

Cole, Thomas and Claudia Edwards. "The 19th Century." *A History of Old Age*, edited by Pat Thane. London: Thames and Hudson, 2005, pp. 211–62.

Conrad, Joseph. *The Selected Letters of Joseph Conrad*, edited by Laurence Davies, Cambridge University Press, 2015.

Csiscery-Ronay, Istvan. *The Seven Beauties of Science Fiction*. Middletown, CT: Wesleyan University Press, 2008.

Daly, Nicholas. *The Demographic Imagination and the Nineteenth-Century City*. Cambridge University Press, 2015.

Dames, Nicholas. *The Physiology of the Novel: Reading, Neural Science, and the Form of Victorian Fiction*. Oxford University Press, 2007.

"Untimely Contextualizations." *Journal of Victorian Culture*, vol. 16, no. 1, 2011, pp. 113–17.

DeAngelis, Ross. "Triangulated Passions: Love, Self-Love, and the Other in Thomas Hardy's *The Well-Beloved*." *Studies in the Novel*, vol. 34, no. 4, 2002, pp. 403–21.

Deleuze, Gilles. *Bergsonism*, translated by Hugh Tomlinson and Barbara Habberjam. New York: Zone, 1991.

Cinema 1: The Movement-Image, translated by Hugh Tomlinson and Barbara Habberjam. London: Athlone, 1986.

Cinema 2: The Time Image, translated by Hugh Tomlinson and Robert Galeta. London: Athlone, 2000.

Difference and Repetition, translated by Paul Patton. New York: Columbia University Press, 1994.

The Logic of Sense, translated by Mark Lester and Charles Stivale. London: Athlone, 1990.

Dickens, Charles. "A Christmas Carol." *A Christmas Carol and Other Stories*. New York: Modern Library, 2001, pp. 1–107.

Dombey and Son. London: Penguin, 2002.

Great Expectations. London: Penguin, 1996.

The Letters of Charles Dickens, edited by Madeline House and Graham Storey, vol. 1. Oxford: Clarendon, 1965.
Little Dorrit. London: Penguin, 2003.
Martin Chuzzlewit. Oxford University Press, 2009.
Master Humphrey's Clock, vol. 1. London and New York: Chapman and Hall, 1840.
The Old Curiosity Shop. London: Penguin, 2000.
Sketches by Boz. London: Penguin, 1995.
Dicker, Ron. "Anthony Cerniello's Aging Simulation Video Will Mesmerize You." *Huffington Post*, 11 September 2013, www.huffingtonpost.com/2013/09/11/anthony-cerniello-aging_n_3906436.html. Accessed 11 April 2018.
Dickson, William. *Rip van Winkle*. American Mutoscope and Biograph, 1903.
Dinshaw, Carolyn. *How Soon is Now? Medieval Texts, Amateur Readers, and the Queerness of Time*. Durham, NC: Duke University Press, 2012.
Doane, Mary Ann. *The Emergence of Cinematic Time: Modernity, Contingency, the Archive*. Cambridge, MA: Harvard University Press, 2002.
Dodsworth, Martin. "Women Without Men at Cranford." *Essays in Criticism*, vol. 13, no. 2, 1963, pp. 132–45.
Dolin, Tim. "Cranford and the Victorian Collection." *Victorian Studies*, vol. 36, no. 2, 1993, pp. 179–206.
Dreher, Nan H. "Redundancy and Emigration: The 'Woman Question' in Mid-Victorian Britain." *Victorian Periodicals Review*, vol. 26, no. 1, 1993, pp. 3–7.
Easton, James. *Human Longevity*. Easton, 1799.
Eliot, George. *Adam Bede*. London: Penguin, 2008.
The Lifted Veil and Brother Jacob. Oxford University Press, 2009.
Middlemarch. London: Penguin, 2003.
Romola. Oxford University Press, 1994.
Scenes of Clerical Life. Oxford University Press, 2009.
Erikson, Eric. *Identity and the Life Cycle*. New York: Norton, 1994.
Erikson, Eric and Joan Erikson. *The Life Cycle Completed*. New York: Norton, 1997.
Ermarth, Elizabeth Deeds. *Realism and Consensus in the English Novel*. Princeton University Press, 1983.
Esty, Jed. *Unseasonable Youth: Modernism, Colonialism, and the Fiction of Development*. Oxford University Press, 2011.
Felski, Rita. *Doing Time: Feminist Theory and Postmodern Culture*. New York University Press, 2000.
The Gender of Modernity. Cambridge, MA: Harvard University Press, 1995.
The Limits of Critique. University of Chicago Press, 2015.
Fenton-Hathaway, Anna. "Gaskell's Detours: How *Mary Barton*, *Ruth*, and *Cranford* Redefined 'Redundancy.'" *Victorian Literature and Culture*, vol. 42, no. 2, 2014, pp. 235–50.

Fisher, Philip. *Hard Facts: Setting and Form in the American Novel.* Oxford University Press, 1985.

Fleissner, Jennifer. *Women, Compulsion, Modernity: The Moment of American Naturalism.* University of Chicago Press, 2004.

Franklin, J. *Jeffrey. Serious Play: The Cultural Form of the Nineteenth-Century Realist Novel.* Philadelphia: University of Pennsylvania Press, 1999.

Gallagher, Catherine. "Formalism and Time." *Modern Language Quarterly*, vol. 61, no. 1, 2000, pp. 229–51.

"George Eliot: Immanent Victorian." *Representations*, vol. 90, 2005, pp. 61–74.

Garcha, Amanpal. *From Sketch to Novel: The Development of Victorian Fiction.* Cambridge University Press, 2009.

Gaskell, Elizabeth. *Cousin Phillis.* Chicago: A. C. McClurg, 1895.

Cranford. Oxford University Press, 2011.

"The Crooked Branch." *Gothic Tales*, edited by Laura Kranzler. London: Penguin, 2004, pp. 227–70.

The Letters of Mrs. Gaskell, edited by J. A. V. Chapple and Arthur Pollard. Cambridge, MA: Harvard University Press, 1967.

Ruth. London: Penguin, 1997.

Genette, Gérard. *Narrative Discourse: An Essay in Method*, translated by Jane Lewin. Ithaca: Cornell University Press, 1983.

George, Henry. *Progress and Poverty: An Inquiry Into the Cause of Industrial Depressions, and of Increase of Want with Increase of Wealth.* New York: Appleton, 1886.

Gilleard, Chris. "Age and Aging Studies: Celebrating the Cultural Turn." *Age, Culture, Humanities*, vol. 1, no. 1, 2014, http://ageculturehumanities.org/WP/aging-and-aging-studies-celebrating-the-cultural-turn. Accessed 11 April 2018.

Gillen, Laura and Diane Martin. "Revisiting Gerontology's Scrapbook: From Metchnikoff to the Spectrum Model of Aging." *The Gerontologist*, vol. 54, no. 1, 2014, pp. 51–8.

Gilmartin, Sophie. *Ancestry and Narrative in Nineteenth-Century British Literature: Blood Relations from Edgeworth to Hardy.* Cambridge University Press, 1998.

Ginsburg, Michal Peled. "Narratives of Survival." *NOVEL: A Forum on Fiction*, vol. 42, no. 3, 2009, pp. 410–16.

Gissing, George. *The Odd Women.* Oxford University Press, 2008.

Godfrey, Esther. *The January–May Marriage in Nineteenth-Century British Literature.* Basingstoke: Palgrave, 2009.

Goldberg, Diego. "The Arrow of Time." Zonezero.com. Accessed 17 June 2018.

Gomel, Elana. "Shapes of the Past and the Future: Darwin and the Narratology of Time Travel." *Narrative*, vol. 17, no. 3, 2009, pp. 334–52.

Graham's Magazine, vol. 43, no. 4, 1853, pp. 447–48.

Gravagne, Pamela. *The Becoming of Age: Cinematic Vision of Mind, Body, and Identity in Later Life.* Jefferson: McFarland, 2013.

Greenslade, William. *Degeneration, Culture and the Novel 1880–1940*. Cambridge University Press, 1994.

Greg, W. R. *Why are Women Redundant?* London: John Childs and Son, 1869.

Greiner, Rae. *Sympathetic Realism in Nineteenth-Century British Fiction*. Baltimore: Johns Hopkins University Press, 2012.

Grosz, Elizabeth. "Bergson, Deleuze and the Becoming of Unbecoming." *parallax*, vol. 11, no. 2, 2005, pp. 4–13.

The Nick of Time: Politics, Evolution, and the Untimely. Durham, NC: Duke University Press, 2004.

Gullette, Margaret Morganroth. *Aged by Culture*. University of Chicago Press, 2004.

Ending Ageism, Or How Not to Shoot Old People. New Brunswick: Rutgers University Press, 2017.

Haggard, H. Rider. *She*. Oxford University Press, 2008.

Halford, Sir Henry. "On the Climacteric Disease." *Essays and Orations, Read and Delivered at the Royal College of Physicians*. London: John Murray, 1831.

Hamilton, Lisa. "New Women and 'Old' Men: Gendering Degeneration." *Women and British Aestheticism*, edited by Talia Schaffer and Kathy Alexis Psomiades. Charlottesville: University of Virginia Press, 1999, pp. 62–80.

Hardy, Barbara. "Martin Chuzzlewit." *Dickens and the Twentieth Century*, edited by John Gross and Gabriel Pearson. Toronto University Press, 1962, pp. 107–20.

Hardy, Thomas. *Collected Letters of Thomas Hardy*, edited by R. L. Purdy and M. Millgate, vol. II. Oxford University Press, 1980.

Far From the Madding Crowd. Oxford University Press, 2002.

"Fellow-Townsmen." *Wessex Tales*, Oxford University Press, 2009, pp. 86–135.

The Mayor of Casterbridge. Oxford University Press, 2008.

The Pursuit of the Well-Beloved and The Well-Beloved. London: Penguin, 1997.

Thomas Hardy: The Complete Poems, edited by James Gibson. Basingstoke: Palgrave, 2001.

Heath, Kay. *Aging by the Book: The Emergence of Midlife in Victorian Britain*. Albany: SUNY, 2009.

Hertz, Neil. *George Eliot's Pulse*. Stanford University Press, 2003.

Hollinger, Veronica. "Deconstructing the Time Machine." *Science-Fiction Studies*, vol. 14, no. 2, 1987, pp. 201–21.

Howard, June. *Form and History in American Literary Naturalism*. Chapel Hill: University of North Carolina Press, 1985.

Hoy, David Couzens. *The Time of Our Lives: A Critical History of Temporality*. Cambridge, MA: MIT Press, 2012.

Hughes, Linda K. and Michael Lund. *Victorian Publishing and Mrs. Gaskell's Work*. Charlottesville: University of Virginia Press, 1999.

Huntington, John. *The Logic of Fantasy: H. G. Wells and Science Fiction*. New York: Columbia University Press, 1982.

Ingham, Patricia. "Notes." *Cranford*. London: Penguin, 2005, pp. 233–57.

Jaffe, Audrey. "Cranford and Ruth." *The Cambridge Companion to Elizabeth Gaskell*, edited by Jill L. Matus. Cambridge University Press, 2007, pp. 46–58.

James, Simon. *Maps of Utopia: H. G. Wells, Modernity, and the End of Culture*. Oxford University Press, 2012.

Jameson, Fredric. *The Antinomies of Realism*. London: Verso, 2013.

Archaeologies of the Future: The Desire Called Utopia and Other Science Fictions. London: Verso, 2007.

Jewusiak, Jacob. "Suspenseful Speculation and the Pleasure of Waiting in *Little Dorrit*." *Victorian Literature and Culture*, vol. 44, no. 2, 2016, pp. 279–96.

Kalina, Noah. "Everyday." *Youtube*, uploaded by Noah Kalina, 27 August 2006, www.youtube.com/watch?v=6B26asyGKDo.

Katz, Stephen. *Disciplining Old Age: The Formation of Gerontological Knowledge*. Charlottesville: University of Virginia Press, 1996.

Kermode, Frank. *The Sense of an Ending: Studies in the Theory of Fiction*. Oxford University Press, 2000.

Kiesel, Alyson. "Meaning and Misinterpretation in Cranford." *ELH*, vol. 71, no. 4, 2004, pp. 1001–17.

Kittler, Friedrich. *Gramophone, Film, Typewriter*, translated by Geoffrey Winthrop-Young and Michael Wutz. Stanford University Press, 1999.

Knezevic, Borislav. "An Ethnography of the Provincial: The Social Geography of Gentility in Elizabeth Gaskell's Cranford." *Victorian Studies*, vol. 41, no. 3, 1998, pp. 405–26.

Krielkamp, Ivan. *Voice and the Victorian Storyteller*. Cambridge University Press, 2005.

Lepine, Anna. "'Strange and Rare Visitants': Spinsters and Domestic Space in Elizabeth Gaskell's *Cranford*." *Nineteenth-Century Contexts*, vol. 32, no. 2, 2010, pp. 121–37.

Levine, Caroline. *Forms: Whole, Rhythm, Hierarchy, Network*. Princeton University Press, 2015.

The Serious Pleasures of Suspense: Victorian Realism and Narrative Doubt. Charlottesville: University of Virginia Press, 2003.

Levine, George. *The Realistic Imagination: English Fiction from Frankenstein to Lady Chatterley*. University of Chicago Press, 1981.

Lewes, George Henry. *The Physiology of Common Life*, vol. II. New York: Appleton, 1875.

Leys, Ruth. "The Turn to Affect: A Critique." *Critical Inquiry*, vol. 37, no. 3, 2011, pp. 434–72.

Lodge, David. *After Bakhtin: Essays on Fiction and Criticism*. London: Routledge, 1990.

"*Jude the Obscure:* Pessimism and Fictional Form." *Critical Approaches to the Fiction of Thomas Hardy*, edited by Dale Kramer. Totowa, NJ: Barnes and Noble, 1979, pp. 193–201.

Looser, Devoney. "Age and Aging Studies, From Cradle to Grave." *Age, Culture, Humanities*, vol. 1, no. 1, 2014, ageculturehumanities.org/WP/age-and-aging-studies-from-cradle-to-grave. Accessed 11 April 2018.

Women Writers and Old Age in Great Britain, 1750–1850. Baltimore: Johns Hopkins University Press, 2008.

Love, Heather. "Close but not Deep: Literary Ethics and the Descriptive Turn." *New Literary History*, vol. 41, no. 2, 2010, pp. 371–91.

Lukács, Georg. *The Theory of the Novel*, translated by Anna Bostock. Cambridge, MA: MIT Press, 1971.

Lupton, Christina. "Theorizing Surfaces and Depths: Gaskell's Cranford." *Criticism*, vol. 50, no. 2, 2008, pp. 235–54.

Macnicol, John. *Neoliberalising Old Age*. Cambridge University Press, 2015.

The Politics of Retirement in Britain, 1878–1948. Cambridge University Press, 1998.

Mangum, Teresa. "Little Women: The Aging Female Character in Nineteenth-Century British Children's Literature." *Figuring Age: Women, Bodies, Generations*, edited by Kathleen Woodward. Bloomington: Indiana University Press, 1998, pp. 59–87.

"The Unnatural Youth of the Old 'New Woman.'" *Interdisciplinary Perspectives on Aging in Nineteenth-Century Culture*, edited by Katharina Boehm, Anna Farkas, and Anne-Julia Zwierlein. London and New York: Routledge, 2014, pp. 75–91.

Marcus, Sharon. *Between Women: Friendship, Desire, and Marriage in Victorian England.* Princeton University Press, 2007.

Massumi, Brian. *Parables for the Virtual: Movement, Affect, Sensation*. Durham, NC: Duke University Press, 2002.

Matthews, Dale. "Dr. Marjory Warren and the Origin of British Geriatrics." *Journal of the American Geriatrics Society*, vol. 32, no. 4, 1984, pp. 253–8.

Matz, Jesse. "The Art of Time, Theory to Practice." *Narrative*, vol. 19, no. 3, 2011, pp. 273–94.

Menke, Richard. *Telegraphic Realism: Victorian Fiction and Other Information Systems.* Stanford University Press, 2008.

Metchnikoff, Élie. *The Nature of Man: Studies in Optimistic Philosophy* [1903]. New York: G. P. Putnam's Sons, 1905.

The Prolongation of Life: Optimistic Studies [1907]. New York: G. P. Putnam's Sons, 1908.

Middeke, Martin. "On Circles and Spirals: Time, Repetition, and Meta-Hermeneutics in Literature." *Symbolism: An International Journal of Critical Aesthetics*, vol. 9, 2009, pp. 103–28.

Miller, Andrew H. *The Burdens of Perfection: On Ethics and Reading in Nineteenth-Century British Literature*. Ithaca: Cornell University Press, 2008.

Novels Behind Plate Glass. Cambridge University Press, 1995.

Miller, D. A. *The Novel and the Police*. Berkeley, CA: University of California Press, 1988.

Miller, J. Hillis. *Fiction and Repetition: Seven English Novels*. Cambridge, MA: Harvard University Press, 1982.

Thomas Hardy: Distance and Desire. Cambridge, MA: Harvard University Press, 1970.

Monod, Sylvère. *Martin Chuzzlewit*. London: Allen and Unwin, 1985.

Moretti, Franco. *The Way of the World: The Bildungsroman in European Culture*, translated by Albert Sbragia. London and New York: Verso, 2000.

Mullen, Mary. "Anachronistic Aesthetics: Maria Edgeworth and the 'Uses' of History." *Eighteenth-Century Fiction*, vol. 26, no. 2, 2013–14, pp. 233–59.

Müller, Johannes. *Elements of Physiology*, translated by W. M. Baly. Philadelphia: Lea and Blanchard, 1843.

Mulroy, David. "Appendix 1: The Riddle of the Sphinx." *Oedipus Rex*. Madison: University of Wisconsin Press, 2011, pp. 91–2.

Mulvihill, James. "Economies of Living in Mrs. Gaskell's Cranford." *Nineteenth-Century Literature*, vol. 50, no. 3, 1995, pp. 337–56.

Nascher, Ignatz. "Geriatrics." *New York Medical Journal*, vol. 90, no. 8, 1909, pp. 358–9.

Geriatrics: The Diseases of Old Age and their Treatment, Including Physiological Old Age, Home and Institutional Care, and Medio-Legal Relations. York, PA: Maple Press, 1914.

Nelson, Claudia. *Precocious Children and Childish Adults: Age Inversion in Victorian Literature*. Baltimore: Johns Hopkins University Press, 2012.

Nieuwenhuis-Mark, Ruth Elaine. "Healthy Aging as Disease?" *Frontiers in Aging Neuroscience*, vol. 3, no. 3, 2011, www.frontiersin.org/articles/10.3389/fnagi.2011.00003/full. Accessed 31 July 2018.

Nightingale, Florence. *Cassandra and Other Selections from Suggestions for Thought*, edited by Mary Poovey. New York University Press, 1993.

Nordau, Max. *Degeneration*. New York: Appleton, 1895.

Oliphant, Margaret. *Hester*. Oxford University Press, 2009.

O'Toole, Tess. "Genealogy and Narrative Jamming in Hardy's *The Well-Beloved*." *Narrative*, vol. 3, no. 1, 1993, pp. 207–22.

Ottaway, Susannah. *The Decline of Life: Old Age in Eighteenth-Century England*. Cambridge University Press, 2004.

Padian, Kevin. "Evolution and Deep Time in Selected Works of Hardy." *Ashgate Research Companion to Thomas Hardy*, edited by Rosemarie Morgan. Farnham: Ashgate, 2010, pp. 217–33.

Parrinder, Patrick. "*News from Nowhere*, *The Time Machine*, and the Break-Up of Classical Realism." *Science Fiction Studies*, vol. 3, no. 3, 1976, pp. 265–74.

Partington, John S. "H. G. Wells: A Political Life." *Utopia Studies*, vol. 19, no. 3, 2008, pp. 517–76.

"The Time Machine: A Polemic on the Inevitability of Working Class Liberation and a Plea for a Socialist Solution to Late-Victorian Capitalist Exploitation." *The Wellsian*, vol. 19, 1996, pp. 12–21.

Pater, Walter. *Studies in the History of the Renaissance*. Oxford University Press, 2010.

Patten, Robert L. "'The Story-Weaver at His Loom': Dickens and the Beginning of the *Old Curiosity Shop*." *Dickens the Craftsman: Strategies of Presentation*, edited by Robert B. Partlow. Carbondale: Southern Illinois University Press, 1970, pp. 44–64.

Philp, Ian. "The Contribution of Geriatric Medicine to Integrated Care for Older People." *Age and Ageing*, vol. 44, no. 1, 2014, pp. 11–15.

Poovey, Mary. *Making a Social Body: British Cultural Formation, 1830–1864*. University of Chicago Press, 1995.

Uneven Developments: The Ideological Work of Gender in Mid-Victorian England. University of Chicago Press, 1988.

Porter, Edwin, director. *The Seven Ages*. Edison Manufacturing Co., 1905.

Quadagno, Jill. *Aging in Early Industrial Society: Work, Family, and Social Policy in Nineteenth-Century England*. New York and London: Academic Press, 1982.

Quetelet, Adolphe. *A Treatise on Man and the Development of his Faculties*. Edinburgh: William and Robert Chambers, 1842.

Radford, Andrew. *Thomas Hardy and the Survivals of Time*. Farnham: Ashgate, 2003.

Rancière, Jacques. *The Intervals of Cinema*. London and New York: Verso, 2014.

Rappoport, Jill. "Conservation of Sympathy in Cranford." *Victorian Literature and Culture*, vol. 36, no. 1, 2008, pp. 95–110.

"Wives and Sons: Coverture, Primogeniture, and Married Women's Property." *BRANCH: Britain, Representation and Nineteenth-Century History*, edited by Dino Franco Felluga, www.branchcollective.org/?ps_articles=jill-rappoport-wives-and-sons-coverture-primogeniture-and-married-womens-property. Accessed 11 April 2018.

Ricoeur, Paul. *Time and Narrative*, translated by Kathleen McLaughlin and David Pellauer, vol. 1. University of Chicago Press, 1984.

Rieder, John. *Colonialism and the Emergence of Science Fiction*. Middletown, CT: Wesleyan University Press, 2008.

Roget, P. M. "Age." *The Cyclopedia of Practical Medicine*, edited by John Forbes, Alexander Tweedie, and John Conolly, vol. 1. London: Sherwood, Gilbert, and Piper Press, 1832, pp. 34–46.

Rose, Michael. *Evolutionary Biology of Aging*. Oxford University Press, 1991.

Rubery, Matthew. *The Novelty of Newspapers: Victorian Fiction After the Invention of the News*. Oxford University Press, 2009.

Sayeau, Michael. *Against the Event: The Everyday and the Evolution of Modernist Narrative*. Oxford University Press, 2013.

Scafella, Frank. "The White Sphinx and *The Time Machine*." *Science-Fiction Studies*, vol. 8, no. 3, 1981, pp. 255–65.

Scarry, Elaine. *Dreaming by the Book*. Princeton University Press, 1999.

Schaffer, Talia. *Romance's Rival: Familiar Marriage in Victorian Fiction*. Oxford University Press, 2016.

Schivelbusch, Wolfgang. *The Railway Journey: The Industrialization of Time and Space in the 19th Century*. Berkeley, CA: California University Press, 1977.

Schor, Hilary. *Scheherezade in the Marketplace*. Oxford University Press, 1992.

Sedgwick, Eve. *Epistemology of the Closet*. Berkeley, CA: University of California Press, 2008.

Touching Feeling: Affect, Pedagogy, Performativity. Durham, NC: Duke University Press, 2003.

Seed, David. "Framing the Reader in Early Science Fiction." *Style*, vol. 47, no. 2, 2013, pp. 137–67.
Segal, Lynne. "The Coming of Age Studies." *Age, Culture, Humanities*, vol. 1, no. 1, 2014, ageculturehumanities.org/WP/the-coming-of-age-studies. Accessed 11 April 2018.
Out of Time: The Pleasures and Perils of Ageing. London and New York: Verso, 2014.
Shakespeare, William. *As You Like It*. Oxford University Press, 2008.
Shaw, Harry. *Narrating Reality: Austen, Scott, Eliot*. Ithaca: Cornell University Press, 1999.
Shouse, Eric. "Feeling, Emotion, Affect." *M/C Journal*, vol. 8, no. 6, 2005, journal.media-culture.org.au/0512/03-shouse.php. Accessed 11 April 2018.
Small, Helen. *The Long Life*. Oxford University Press, 2010.
"The Unquiet Limit: Old Age and Memory in Victorian Narrative." *Memory and Memorials, 1789–1914: Literary and Cultural Perspectives*, edited by Matthew Campbell, Jacqueline M. Labbe, and Sally Shuttleworth. London and New York: Routledge, 2000, pp. 60–79.
Soloway, Richard. *Demography and Degeneration: Eugenics and the Declining Birthrate in Twentieth-Century Britain*. Chapel Hill: University of North Carolina Press, 1995.
Sontag, Susan. "The Double Standard of Aging." *The Saturday Review*, 23 September 1972, pp. 29–38.
Spacks, Patricia Meyer. *The Adolescent Idea: Myths of Youth and Adult Imagination*. New York: Basic Books, 1981.
Gossip. New York: Knopf, 1985.
Stearns, Peter. *Be a Man! Males in Modern Society*. New York: Holmes and Meier, 1990.
Steinlight, Emily. "Dickens's 'Supernumeraries' and the Biopolitical Imagination of Victorian Fiction." *NOVEL: A Forum on Fiction*, vol. 43, no. 2, 2010, pp. 227–50.
Stevenson, Robert Louis. *The Strange Case of Dr. Jekyll and Mr. Hyde*. Mineola, NY: Dover, 1991.
Stewart, Garrett. *Dickens and the Trials of Imagination*. Cambridge, MA: Harvard University Press, 1974.
Stoker, Bram. *Dracula*, edited by Nina Auerbach and David Skal. New York: Norton, 1997.
Stoneman, Patsy. *Elizabeth Gaskell*. Manchester University Press, 2006.
Stover, Leon. "Introduction." *The Time Machine: An Invention: A Critical Text of the 1895 London First Edition, with an Introduction and Appendices*, edited by Leon Stover. Jefferson: McFarland, 1996, pp. 1–17.
Suvin, Darko. *Metamorphoses of Science Fiction: On the Poetics and History of a Literary Genre*. New Haven: Yale University Press, 1979.
Swann, Charles. "Déjà Vu: Déjà Lu: 'The Lifted Veil' as an Experiment in Art." *Literature and History*, vol. 5, 1959, pp. 40–57.

Tennyson, Alfred Lord. "Ulysses." *Selected Poems*, edited by Christopher Ricks. London: Penguin, 2007, pp. 49–50.

Thane, Pat. *Old Age in English History: Past Experiences, Present Issues*. Oxford University Press, 2000.

Thompson, E. P. "Time, Work-Discipline, and Industrial Capitalism." *Past and Present*, vol. 38, 1967, pp. 56–97.

Thomson, David. "The Welfare of the Elderly in the Past: A Family of Community Responsibility?" *Life, Death, and the Elderly*, edited by Margaret Pelling and Richard M. Smith. London and New York: Routledge, 1991, pp. 194–221.

Tornstam, Lars. "Gero-Transcendence: A Theoretical and Empirical Exploration." *Aging and the Religious Dimension*, edited by L. Eugene Thomas and Susan Eisenhandler. Westport, CT: Greenwood, 1994, pp. 203–26.

Trollope, Anthony. *The Fixed Period*. Edinburgh: Blackwood, 1882.

Turner, George. "Case for State Pensions in Old Age." *Fabian Tract*, vol. 73, Fabian Society, 1897.

Turner, Mark. "'Telling of my weekly doings': The Material Culture of the Victorian Novel." *A Concise Companion to the Victorian Novel*, edited by Francis O'Gorman. Malden, MA: Blackwell, 2005, pp. 113–33.

Uglow, Jenny. *Elizabeth Gaskell: A Habit of Stories*. London: Faber and Faber, 1993.

Warren, Marjory. "Care of the Chronic Aged Sick." *Lancet*, vol. 247, 1946, pp. 841–3.

"Care of the Chronic Sick: A Case for Treating the Chronic Sick in Blocks in a General Hospital." *British Medical Journal*, vol. 2, no. 2, 1943, pp. 822–3.

Weismann, August. *Essays Upon Heredity and Kindred Biological Problems* [1889]. Oxford: Clarendon, 1891.

Wells, H. G. "Death." *H. G. Wells: Early Writings in Science and Science Fiction*, edited by Robert Philmus and David Hughes, Berkeley, CA: University of California Press, 1975, pp. 136–9.

Experiment in Autobiography. London: Macmillan, 1934.

The Food of the Gods: And How It Came to Earth. New York: Charles Scribner's Sons, 1904.

In the Days of the Comet. New York: Century Co., 1906.

"The New Accelerator." *The Country of the Blind and Other Selected Stories*, edited by Patrick Parrinder. London: Penguin, 2007, pp. 296–310.

New Worlds for Old: A Plain Account of Modern Socialism. London: Archibald Constable, 1908.

The Sleeper Awakes. London: Penguin, 2005.

"The Story of the Late Mr Elvesham." *The Country of the Blind and Other Selected Stories*, edited by Patrick Parrinder. London: Penguin, 2007, pp. 120–36.

The Time Machine: An Invention: A Critical Text of the 1895 London First Edition, with an Introduction and Appendices, edited by Leon Stover. Jefferson: McFarland, 1996.

The War in the Air: And Particularly How Mr. Bert Smallways Fared While It Lasted. London: MacMillan, 1908.
The War of the Worlds. London: Penguin, 2005.
"Zoological Retrogression." *H. G. Wells: Early Writings in Science and Science Fiction*, edited by Robert Philmus and David Hughes. Berkeley, CA: University of California Press, 1975, pp. 158–68.
Wells, H. G., Julian Huxley, and G. P. Wells. *The Science of Life*, vol. 1. New York: Doubleday, 1931.
Wicke, Jennifer. "The Same and the Different: Standards and Standardization in Thomas Hardy's *Tess of the d'Urbervilles*." *Tess of the d'Urbervilles*, edited by John Paul Riquelme. Boston: Bedford, 1998, pp. 571–89.
Wilde, Oscar. *The Picture of Dorian Gray.* Ware: Wordsworth, 2001.
Wittenberg, David. *Time Travel: The Popular Philosophy of Narrative.* New York: Fordham, 2013.
Woloch, Alex. *The One vs. the Many: Minor Characters and the Space of the Protagonist in the Novel.* Princeton University Press, 2003.
Woodward, Kathleen. *Aging and its Discontents: Freud and Other Fictions.* Bloomington: Indiana University Press, 1991.
"The Look and the Gaze: Narcissism, Aggression, and Aging." *SubStance*, vol. 18, no. 1, 1989, pp. 74–88.
Statistical Panic: Cultural Politics and the Poetics of the Emotions. Durham, NC: Duke University Press, 2009.
Woolf, Virginia. *Between the Acts.* New York: Harcourt Brace Jovanovich, 1970.
"The Cinema." *Selected Essays*, edited by David Bradshaw. Oxford University Press, 2008, pp. 172–6.
The Diary of Virginia Woolf, edited by Anne Olivier Bell. 5 vols. San Diego: Harcourt Brace, 1977–84.
Jacob's Room. London: Penguin, 1992.
Orlando. New York: Harcourt Brace Jovanovich, 1956.
A Room of One's Own. New York: Harcourt Brace Jovanovich, 1989.
Selected Diaries. London: Vintage, 2008.
Three Guineas. New York: Harcourt Brace Jovanovich, 1966.
To the Lighthouse. New York: Harcourt Brace Jovanovich, 1981.
The Waves. New York: Harcourt Brace Jovanovich, 1959.
The Years. New York: Harcourt Brace Jovanovich, 1965.
Woolfe, Patricia A. "Structure and Movement in Cranford." *Nineteenth-Century Fiction*, vol. 23, no. 2, 1968, pp. 161–76.
Yahav, Amit. "Sonorous Duration: *Tristram Shandy* and the Duration of Novels." *PMLA*, vol. 128, no. 4, 2013, pp. 872–87.
Zemka, Sue. *Time and the Moment in Victorian Literature and Culture.* Cambridge University Press, 2012.
Zimmerman, Virginia. *Excavating Victorians.* Albany: SUNY Press, 2008.

Index

CAMBRIDGE STUDIES IN NINETEENTH-CENTURY LITERATURE AND CULTURE

General editor
GILLIAN BEER, *University of Cambridge*

Titles published

1. *The Sickroom in Victorian Fiction: The Art of Being Ill*
MIRIAM BAILIN, *Washington University*

2. *Muscular Christianity: Embodying the Victorian Age* edited by
DONALD E. HALL, *California State University, Northridge*

3. *Victorian Masculinities: Manhood and Masculine Poetics in Early Victorian Literature and Art*
HERBERT SUSSMAN, *Northeastern University, Boston*

4. *Byron and the Victorians*
ANDREW ELFENBEIN, *University of Minnesota*

5. *Literature in the Marketplace: Nineteenth-Century British Publishing and the Circulation of Books* edited by
JOHN O. JORDAN, *University of California, Santa Cruz* and Robert L. Patten, *Rice University, Houston*

6. *Victorian Photography, Painting and Poetry*
LINDSAY SMITH, *University of Sussex*

7. *Charlotte Brontë and Victorian Psychology*
SALLY SHUTTLEWORTH, *University of Sheffield*

8. The Gothic Body: Sexuality, Materialism and Degeneration at the *Fin de Siècle*
KELLY HURLEY, *University of Colorado at Boulder*

9. *Rereading Walter Pater*
WILLIAM F. SHUTER, *Eastern Michigan University*

10. *Remaking Queen Victoria* edited by
MARGARET HOMANS, *Yale University* and Adrienne Munich, *State University of New York, Stony Brook*

11. *Disease, Desire, and the Body in Victorian Women's Popular Novels*
PAMELA K. GILBERT, *University of Florida*

12. *Realism, Representation, and the Arts in Nineteenth-Century Literature*
ALISON BYERLY, *Middlebury College, Vermont*

13. *Literary Culture and the Pacific*
VANESSA SMITH, *University of Sydney*

14. *Professional Domesticity in the Victorian Novel: Women, Work and Home*
MONICA F. COHEN

15. *Victorian Renovations of the Novel: Narrative Annexes and the Boundaries of Representation*
SUZANNE KEEN, *Washington and Lee University, Virginia*

16. *Actresses on the Victorian Stage: Feminine Performance and the Galatea Myth*
GAIL MARSHALL, *University of Leeds*

17. *Death and the Mother from Dickens to Freud: Victorian Fiction and the Anxiety of Origin*
CAROLYN DEVER, *Vanderbilt University, Tennessee*

18. *Ancestry and Narrative in Nineteenth-Century British Literature: Blood Relations from Edgeworth to Hardy*
SOPHIE GILMARTIN, *Royal Holloway, University of London*

19. *Dickens, Novel Reading, and the Victorian Popular Theatre*
DEBORAH VLOCK

20. *After Dickens: Reading, Adaptation and Performance*
JOHN GLAVIN, *Georgetown University, Washington D C*

21. *Victorian Women Writers and the Woman Question*
edited by
NICOLA DIANE THOMPSON, *Kingston University, London*

22. *Rhythm and Will in Victorian Poetry*
MATTHEW CAMPBELL, *University of Sheffield*

23. *Gender, Race, and the Writing of Empire: Public Discourse and the Boer War*
PAULA M. KREBS, *Wheaton College, Massachusetts*

24. *Ruskin's God*
MICHAEL WHEELER, *University of Southampton*

25. *Dickens and the Daughter of the House*
HILARY M. SCHOR, *University of Southern California*

26. *Detective Fiction and the Rise of Forensic Science*
RONALD R. THOMAS, *Trinity College, Hartford, Connecticut*

27. *Testimony and Advocacy in Victorian Law, Literature, and Theology*
JAN-MELISSA SCHRAMM, *Trinity Hall, Cambridge*

28. *Victorian Writing about Risk: Imagining a Safe England in a Dangerous World*
ELAINE FREEDGOOD, *University of Pennsylvania*

29. *Physiognomy and the Meaning of Expression in Nineteenth-Century Culture*
LUCY HARTLEY, *University of Southampton*

30. *The Victorian Parlour: A Cultural Study*
THAD LOGAN, *Rice University, Houston*

31. *Aestheticism and Sexual Parody 1840–1940*
DENNIS DENISOFF, *Ryerson University, Toronto*

32. *Literature, Technology and Magical Thinking, 1880–1920*
PAMELA THURSCHWELL, *University College London*

33. *Fairies in Nineteenth-Century Art and Literature*
NICOLA BOWN, *Birkbeck, University of London*

34. *George Eliot and the British Empire*
NANCY HENRY *The State University of New York, Binghamton*

35. *Women's Poetry and Religion in Victorian England: Jewish Identity and Christian Culture*
CYNTHIA SCHEINBERG, *Mills College, California*

36. *Victorian Literature and the Anorexic Body*
ANNA KRUGOVOY SILVER, *Mercer University, Georgia*

37. *Eavesdropping in the Novel from Austen to Proust*
ANN GAYLIN, *Yale University*

38. *Missionary Writing and Empire, 1800–1860*
ANNA JOHNSTON, *University of Tasmania*

39. *London and the Culture of Homosexuality, 1885–1914*
MATT COOK, *Keele University*

40. *Fiction, Famine, and the Rise of Economics in Victorian Britain and Ireland*
GORDON BIGELOW, *Rhodes College, Tennessee*

41. *Gender and the Victorian Periodical*
HILARY FRASER, *Birkbeck, University of London*
JUDITH JOHNSTON and STEPHANIE GREEN, *University of Western Australia*

42. *The Victorian Supernatural*
edited by
NICOLA BOWN, *Birkbeck College, London*
CAROLYN BURDETT, *London Metropolitan University* and
PAMELA THURSCHWELL, *University College London*

43. *The Indian Mutiny and the British Imagination*
GAUTAM CHAKRAVARTY, *University of Delhi*

44. *The Revolution in Popular Literature: Print, Politics and the People*
IAN HAYWOOD, *Roehampton University of Surrey*

45. *Science in the Nineteenth-Century Periodical: Reading the Magazine of Nature*
GEOFFREY CANTOR, *University of Leeds*
GOWAN DAWSON, *University of Leicester*
GRAEME GOODAY, *University of Leeds*
RICHARD NOAKES, *University of Cambridge*
SALLY SHUTTLEWORTH, *University of Sheffield* and
JONATHAN R. TOPHAM, *University of Leeds*

46. *Literature and Medicine in Nineteenth-Century Britain from Mary Shelley to George Eliot*
JANIS MCLARREN CALDWELL, *Wake Forest University*

47. *The Child Writer from Austen to Woolf*
edited by
CHRISTINE ALEXANDER, *University of New South Wales* and
JULIET MCMASTER, *University of Alberta*

48. *From Dickens to Dracula: Gothic, Economics, and Victorian Fiction*
GAIL TURLEY HOUSTON, University of New Mexico

49. *Voice and the Victorian Storyteller*
IVAN KREILKAMP, *University of Indiana*

50. *Charles Darwin and Victorian Visual Culture*
JONATHAN SMITH, *University of Michigan-Dearborn*

51. *Catholicism, Sexual Deviance, and Victorian Gothic Culture*
PATRICK R. O'MALLEY, *Georgetown University*

52. *Epic and Empire in Nineteenth-Century Britain*
SIMON DENTITH, *University of Gloucestershire*

53. *Victorian Honeymoons: Journeys to the Conjugal*
HELENA MICHIE, *Rice University*

54. *The Jewess in Nineteenth-Century British Literary Culture*
NADIA VALMAN, *University of Southampton*

55. *Ireland, India and Nationalism in Nineteenth-Century Literature*
JULIA WRIGHT, *Dalhousie University*

56. *Dickens and the Popular Radical Imagination*
SALLY LEDGER, *Birkbeck, University of London*

57. *Darwin, Literature and Victorian Respectability*
GOWAN DAWSON, *University of Leicester*

58. *'Michael Field': Poetry, Aestheticism and the Fin de Siècle*
MARION THAIN, *University of Birmingham*

59. *Colonies, Cults and Evolution: Literature, Science and Culture in Nineteenth-Century Writing*
DAVID AMIGONI, *Keele University*

60. *Realism, Photography and Nineteenth-Century Fiction*
DANIEL A. NOVAK, *Lousiana State University*

61. *Caribbean Culture and British Fiction in the Atlantic World, 1780–1870*
TIM WATSON, *University of Miami*

62. *The Poetry of Chartism: Aesthetics, Politics, History*
MICHAEL SANDERS, *University of Manchester*

63. *Literature and Dance in Nineteenth-Century Britain: Jane Austen to the New Woman*
CHERYL WILSON, *Indiana University*

64. *Shakespeare and Victorian Women*
GAIL MARSHALL, *Oxford Brookes University*

65. *The Tragi-Comedy of Victorian Fatherhood*
VALERIE SANDERS, *University of Hull*

66. *Darwin and the Memory of the Human: Evolution, Savages, and South America*
CANNON SCHMITT, *University of Toronto*

67. *From Sketch to Novel: The Development of Victorian Fiction*
AMANPAL GARCHA, *Ohio State University*

68. *The Crimean War and the British Imagination*
STEFANIE MARKOVITS, *Yale University*

69. *Shock, Memory and the Unconscious in Victorian Fiction*
JILL L. MATUS, *University of Toronto*

70. *Sensation and Modernity in the 1860s*
NICHOLAS DALY, *University College Dublin*

71. *Ghost-Seers, Detectives, and Spiritualists: Theories of Vision in Victorian Literature and Science*
SRDJAN SMAJIĆ, *Furman University*

72. *Satire in an Age of Realism*
AARON MATZ, *Scripps College, California*

73. *Thinking About Other People in Nineteenth-Century British Writing*
ADELA PINCH, *University of Michigan*

74. *Tuberculosis and the Victorian Literary Imagination*
KATHERINE BYRNE, *University of Ulster, Coleraine*

75. *Urban Realism and the Cosmopolitan Imagination in the Nineteenth Century: Visible City, Invisible World*
TANYA AGATHOCLEOUS, *Hunter College, City University of New York*

76. *Women, Literature, and the Domesticated Landscape: England's Disciples of Flora, 1780–1870*
JUDITH W. PAGE, *University of Florida*
ELISE L. SMITH, *Millsaps College, Mississippi*

77. *Time and the Moment in Victorian Literature and Society*
SUE ZEMKA, *University of Colorado*

78. *Popular Fiction and Brain Science in the Late Nineteenth Century*
ANNE STILES, *Washington State University*

79. *Picturing Reform in Victorian Britain*
JANICE CARLISLE, *Yale University*

80. *Atonement and Self-Sacrifice in Nineteenth-Century Narrative*
JAN-MELISSA SCHRAMM, *University of Cambridge*

81. *The Silver Fork Novel: Fashionable Fiction in the Age of Reform*
EDWARD COPELAND, *Pomona College, California*

82. *Oscar Wilde and Ancient Greece*
IAIN ROSS, *Colchester Royal Grammar School*

83. *The Poetry of Victorian Scientists: Style, Science and Nonsense*
DANIEL BROWN, *University of Southampton*

84. *Moral Authority, Men of Science, and the Victorian Novel*
ANNE DEWITT, *Princeton Writing Program*

85. *China and the Victorian Imagination: Empires Entwined*
ROSS G. FORMAN, *University of Warwick*

86. *Dickens's Style*
DANIEL TYLER, *University of Oxford*

87. *The Formation of the Victorian Literary Profession*
RICHARD SALMON, *University of Leeds*

88. *Before George Eliot: Marian Evans and the Periodical Press*
FIONNUALA DILLANE, *University College Dublin*

89. *The Victorian Novel and the Space of Art: Fictional Form on Display*
DEHN GILMORE, *California Institute of Technology*

90. *George Eliot and Money: Economics, Ethics and Literature*
DERMOT COLEMAN, *Independent Scholar*

91. *Masculinity and the New Imperialism: Rewriting Manhood in British Popular Literature, 1870–1914*
BRADLEY DEANE, *University of Minnesota*

92. *Evolution and Victorian Culture*
edited by
BERNARD LIGHTMAN, *York University, Toronto* and
BENNETT ZON, *University of Durham*

93. *Victorian Literature, Energy, and the Ecological Imagination*
ALLEN MACDUFFIE, *University of Texas, Austin*

94. *Popular Literature, Authorship and the Occult in Late Victorian Britain*
ANDREW MCCANN, *Dartmouth College, New Hampshire*

95. *Women Writing Art History in the Nineteenth Century: Looking Like a Woman*
HILARY FRASER *Birkbeck, University of London*

96. *Relics of Death in Victorian Literature and Culture*
DEBORAH LUTZ, *Long Island University, C. W. Post Campus*

97. *The Demographic Imagination and the Nineteenth-Century City: Paris, London, New York*
NICHOLAS DALY, *University College Dublin*

98. *Dickens and the Business of Death*
CLAIRE WOOD, *University of York*

99. *Translation as Transformation in Victorian Poetry*
ANNMARIE DRURY, *Queens College, City University of New York*

100. *The Bigamy Plot: Sensation and Convention in the Victorian Novel*
MAIA MCALEAVEY, *Boston College, Massachusetts*

101. *English Fiction and the Evolution of Language, 1850–1914*
WILL ABBERLEY, *University of Oxford*

102. *The Racial Hand in the Victorian Imagination*
AVIVA BRIEFEL, *Bowdoin College, Maine*

103. *Evolution and Imagination in Victorian Children's Literature*
JESSICA STRALEY, *University of Utah*

104. *Writing Arctic Disaster: Authorship and Exploration*
ADRIANA CRACIUN, *University of California, Riverside*

105. *Science, Fiction, and the Fin-de-Siècle Periodical Press*
WILL TATTERSDILL, *University of Birmingham*

CPSIA information can be obtained
at www.ICGtesting.com
Printed in the USA
BVHW041006061021
618259BV00015B/304

9 781108 713221